Urban Bridges, Global Capital(s)
Trans-Mediterranean Francosphères

Urban Bridges, Global Capital(s)

Trans-Mediterranean Francosphères

Edited by
Claire Launchbury
and
Megan C. MacDonald

LIVERPOOL UNIVERSITY PRESS

First published 2021 by
Liverpool University Press
4 Cambridge Street
Liverpool
L69 7ZU

Copyright © 2021 Liverpool University Press

The right of Claire Launchbury and Megan C. MacDonald to be identified as the editors of this book has been asserted by them in accordance with the Copyright, Designs and Patents Act 1988.

All rights reserved. No part of this book may be reproduced, stored in a retrieval system, or transmitted, in any form or by any means, electronic, mechanical, photocopying, recording, or otherwise, without the prior written permission of the publisher.

British Library Cataloguing-in-Publication data
A British Library CIP record is available

ISBN 978-1-78962-811-1

Typeset by Carnegie Book Production, Lancaster
Printed and bound by CPI Group (UK) Ltd, Croydon CR0 4YY

Contents

Acknowledgements   vii

Introduction: Urban Bridges, Global Capital(s)   1
   Claire Launchbury and Megan C. MacDonald

Part I: Writing Capital(s), Narrating the City: Mediterranean *allers-retours*

1 The *Flâneuses* of Tunis: Reading the City in the Life Narratives of Kaouthar Khlifi and Dora Latiri   17
   Rania Said

2 City Speak: Nice through the Eyes of Jean Vigo, Jacques Demy and Emmanuel Roblès   37
   Christa Jones

3 Moroccan Narratives of Dystopia: Representations of Tangier in Leïla Kilani's film *Sur la planche*   53
   Marzia Caporale

4 Cultural Capitals in Crisis: Meditating on the Mediterranean and Memory between Paris and Athens in *La clarinette* by Vassilis Alexakis   67
   Alison Rice

Part II: Marseille *Multiples*: Capital of Culture

5 Screening Cosmopolitan and Mediterranean Marseille   85
   Ipek Çelik Rappas

6 Shaping Mediterranean Geographies: The Museum of
European and Mediterranean Civilizations in Marseille and
the Making of Identity 101
Angela Giovanangeli

7 Marseille Provence 2013: A Social Facelift for an Old Lady? 121
Agnès Peysson-Zeiss

8 Bridges and Fault Lines in the Mediterranean City:
Neighbourhood Memory in an Urban Walk in Marseille 135
Mark Ingram

Part III: Mediterranean Beyonds

9 Between the Comoros Islands and Marseille:
Trans-Mediterranean Bridging Narratives in the Works of
Salim Hatubou 155
Silvia Baage

10 Trans-Mediterranean *Beyroutes* 175
Claire Launchbury

11 Multilingual Pilgrimages: Language and
Trans-Mediterranean Cultural Identity in Ismaël Ferroukhi's
Le Grand Voyage 199
Gemma King

12 Bare Life At Sea: Mediterranean Crossings, Istanbul Limbo 213
Megan C. MacDonald

Notes on Contributors 233

Index 239

Acknowledgements

The editors are very grateful to the anonymous readers of the proposal. We would like to acknowledge the support of Stuart Taberner and the AHRC for the ACLA seminar at NYU in 2014, which launched this project, and colleagues at the School of Languages, Cultures and Societies at Leeds, Charles Forsdick (Liverpool), Chloe Johnson, Anthony Cond and the editorial staff at Liverpool University Press.

Introduction:
Urban Bridges, Global Capital(s)

Claire Launchbury and Megan C. MacDonald

A space of cultural exchange, linguistic negotiation, multiple migrations and diverse identities, the trans-Mediterranean is also identified by long-existing trade links between the major, and ancient, cities situated on its coasts. From Athens to Casablanca, Nice to Tunis, these cities, administrative capitals in their own right, often rival their inland designated counterparts as places of cosmopolitan capital and exchange. Our collection reflects upon the different and often competing transnational spheres and borders—linguistic, religious, political—focusing on the concept of 'bridging' across and between Mediterranean urban centres. We locate as case studies of transcultural exchange texts which originate, or are located in, voyages to and from these centres. Our aim is twofold: to recalibrate francophone studies within a Mediterranean frame, and to rethink Mediterranean case studies in an interdisciplinary manner. This project first took shape at the American Comparative Literature Association's (ACLA) 2014 Conference, 'Capitals', where Claire Launchbury organized the panel 'Trans-Mediterranean Capitals: Bridging Narratives'. Since then, we have opened it up to additional interlocutors, in order to think about francophone voices from the perspectives of the Mediterranean and the French metropole.

This collection also responds to increased attention on the Mediterranean as a space of exchange and interrogation in contemporary literary studies.[1] The Mediterranean has already been institutionalized in certain disciplines; historians, for example, have

---

1 Sharon Kinoshita (2014) has forged a path for the literary Mediterranean in medieval francophone studies.

grappled with and attempted to move beyond the seemingly ossified shadow of Fernand Braudel and his seminal Mediterranean works from the middle of the last century. More recently, it has come to the fore in literary and cultural studies. We therefore launch this collection as one in conversation with the work of thinkers such as Edwige Tamalet-Talbeyev, Claudia Esposito, Iain Chambers, Claudio Fogu, yasser elhariry, Hakim Abderrezak, Olivia C. Harrison, and Madeleine Dobie, to name but a few. Fogu offers the following challenge when considering the Mediterranean as a space of enquiry: 'Contrary to the clearly marked geographical boundaries of the Mediterranean Sea, the flow of metaphors around the theme of Mediterranean-ness is virtually infinite, and may indeed be without parallel in other cultural contexts' (2010: n. pag.). This idea of a limited geographical Mediterranean space goes against Braudel's conception, where:

> From the Black Sea to the Straits of Gibraltar, the Mediterranean's northern waters wash the shores of Europe. Here again, if he [sic] wants to establish boundaries, the historian will have more hesitation than the geographer. 'Europe, a confused concept,' wrote Henri Hauser. It is a twofold or even threefold world, composed of peoples and territories with whom history has dealt very differently. The Mediterranean, by its profound influence over southern Europe, has contributed in no small measure to prevent the unity of that Europe, which it has attracted towards its shores and then divided to its own advantage. (1996: 188)

As literary geographers, we expand the Mediterranean, adding to the pool of metaphors: the figure of the *passerelle* represents the passage between these locations, and the *navette* enables transcultural dialogue.[2] A *passerelle* is a gangway, the plank mediating the movement from land to sea, and vice versa. It signifies journey beginnings, and their endings. Used as a theatrical term, it is a catwalk enabling movement between orchestra and stage: a Mediterranean theatre. The *navette* refers to a small boat making regular trips, a shuttle, as well as a weaving metaphor: the part of the loom moving back and forth over the architecture of a woven work in progress. Here we use it as both metaphor and reading methodology. The chapters in this collection move between shifting and competing notions of centre and periphery, travelling between texts and locations, transporting

---

2 For example, the *Dictionnaire des mots français d'origine arabe* by Saleh Guemriche (2007), with a preface by Assia Djebar, works to revise the colonial linguistic traffic between France, North Africa and the eastern Mediterranean.

Introduction

cultural and textual baggage, and leaving other things behind: a metaphor for Mediterranean futurity, watermarks and wakes. The *navette* privileges juxtaposition, putting these texts and locations into communication with one another, shoving off together, making them move. The *passerelle* and the *navette* work together to weave across Mediterranean space, leaving in their wake a constellation of threads, a flexible matrix linking Mediterranean capitals, formally recognized or otherwise. The movement creates the space of the trans-Mediterranean.[3] As Hakim Abderrezak cautions in *Ex-Centric Migrations: Europe and the Maghreb in Mediterranean Cinema, Literature, and Music*: 'The Mediterranean has emerged as a privileged site for exploring global dynamics, containing both proximity and distance, constituting a link but also an obstacle, and a barrier' (2016: 61). We see one version of this capacity for disconnection in Rice's contribution to this volume, where the Greek bridge of hospitality begins to break down once the famously hospitable Athens is reread in light of the current and ongoing Mediterranean refugee crisis.

In order to stem the potentially infinite 'flow of metaphors' linked to the Mediterranean, we settled on the term *francosphère*, which speaks to language and geography, as well as history. It is more helpful, we believe, than making a distinction between French and francophone, particularly when the latter becomes a shorthand for emerging, non-Metropolitan cultural production. In this way, the term sidesteps the more loaded colonial language that has marked some aspects of French Studies. Attending to the comparative difference between what we understand as the *francosphère* and Anglosphere is particularly productive.[4] The transnational focus builds upon our belief that, far from being wedded to a nation state, the *francosphère* represents a mutable location in which to articulate of a mode of inquiry in order to assess how cultural discourses in French operate and interact across the many bridges which connect across the Mediterranean basin. Many of our contributions point to how traditional metaphors of centre and periphery are superseded by a plurality of voices, networks of relationships where the *francosphères* (deliberately plural) of the Mediterranean coexist among other transnational linguistic clusters.

3 This reading methodology is inspired by Gayatri Spivak's reading of Jacques Derrida's *Glas*. For more on the *navette*, see MacDonald (2013: 58–68).

4 The journal *Francosphères*, for example, sees its 'overall aim' as 'to advance a dialogue about what it means to work in "French" Studies in the 21st Century', http://online.liverpooluniversitypress.co.uk/loi/franc.

Where, What and Who Is the Mediterranean?

Following Jacques Derrida's peregrinations in *L'Autre Cap* (1991), our collection interrogates the what of Europe; the when or where of Paris; the who of the Mediterranean. Or might the Mediterranean fall under the rubric of 'paleonomy', that is, as Michael Naas recalls Derrida's words in *Positions*: 'the "strategic" necessity that requires the occasional maintenance of an *old name* in order to launch a new concept' (1992: xliii)? The Mediterranean is also a disquieting and dangerous place as refugees flee and borders tighten. Iain Chambers describes a 'fluid and fluctuating' map of the Mediterranean as a postcolonial sea where there are 'deeper and more dispersive currents which draw us back in time while simultaneously projecting a radically different understanding of the present and its potential futures' (2008: 2).

Taking this forward, we understand the Mediterranean as *an old name to launch a new concept* and the essays in the book each reflect on this in different ways. Issues concerning identity are challenged, since a Metropolitan, European, Arab or African identity may be preferred over a Mediterranean one. As borders become reinforced in the region, trans-Mediterranean bridging narratives may be thwarted, especially by those who write across Europe, Africa and Southwest Asia, in the face of the contemporary refugee crisis. Finally, chapters explore what it means to define a Mediterranean city—such as Marseille as European Capital of Culture—and interrogate how this feeds into the cultural production of a city whose multi-ethnic identities are as outward-looking towards North Africa as they are inward towards the French capital. In this way, Marseille becomes a node, a site *par excellence* of trans-Mediterranean passages. Marseille seen in this light, put into conversation with unexpected interlocutors (such as the Comoros Islands), resituates Mediterranean *francosphères* through an examination of its new sites and the relationships between them.

The book is organized in three parts, offering an original examination of cultural production and flows between urban capitals and 'capital' in and of a selection of Mediterranean cities and sites. The connections forged here are man-made, via literature, political considerations and cultural movements. This is a specific choice and moves away from the work on the natural world of the Mediterranean which not only privileges the geographic, but focuses on much earlier periods.

Introduction

Part I: Writing Capital(s), Narrating the City: Mediterranean *allers-retours*

Part I addresses Tunis, Nice, Tangier, Athens and Paris, where each city offers rich urban landscapes that are undone or revitalized through literary and cinematic lenses. Tunis and its relationship to its Mediterranean environment is explored by two women writers, promoting urban *flâneries* in order to revive the city through crisscrossing it, and distinguishing it from other Arab and European capitals. As France's second largest Mediterranean city, and latecomer to the French national fabric, the city of Nice is another crossroads. The study of two films and a novel offers a palimpsestic look at Nice's antecedents and its contemporary role in producing the Mediterranean. Each chapter renders Mediterranean cities visible in alternative ways, strongly suggesting that rewriting the city may change the city itself.

Moving to consider *allers-retours*, Part I turns to travel in several directions—from Paris to Athens, and *between* France and North Africa. Derrida's *L'Autre cap* is brought into play, as the Greek economic crisis positions Athens and Paris in a dialogue where cultural capital is produced in spite of the economic crisis. Tangier on screen locates post-Arab Spring Morocco as a site of globalization, foreign investment, trade and the everyday reality of gendered labour for working Moroccan women. Here, Mediterranean and capital flows are often only in one direction.

Rania Said examines gendered urban *flânerie* and the dynamics of identity formation and linguistic hybridity in the work of two Tunisian women writers in Chapter 1, 'The *Flâneuses* of Tunis: Reading the City in the Life Narratives of Kaouthar Khlifi and Dora Latiri'. Tunis is a relational urban space in Said's reading, in conversation with its suburbs and the Mediterranean environment, where narratives produce the city and the self. The Tunis on offer in Khlifi's and Latiri's work breaks with what Yasser Elsheshtawy (2004) calls 'the narrative of loss' which, for decades, has characterized the discourse on Arab-majority cities. The two texts bookend the 2011 uprisings in Tunisia, and both authors construct a Tunis that is alive, cosmopolitan and theatrical, a stage on which to perform simultaneous cultures and historical moments. By portraying the complexity of the city's interstitial position, these two narratives challenge the defeatist discourses that have reduced Arab-majority cities to either relics of their glorious medieval past, or to struggling victims of colonial history. Said's reading offers a genealogy of the *flâneur* and takes it travelling: from European spaces to Tunis, from gendered male to female *flâneuse*. This both challenges orientalist readings of wandering in cities on southern Mediterranean shores and displaces the hegemonic gendered European metropolis as the site of wandering *par excellence* via the 'narrator-*flâneuse*' in each text.

In Chapter 2, 'City Speak: Nice through the Eyes of Jean Vigo, Jacques Demy and Emmanuel Roblès', Christa Jones begins by looking at Jean Vigo's 1930 short silent documentary 'A propos de Nice', where Nice is the main character, in order to unpack and interrogate the various clichés and fantasies associated with this Mediterranean city. She then moves ahead 30 years with a reading of Jacques Demy's film *La Baie des Anges* (1963), followed by Emmanuel Roblès's crime novel of the same period *La Remontée du fleuve* (1966). Historically a cosmopolitan city, Nice is France's second largest Mediterranean city, and is also known as Niça, Nissa or Nizza. It only became a part of France in 1860, and enjoys a historical and cultural proximity to Italy, as well as being at the crossroads of multiple cultures, migrations and identities. Vigo's film is one in motion, where people and capital are constantly moving, each according to her social class, a kaleidoscope of spectacles transmitted by Vigo's 'merciless camerawork' (Jones) where Vigo mocks the leisure classes: leisure juxtaposed with a smoking factory tower. In Demy's film, Nice is temporary, 'a transitory mirage' (Jones), perhaps best personified by its famous *carnaval*, where roles and hierarchies are upended for a limited period of time. Roblès's novel *La Remontée du fleuve* opens in winter right after *carnaval*, working against Nice's reputation as a place of holidaying, decadence and sun. Jones convincingly argues that Nice is a city of capital and bridging narratives, embodied by overt displays of wealth, casinos and the physical bridge, 'the emblematic Promenade des Anglais, a runway to human monetary success, human passion and moral depravity'.

Marzia Caporale assesses how Morocco is today a fluid society oscillating between tradition and modernity, adherence to its national identity and a strong determination to open up to the world and to move towards globalization. Arguing that the northern port city of Tangier, strategically located on the Strait of Gibraltar and historically considered a principal gateway to the Mediterranean, reproduces within its microstructure the struggles of the country as a whole. More liberal open than other Moroccan cities, its cultural vibrancy has been the staging post for writers and film-makers. This has resulted, due to its notoriety for international trafficking, in the filming of several spy

Introduction 7

dramas by Anglo-American film-makers. Caporale reads Leïla Kilani's debut feature *Sur la planche*, as an exemplar of the aporia between the promising presence of foreign investors on Moroccan soil and the harsh everyday reality that relegates most Moroccans, and particularly women, to the condition of victims to the rules of a new exploitative capitalist economy. Caporale argues that in *Sur la planche* the contract between social subject and urban environment is portrayed as an illusory utopic construct, as access to parts of the city is brokered and restricted by Western capital flow to all but the most economically mobile of citizens.

Alison Rice begins Chapter 4, 'Cultural Capitals in Crisis: Meditating on the Mediterranean and Memory between Paris and Athens in *La clarinette* by Vassilis Alexakis' with Derrida's distinction between *capital* and *capitale*. This allows for a double bridge between two capitals—Athens and Paris—and comparisons between their economic situation, as explored by Greek-born francophone writer Vassilis Alexakis in *La clarinette*. Rice turns to Derrida's *De l'hospitalité* in order to situate the alienation and challenges that the 'foreigner' can face in a legal setting in a language not her own, exploring whether or not a Mediterranean Athens could travel via francophone literary bridges to Paris.

Writing in two languages, Alexakis translates his own work from Greek to French and vice versa. This, too, is an act of bridging, and 'a conscious desire to unite the two locations' (Rice). He points out a number of French influences in Athens, and wonders if he doesn't favour French words of Greek origin (*médusé*, *épopée*, but also *xénophobie*) when writing in French.[5] Venturing into a territory where he suggests that what unites Paris and Athens, or France and Greece, is a crisis of cultural capital, Alexakis then explores memory lapses, memory loss and the loss of loved ones. Meditations on hospitality lead to explorations on the word *xénophobie*, and what Alexakis considers as its relatively recent entry into the Greek language. Rice deftly uses

---

5 This tendency recalls another Mediterranean thinker, Frantz Fanon, who, though he didn't speak Arabic, often inserted French words connected to the Arabic language in his writing. For a detailed discussion, see Edwards (2002). This attention to strangeness and in/hospitality in language also includes Mediterranean thinkers (and Algerians), Jacques Derrida (*Monolingualism of the other*), Hélène Cixous ('Mon Algériance') and Assia Djebar ('Le Voyage des mots arabes dans la langue française'). For a more detailed discussion of Cixous and Derrida in a Mediterranean frame, see MacDonald (2017).

the moment to revisit Derrida's *De l'hospitalité*, and his exploration of the Greek limits of hospitality. In this way, we might consider Derrida as one point in a Mediterranean triangle, connecting Greece, France and Algeria. Alexakis is horrified by the treatment of foreigners in today's Greece—locked up without recourse, and in the case of those unlawfully imprisoned in the Kypseli *commissariat*, 'enfermées dans une cave qui est une sorte de tombeau' (Alexakis quoted in Rice). Here we can cite refugees who fled Greek hotspots in 2017 in order to try and make the dangerous Black Sea crossing from Turkey into Romania, who claimed: 'We are already dead' (Hilton and Cupolo, 2017: n. pag.). Forgetting and remembering the place, language, body and rights of the other is a Mediterranean project.

Part II: Marseille *Multiples*: Capital of Culture

Part II, 'Marseille Multiples: Capital of Culture', is a cross-disciplinary examination exclusively focusing on Marseille. Following its designation as European Capital of Culture in 2013, both currency and cultural projects flowed. Of particular focus is the Musée des Civilisations de l'Europe et de la Méditerranée (MuCEM), and how, as a museum in provincial France, MuCEM both sits on the site of multiple migrations (Marseille's Vieux-Port) and projects Mediterranean identities inland towards Europe and elsewhere. Other projects of Marseille's cultural capital tenure included what Peysson-Zeiss refers to a 'facelift' or regeneration of old industrial areas, in the hope of making them shiny commercial and residential quarters. Who is included in this new Marseille, where often *culture* becomes *rupture*?

Marseille is influenced not only by its reputation in film, but also through the structure of the film industry itself. Its current position as 'the' Mediterranean city *par excellence* is the result of over two decades of planning. And this very positioning of Marseille is due to two cinematic styles, as Çelik Rappas argues, which locate it as both transnational capital and Mediterranean centre. Another Marseille is on offer through ethnographic interviews in low-income neighbourhoods in Ingram's contribution, where Marseille residents create site-specific performances. The urban walk initiative probes and crosses Marseille neighbourhoods, asking, How and to what extent is 'the Mediterranean' important to these city dwellers? The city is at once hyper-local and international, trans-Mediterranean and neighbourhood-specific, and sometimes even a globally articulated process.

Ipek Çelik Rappas creates a cinematic genealogy of Marseille's role in Mediterranean narratives leading up to, and during, Marseille's 2013 status as European Capital of Culture, one which privileged the Mediterranean, in 'Screening Cosmopolitan and Mediterranean Marseille'. While the French media portrays Marseille as 'the chaotic product of multiculturalism and migration', its self-presentation (sometimes top-down) in relation to the European Capital of Culture is one of 'an orderly cosmopolitanism inherited from cross-cultural experiences with other Mediterranean cities' (Çelik Rappas). In Malek Bensmaïl's film *Ulysse le brûleur de frontières et la mer blanche du milieu*, Çelik Rappas argues, Marseille itself is symbolized as a boat. Here a boat onscreen is like a Mediterranean chronotope, a visual bridging narrative connecting space/time in the Mediterranean basin. Marseille is depicted as 'a distant utopia' in comparison to the other Mediterranean cities. It is unproblematically depicted as 'well-connected' and 'transnational', 'devoid of the problems' depicted in other Mediterranean cities. This attitude is the product of urban reconstruction in Marseille, specifically the French government's L'Euroméditerranée project (1995–2012), which invested over 50 million euros in the city. Investigating what is at stake in the depiction of Marseille through different cinematic styles, Çelik Rappas deliberates on whether Marseille is France's Mediterranean hub or a transnational Mediterranean space in its own right.

Angelia Giovangeli, by taking us to MuCEM, also deliberates on how regional, national and Mediterranean identities are formulated, specifically by analysing how the museum participates in formulating Mediterranean identity through its curatorial practice and how as a regional museum it becomes the location for competing narratives of identity. Investigating the historical development of the project whose central collection was originally housed in the Musée National d'Arts et Traditions Populaires, Giovanangeli then examines the location of the project within the city, which is, importantly, by the sea, before showing through personal observations of the site how the city, the nation and supra-national organization of the European Union are all contributing in different ways to the institution right down to curatorial display. The strategic impetus of Sarkozy's ultimately abandoned plan for a French-led Mediterranean Union also played its part in the concept highlighting the desire for a 'new' transnational Mediterranean harnessed to the French metropole but looking outward beyond the Hexagon frame.

In her chapter, 'Marseille Provence 2013: A Social Facelift for an Old Lady?', Agnès Peysson-Zeiss focuses on Marseille's tenure as European City of Culture, in particular the Euroméditerranée regeneration projects in the Joliette district of the city. The City of Culture scheme is designed to encourage both capital flow and civic pride with legacy projects continuing long after the short year of tenure. With a rich history of French literary culture underpinning the identity of Marseille, the city has also in parallel developed a grassroots cultural identity in which hip-hop is central and which has been sharply critical of the effects and affects of regeneration in the city. The documentary *Capitale de la Rupture* (2012) by Keny Arkana proves central to the analysis portraying how local populations risk being left behind in the smartening 'facelift' but, as Peysson-Zeiss concludes, significant if not sufficient attempts have been made to provide access to employment, training and education alongside the redevelopment.

Staying within the urban fabric of Marseille, Mark Ingram assesses, again through the influence of the 2013 Capital of Culture, the same low-income districts of the city, focusing on site-specific performance undertaken within them, in 'Bridges and Fault Lines in the Mediterranean City: Neighbourhood Memory in a Urban Walk in Marseille'. Drawing on ethnographic fieldwork conducted between 2007 and 2015, Ingram offers a unique perspective on the 'trans-Mediterranean' nature of Marseille and shows how the making of a city as a distinctive place is an international and sometimes globally articulated process. The heritage at stake here, unlike the broad ambitions of MuCEM, is the memory of marginalized and popular neighbourhoods. Through the testimony of 'Safia', Ingram investigates how community-based theatre, including site-specific performance and urban walks, operates to curate memory, of both neighbourhood and the Mediterranean (understood by Safia as a legacy of family from Algeria). Again, the place of Marseille as one of tension between popular local neighbourhood and Mediterranean node underpins how people remember and identify with the city.

Introduction 11

Part III: Mediterranean Beyonds

The four chapters in this final section fan out from France. Here, the notion of connecting seas comes into play, where literary works by authors who settle in Mediterranean urban centres travel in from outside the Mediterranean, finding a place there. Writers whose origins are outside Hexagonal France produce francophone texts in Mediterranean capitals, postcolonial products of neocolonial politics. Comorian protagonists find themselves in urban Marseille narratives, and these texts and authors shuttle between the Mediterranean and elsewhere, promoting trans-Mediterranean spheres. Moving east from France towards Mecca, a road movie traverses linguistic spaces and Mediterranean stopovers. Claire Launchbury's tracing of trans-Mediterranean 'Beyroutes' demonstrates the multiple urban paradoxes at work in a city that is both adrift yet a centre for transnational capital exchange. Navigating, or, more tellingly, *orienting* oneself in Beirut brings up questions about citizenship, surveillance and the accidental monuments encountered in the Lebanese capital. Twenty-first-century francophone cinema overflows with multilingualism, linking immigration and naturalization, 'integration' and the nature of difference. Yet, as Gemma King highlights, a film such as Ismaël Ferroukhi's *Le Grand Voyage* (2004) foregrounds the potential of even the most historically disenfranchised languages to empower their speakers. By way of conclusion, Megan C. MacDonald examines Mediterranean bodies in limbo on the Black Sea, via an archival document connecting bare life at sea and 'stowaway time', following S.A. Smythe's words: 'It would be a helpful provocation to examine the farce of the recurrent practice of enumeration, of counting people without being accountable to them' (2018: n. pag.).

In Silvia Baage's contribution, extra-Mediterranean narratives travel from the Comoros Islands and *become* bridging narratives in Salim Hatubou's diasporic works in Marseille, in 'Between the Comoros Islands and Marseille: Trans-Mediterranean Bridging Narratives in the Works of Salim Hatubou'. Baage's insistence on including Hatubou's work in trans-Mediterranean *francosphères* further opens up the Mediterranean, where Marseille-as-diaspora becomes linked with one of its antecedents, the Comoros Islands. Baage calls Hatubou an 'exemplary case of a non-Mediterranean migrant', one who focuses on the journey to the Mediterranean and Marseille, the expectations of an Eldorado and the often-bitter reality that greets migrants. Like Rania Said's argument about the *flâneuses* of Tunis, Baage's reading also extracts Marseille as a character in the novels, one which, like in Said's reading, is constructed through space and time, negotiates mobility and modernity, and is traced out through walking the city.

It is the very process of movement itself that, for Baage, 'creates an important link between two bodies of water that are not normally connected'. Baage draws on connecting seas, and distinguishes between the Mediterranean as a body of water and as a space defined through human interactions. This very connection, she argues, 'has interesting implications for literary works produced by contemporary diasporic authors' who nevertheless maintain ties with their place of birth. This connecting also means that Comorian voices are heard in Marseille (where many Comorian immigrants settle), and that Marseille and the wider Mediterranean is then folded back into the Indian Ocean.

Beirut is a series of urban paradoxes, as Claire Launchbury demonstrates in her chapter. A city which is simultaneously adrift, free-floating in the Mediterranean which borders its shores yet functions as the hub for transnational capital and its exchanges. In thinking through how to both navigate the city and reclaim it, this chapter addresses attempts to tame urban space semantically through an agenda of familiarization and how its pervasive official and unofficial securitization and surveillance makes for alert citizens with adept urban ruses offering up scope for the examination of different ways of seeing and understanding the city. She also discusses how capital flows have influenced urban dynamics from independence through to the present, attentive to multiple layers of mediation between knowledge and power, language and metropole in the Lebanese capital.

Gemma King introduces analysis of the rich multilingualism at work in the trans-Mediterranean through Ferroukhi's film *Le Grand Voyage* (2004) and how it functions to renegotiate power dynamics within the Mediterranean *francosphère*, resetting the boundaries of the Hexagon and, indeed, Europe as mutable. These new dynamics, present in this film in particular, and contemporary French film in general, refuse to shy away from contested cultural identities across generations of migrant families. King shows how this is demonstrated through a father and son's relationships to language via the different multilingual capital each hold. King's analysis shows how the usual dynamics of multilingual films in French privilege fluency in the language as the means to open doors, and find a place in society, yet in *Le Grand Voyage* this is offset by the father's ease in Arabic facilitating their journey to Mecca to perform *hajj*, demonstrating a more progressive representation of language relations. The film goes on to represent the Mediterranean as 'a non-linear space transcendent of simplistic postcolonial configurations'

(p. 210). King highlights the plurality of voices and spaces, moving beyond traditional and increasingly redundant metaphors of periphery and centre.

Megan C. MacDonald's contribution, 'Bare Life at Sea: Mediterranean Crossings, Istanbul Limbo', functions as a conclusion to the collection. This ethnographic approach examines a 2017 news story about stowaways on a Black Sea ferry in perpetual transit between Turkey and Ukraine. These stowaways inhabit the space of bare life at sea, collapsing the difference between containment and expulsion, international marine law and the ferry as a floating camp both inside and outside of the law. MacDonald pushes at the limit of Mediterranean geographies, asking if a clandestine Mediterranean presence on the Black Sea constitutes a Mediterranean story. She examines the unnamed stowaways via their archival traces, and a connecting seas approach limns the Bosphorus as a Mediterranean literary space, making connections between the time of the stowaway, and archives further out to sea.

Together these three interlinked but distinct parts of our collection offer a showcase of the research and thought at work in the capital flows and capital centres of the trans-Mediterranean *francosphère*. Exposing new relationships and connections—both cultural and capital—between the transnational nodes of this complex geopolitical region pushes at the seams of Mediterranean borders, the *francosphère* and contemporary French and francophone studies.

Bibliography

Abderrezak, Hakim. 2016. *Ex-centric migrations: Europe and the Maghreb in Mediterranean cinema, literature, and music*. Indianapolis: Indiana University Press.

Braudel, Fernand. 1996. *The Mediterranean and the Mediterranean world in the age of Philip II, Vol. 1*. Reprint, Berkeley: University of California Press.

Chambers, Iain. 2008. *Mediterranean crossings: The politics of an interrupted modernity*. Durham: Duke University Press.

Edwards, Brian T. 2002. Fanon's al-Jaza'ir, or Algeria translated. *Parallax* 8(2): 99–115.

Elsheshtawy, Yasser. 2004. *Planning the Middle Eastern city: An urban kaleidoscope in a globalizing world*. London: Routledge.

Fogu, Claudio. 2010. From *Mare Nostrum* to *Mare Aliorum*: Mediterranean theory and Mediterraneism in contemporary Italian thought. *California Italian Studies* 1(1). http://escholarship.org/uc/item/7vp210p4.

Guemriche, Saleh. 2007. *Dictionnaire des mots français d'origine arabe*. Paris: Seuil.
Hilton, Jodi and Diego Cupolo. 2017. Old route, new dangers: Migrant smugglers revive Black Sea route to Europe. *IRIN News*, 16 October. https://www.irinnews.org/feature/2017/10/16/old-route-new-dangers-migrant-smugglers-revive-black-sea-route-europe.
Kinoshita, Sharon. 2014. Mediterranean literature. In Peregrine Horden and Sharon Kinoshita, eds., *A companion to Mediterranean history*, 314–29. Chichester: Wiley-Blackwell.
MacDonald, Megan C. 2013. The Trans-Mediterranean *navette*: Assia Djebar and the *Dictionnaire des mots français d'origine Arabe. Contemporary French and Francophone Studies* 17(1): 58–68.
———. 2017. Haunting correspondences and elemental scenes: Weaving Cixous after Derrida. In Elizabeth Berglund Hall, Frédérique Chevillot, Eilene Hoft-March and Maribel Penalver Vicea, eds. *Cixous after/depuis 2000*, 36–54. Amsterdam: Brill Rodopi.
Naas, Michael B. 1992. Introduction: For Example. In Jacques Derrida, *The other heading: Reflections on today's Europe*, vii–lix. Bloomington: Indiana University Press.
Smythe, S.A. 2018. The black Mediterranean and the politics of the imagination. *Middle East Research and Information Project* 48(286). https://www.merip.org/mer/mer286/black-mediterranean-politics-imagination.

PART I

Writing Capital(s), Narrating the City: Mediterranean *allers-retours*

1

The *Flâneuses* of Tunis

Reading the City in the Life Narratives of Kaouthar Khlifi and Dora Latiri

Rania Said

This chapter examines urban *flânerie* in the work of two Tunisian women authors: *Ce que Tunis ne m'a pas dit* (2008) by Kaouthar Khlifi and *Un amour de tn* (2013) by Dora Latiri. More particularly, it studies the representation of the city of Tunis in relation to its suburbs and its Mediterranean environment. It also analyses the dynamics of identity formation and the linguistic hybridity that inform the narrative production of both the city and the self. I argue that the Tunis of these two narratives breaks with what Yasser Elsheshtawy (2004: 3) calls 'the narrative of loss' which has characterized the discourse on Arab-majority cities for decades now. The two authors construct a Tunis that is alive, cosmopolitan and theatrical. Lying at the intersection of several cultures and several histories, Tunis is pictured as a stage upon which simultaneous performances, both traditional and modern, are being played. By portraying the complexity of the city's interstitial position, these two narratives challenge the defeatist discourses that have reduced Arab-majority cities to relics of their glorious medieval past or to struggling victims of colonial history.

For both authors, the rewriting of the Arab-majority city as a dynamic and cosmopolitan entity is powered by the act of *flânerie*, a cultural and literary tradition with strong French roots and influences. *Flânerie* as a paradigm is often associated with the study of urban life in modern Western metropolises; more particularly Paris, but also London, Berlin and New York City in the late nineteenth and early twentieth century. The first theorists of *flânerie* were Charles Baudelaire in his essay 'The Painter of Modern Life' (1859), Victor Fournel in *Ce qu'on voit dans les rues de Paris* (1867) and Walter Benjamin in his essays on Paris and

Baudelaire. For decades *flânerie*, as an artistic act and as a paradigm, was focused on the subject position of the bourgeois male *flaneur*, who walked around the modern commodified urban space and gazed at the city and its subjects before transforming them into art.

With the publication of Janet Wolff's 1985 article 'The Invisible *Flâneuse*: Women and the Literature of Modernity' and Griselda Pollock's 1988 essay 'Modernity and the Spaces of Femininity', *flânerie* studies finally received a much-needed feminist revision. Both essays critiqued the 'invisibility' of the female *flâneuse* in the discourses of the humanities and studied gender segregation in European cities. Wolff's early work, and to a lesser degree Pollock's, was criticized for being under the influence of the theory of 'separate spheres' (D'Souza and McDonough, 2006: 11). This theory stipulates that early modern European spaces were divided into a public/male sphere and a private/female sphere. Cultural theorists and historians have in the past two decades demonstrated that the borders between the two spheres were not as rigid as the theory would have us believe and that navigating them involved a constant negotiation of social roles.

A key revision of Wolff's and Pollock's work can be found in Elizabeth Wilson's 1992 essay 'The Invisible Flâneur'. The essay builds upon the critique of the theory of separate spheres and rejects the assumption that the *flâneur* embodies 'the triumph of masculine power or the male gaze' (Wilson, 1992: 109). For Wilson, the overdependence of some feminists on 'the conscious desire and potential mastery' of this gaze is a reductive reading of Lacanian theory that can only lead to the imprisonment of women in 'the straitjacket of otherness' (1992: 102). She reminds us that the Lacanian male gaze also embodies 'an unconscious significance' which is to 'annihilate the threat that woman (as castrated, and possessing a sinister genital organ) poses' (Wilson, 1992: 102). Rejecting the dichotomies of gender and space that she found in early feminist readings of *flânerie*, Wilson conceptualizes the *flâneur* as above all 'a mythological or allegorical figure' who represented an ambivalent response to the new violent realities of European modernity (1992: 93). According to Wilson (1992: 109, 95), both the *flâneur* and his writings were subject to the fragmentations caused by the increased anonymity of the urban subject and the commodification of urban space. Her conclusion is that it was the *flâneur*, the ambivalent figure of European modernity, not the *flâneuse*, who was constantly under the threat of erasure by the powers of urban life (Wilson, 1992: 110).

The hegemony of the European metropolis in *flânerie* studies continues to this day despite an increased attention to the figure of the postcolonial *flâneur*. The postcolonial *flâneur*, a term first explored by Adebayo Williams in his 1997 essay, 'The Postcolonial Flâneur and Other Fellow Travelers: Conceits for a Narrative of Redemption', is visible mostly as a male wanderer in Western metropolises. Critics who have studied this figure and its potential for contrapuntal readings of the Western city did so by focusing on works such as Teju Cole's *Open City* (see Hartwiger, 2016) or Ramsey Nasr's Antwerp poetry (see Minnard, 2013). More recently, Isabella Carrera Suarez (2015: 853) shifted the focus to women 'postcolonial post-diasporic pedestrian' figures and argued that these figures are more embodied in their cities than the European modernist *flaneur*, whom she thinks of as a distant observer of the city. In Carrera Suarez's article, Singapore emerges as a site of *flânerie* but is very much overshadowed by the presence of London, Toronto and Sydney. It is this general invisibility of the non-Western city in *flânerie* studies that make the Tunisois *flâneries* of Kaouthar Khlifi and Dora Latiri even more significant. These texts not only expose us to a marginalized postcolonial city but also herald a new era in autobiographical engagement with urban life in Arab-majority cities. We are out of the Western city with its neoliberal fables about mobility and access, and we are also out of the harems of Mernissi's and Djebar's autofiction. What we are introduced to in the *flâneries* of Kaouthar Khlifi and Dora Latiri is a postcolonial capital city that is vibrant and in constant flux but also divided across class and regional lines.

Downtown Tunis, the Avenue and the Suburbs in *Ce que Tunis ne m'a pas dit*

In this book, the narrator-*flâneuse* walks around downtown Tunis to escape the dullness of her suburban life. Her *flâneries* are mostly concentrated in the avenue Habib Bourguiba,[1] the main artery of the downtown area. The Tunis that emerges out of her wanderings is a city of daily metamorphoses and one that combines secular and non-secular features. Portraying the city in flux challenges the Orientalist imaginary that has long reduced Arab-majority cities to calcified images of their

---

1 This main axis of downtown Tunis is commonly known as 'l'Avenue'. It is also called 'avenue Habib Bourguiba' after the first president of Tunisia. Following the uprising of 2011, it was officially renamed 'Avenue 14 Janvier' in commemoration of Zine El Abidine Ben Ali's ousting.

medieval past or to cities in which Islam is 'the only cause of urban form' (Abu-Lughod, 1987: 162). Moreover, contrary to much of Arabic urban literature, the narrator's city is far from alienating. It is a source of renewal and artistic inspiration.

The narrator's long and repeated walks downtown allow her to notice the changes that the city experiences from the early morning to late at night. These solitary walks awaken the narrator's senses and render her more attuned to the city's varied colours, smells and noises. As a result, the Tunis of the narrative appears not just as a visual landscape, but as a 'polysensorial' territory, with its own 'smellscape' and 'soundscape', to use Bertrand Westphal's geocritical terminology (2007: 209). The stimulation of the senses does not turn the narrator into a blasé city dweller, as predicted by Simmel in 'The Metropolis and Mental Life' (1969: 51). On the contrary, it connects her even more to her city, by preparing her for a sensuous engagement with its streets. The narrator speaks of this engagement as an invitation from 'Des rues qui veulent coûte que coûte qu'on les traverse. Comme une dette qu'on s'acquitte. Ou une femme qu'on honore. C'est une question presque libidinale. Et c'est peut-être le début de quelque chose. D'une rencontre ou d'une passion …' (Khlifi, 2008: 125). At the invitation of her city, the *flâneuse* takes on the double role of lover and explorer. She reverses the traditional gender and culture hierarchies of literary *flâneries* and Western travel narratives. The gaze is no longer masculine, exoticizing and pioneering. It becomes feminine, local and libidinal.

Let us now look at examples of the narrator's polysensorial construction of the cityscape. To map the cityscape in downtown Tunis in the early hours of the day, the narrator uses the following synesthetic image, 'les premiers rayons de lumière sont déjà à l'œuvre. Ils s'entendent dans les échos des pas pressés des premiers travailleurs de l'aube qui battent le trottoir' (Khlifi, 2008: 34). This image, which combines the visual and the auditory in an unexpected way, highlights the vitality of the city, but also shows the narrator's appreciation of these early morning workers, a class to which she does not belong, but towards which she feels considerable guilt. The narrator creates multiple tableaux of downtown Tunis and the suburbs using this kind of polysensoriality. The outcome of these tableaux is a 'sensorial geography'[2] powerful enough to map the spatial and social relations of the capital in the few years preceding the 2011 uprising.

2 The term is borrowed from the cultural geographer Paul Rodaway (1994: 37), who called for a sensuous geography that can provide us with a holistic rendering

After the surrealist image of the sun's rays echoing in the workers' footsteps, the soundscape and landscape produced by the narrator become more realist. The *flâneuse* overhears the excited screams of children going to school against a backdrop of young street vendors running away from the police (Khlifi, 2008: 34). She listens to the daring invitations of bearded religious men selling racy lingerie out in the open (Khlifi, 2008: 34). She is also attentive to the scent of basil nuancing the stench of blood coming out of the neighbouring butcher shops (Khlifi, 2008: 35). She notes how the happy music of the national radio station accompanies both the voices of impoverished street vendors singing the praises of their bread and the opening clack of the metal shutters of downtown stores (Khlifi, 2008: 35). This 'sensuous geography' maps most of the contradictions of the city in relation to class, ideology and urban planning.

The figure of the informal vendor appears twice in the narrator's rendition of Tunis in the morning, but it will also appear at other occasions in the narrative. This figure points at the uneasy coexistence of two parallel economic structures. The first is that of commodity capitalism comfortably housed in the protected boutiques and stores lining up the Avenue and its side streets. Most street vendors are migrants from the downtrodden Tunisian interior. This interior was left 'undeveloped' because of the concentration of trade on the coast. A few years later, in 2011, the informal vendor would become a symbolic figure of the Tunisian uprising, after a street vendor from Sidi Bouzid set himself on fire and ignited a wave of social unrest.[3] The literature on 'developing' cities often romanticizes informal street vendors and praises their ability to feed off the capitalist system. Some commentators on Cairo, like Joseph Dana (2014), for example, hail informal commerce as a sign of healthy 'D.I.Y. urbanism' or a tactic developed by the marginalized to take back control of their city.

It is necessary to mention, however, that in the case of Tunis, even informal trade was controlled by the 'state', which was itself controlled by crony capitalists belonging to Ben Ali's family. The narrator, of course, could not have gone this far with her social commentary,

---

of the environment and facilitate our orientation in space and awareness of spatial relationships.

3   This is in reference to the suicide of Mohamed Tarek Bouazizi, an unlicensed street vendor who set himself on fire in front of the regional governor's office after a policewoman confiscated his goods. Bouazizi was from Sidi Bouzid, a state in west central Tunisia.

given the oppressive atmosphere in which she wrote the narrative. Her remedy for this lack of freedom was the multiplication of tableaux of contrasting colours and structures to shock the reader into noticing the gaps and the layers that constitute the capital. The reader, whether local or foreign, undergoes a process of defamiliarization that can help her see its complexity.

To further underscore this complexity, the narrator-*flâneuse* contrasts the unnamed suburbs where she lives with downtown Tunis. For the narrator, the suburbs are the main cause of the ennui that is gripping her. Downtown Tunis, on the other hand, despite all its glaring class issues, represents a cure for her soul. For Khlifi, alienation is only a product of suburban life because suburbia is 'sans mémoire', whereas the city, and more particularly L'Avenue, is 'le lieu qui conserve le mieux les réminiscences immatérielles de l'histoire nouvelle du pays' (2008: 119–62). The narrator's suburbs were born out of 'une politique dite de dégourbification [slum clearance]', but ended up being seized by an upper middle class that constantly mimicked the French way of life. The narrator needs the power of memory to feed her creativity. Her suburbs did not grow organically, and therefore lacked the cultural sedimentation that could invigorate her writing.

Khlifi dedicates an important part of her narrative to lampooning the *petit bourgeois* suburbs where she lives. Her narrative about the suburban inhabitants is infused with a strong satirical tone. In these wealthy suburbs, we are told, women are French 'jusqu'au bout des ongles', and one is always subject to 'des *merci* et des *pardon* et des r jamais roulés' (Khlifi, 2008: 131–32). Curiously, here the narrator writing in French finds other people's use of it laughable and out of context. This might be due to her bourgeois guilt, which I will address in more detail later in the chapter. Besides the people themselves, the architecture of these suburbs reveals unhealthy symptoms of introversion and amnesia. The narrator's depiction of the architecture of her suburbs relies on an arsenal of dystopian imagery in which the negation of the cultural takes centre stage. For example:

> Dehors rien ne rappelle rien et le pouls est faible. Tout est pierre, tout est construction, tout est luxe. Ma cité n'a pas de théâtre, ni de cinéma, ni de galeries d'art, ni de cimetières d'ailleurs. L'amnésie précède parfois la constitution même du souvenir. On ne peut rendre une âme que l'on ne s'est pas encore procurée […] D'ailleurs, [ma cité] vient à peine d'avoir des rues. Des rues dont les noms renvoient à ses nouvelles républiques nées il y a quelque peu, à l'ère de l'écologique et du tout humanitaire. Aucun morceau d'histoire n'est passé par là. Aucun évènement, aucune

manifestation. Aucune atmosphère dans l'air, aucune magie, aucun rappel, aucun renvoi. Même le ciel n'y est presque pas. Il faut le chercher d'une élévation de mur une autre. (Khlifi, 2008: 129)

The list of negations is too long to be reproduced in full here. This sombre image of Tunisian suburbia reflects the economic rise of upper middle-class city dwellers, whose relationship with space is extremely individualistic. The obvious lack of space-planning and place-making in these suburbs is at odds with the orderliness that is generally associated with the suburbs in the North American context. This is most likely due to the spread of corruption among public officials. The narrator already hinted at this when she presented her suburbs as the product of a hijacked project of *dégourbification*. Built for and by business-minded petit bourgeois, the *cité* provides no meaningful public spaces and therefore no possibilities for community building. It is this extreme isolation that causes the narrator flee the suburbs for downtown Tunis in order to perform the *flâneries* necessary for her sanity and her creativity.

The daily spectacle unfolding on the avenue Habib Bourguiba provides the narrator with the material she needs to develop her writing, and with the energy she needs to reconnect with her city. The Avenue, with its outdoor cafés, wide sidewalks and the large steps of some of its buildings, provides an open space for people-watching and for personal performances of subjectivity. Pedestrians are able to showcase their difference, which would have otherwise been crushed, either by the dull rhythms of suburbia or by the demands of urban working-class life. The narrator celebrates the Avenue's theatricality:

[C]'est là où on peut encore avoir l'illusion d'appartenir à une autre époque, d'avoir un autre âge, une autre conscience. C'est là où on se permet encore le plus d'être saoul dans la rue, d'être fou quand on veut, putain et respectée, ou encore, libre comme un clochard. On exagère son maquillage, son extravagance, sa misère ou son esprit dérange. (Khlifi, 2008: 62)

The Avenue creates an atmosphere of enchantment in which morality is quieted and ideologies mix. The narrator credits the Avenue's rich history for this power of fabulation. Knowing that this power emanates from the palimpsestic nature of the Avenue itself, the narrator tries to engage with the old and new monuments that house it.

She enters into conversation with two colonial monuments, the Municipal Theatre, an Art Nouveau building dating back to 1901, and Saint-Vincent-de-Paul, a Catholic cathedral built in 1897. The narrator constructs this colonial heritage as a haunted space, 'un peu comme les demeures qu'on ne revisite plus dès que meurent le dernier des parents' (Khlifi, 2008: 42). Both buildings are described as mostly silent; however, the narrator believes that each possesses an enduring prophetic power. She feels the power of the message in the tolling of the cathedral bells and in the rare sound of artists' footsteps on the theatre's stage. She does not tell us what these prophecies are about, but we can assume that the spectre haunting these two buildings is that of 'une France d'autrefois' (Khlifi, 2008: 43). A France that came, saw, conquered, but eventually left. This spectre, much like the spirit of Shelley's Ozymandias, is there to warn against the changing currents of history. Could this be a daring allusion to Ben Ali's regime? I think this reading is valid, especially if we connect it to the narrator's conversation with the newer monuments.

The newer monuments that she converses with are the statue of Ibn Khaldun erected by Bourguiba in 1978 to replace the colonial site of the Unknown Soldier, and the clock tower commissioned by Ben Ali to replace Bourguiba's equine statue. While this national history of violent erasures is not explicitly mentioned in the text, the narrator does her best to underscore the regime's strong presence on the Avenue. For example, the statue of Ibn Khaldun reading his *Muqaddimah* makes her lament the passing of 'le temps des prolégomènes' and the spread of 'mutisme' in these 'temps durs' (Khlifi, 2008: 43). She then starts wondering about the meaning of 'temps durs' for someone with her class privilege. Moreover, the narrator interprets the clock tower, which used to be called 'Horloge 7 Novembre'[4] as a symbol of resignation to time (Khlifi, 2008: 46). This vocabulary of silence, prophecies and hard times demonstrates that the narrator's *flâneries* in the capital awaken not just her senses but also her desire to be a political being.

La Goulette and Cosmopolitan Tunisia in *Un amour de tn*

In a paper given at the 2015 Northeast Modern Languages Association (NeMLA) conference, Latiri classifies her text as a travel narrative, even though the title of the book classifies it as 'un carnet photographique

---

[4] 7 November 1987 is the day Ben Ali became president after his coup d'état against Bourguiba. The date became an essential part of Ben Ali's propaganda machine.

de retour au pays natal' (2015: n. pag.). This double labelling makes the reader aware of the narrator's in-betweenness and of the transitory nature of her presence in Tunisia. This in-betweenness endows the narrative with what Westphal (2007: 209) calls an 'allogeneous' focalization, or a focalization that is neither that of a local nor that of a foreigner. The narrator can no longer claim to be a local like Khlifi, not only because she emigrated a long time ago, but also because her native land has undergone an important metamorphosis since she left.

The 2011 uprising led to the collapse of several boundaries, especially those imposed on freedom of expression. The narrator's return visit is then partly motivated by a nostalgia for her Tunisian childhood and partly by a desire to experience a 'freer' Tunisia. These two intersecting desires affect the narrative structure in considerable ways. The text of *Un amour de tn* unfolds according to the logic of Proustian associative memory. The narrator's walks or taxi rides put her in contact with spaces, objects and people that take her back in time to memories in Tunis and other world cities. The photographs buttress the text by documenting some of the most important moments of this journey.

Unlike Khlifi, whose *flâneries* are a flight from the suburbs, Latiri performs her *flâneries* in the heart of the *banlieue nord*. Armed with a camera, the narrator revisits her newly liberated native land with the eyes of a curious expatriate. La Goulette is the main harbour of the capital Tunis. It has always attracted migrants from the southern Mediterranean, especially from Sicily. Up until the early days of independence, La Goulette was also home to a large Jewish community. However, the cosmopolitan character of this seaside suburb was severely damaged after independence, following waves of migrations, to Europe and Israel. The rise of anti-Semitism after the humiliating defeat of the Arab armies in the Six Day War of 1967 is often cited as a cause for this exodus; however, the strict economic policies of the newly independent Tunisia, as well as the gradual Arabization of the administration, are more likely to have been the main push factors. The narrator's *flâneries* are an attempt to uncover these different cultural layers that constitute La Goulette, in the hope of retrieving a certain Tunisois cosmopolitanism and of reconnecting with her 'amour de tn'.

The narrator's walks take her to a number of non-Islamic sacred spaces in La Goulette, which she enters not as a tourist or a community member, but as a woman of multiple intellectual and spiritual references. Her focus in these sacred spaces is more on the interiority of the building than on their outward architectural appearance. This perspective might be at odds with the traditional conceptualization of *flânerie*, in which the *flâneur* is more occupied with the streets and with anonymous passers-by than with the inside of the buildings he encounters on his walks. But for the narrator, the exploration of the interior of these 'othered' buildings is a necessary step to reconnect with her city. Her photographic documentation of all of these spaces always zooms in on one detail, for example an icon of the Virgin Mary, a wall of dedications to a saint or a rabbi's pulpit. Perhaps this kind of focus is the narrator's way to prove that there is life inside these buildings, that these spaces are not architectural oddities in the cityscape, but are an essential part of La Goulette.

While the narrator's visits to the churches of La Goulette are characterized by a sense of familiarity due to her childhood friendships with Christian girls, her visits to the synagogue are marked by a sense of wonder and a desire for knowledge. The narrator confesses never having gone to the synagogue until she became interested in Tunisian 'minorities' (Latiri, 2013: 106). The synagogue soon evolves from a mere object of academic study to a space where she can share her spirituality with Tunisians of different faiths. She remembers that during her first visit, 'les juifs de La Goulette ont récité le Kaddish des morts' in honour of her father, who had just passed away (Latiri, 2013: 106). Entry into the synagogue also allows her to discover many affinities between Islamic and Tunisian culture. These similarities range from the argument against a female priesthood to the song of the Hilloula, that the narrator compares to 'la prière Allah Allah Allah' (Latiri, 2013: 8). Despite these similarities, the narrator is careful not to paint a utopian picture of La Goulette. She writes, hinting at the fact that the synagogue may not really be at ease in its environment, 'A La Goulette, la synagogue est discrète, il faut connaitre pour la retrouver ou bien vous y allez avec des amis' (Latiri, 2013: 105). Both the narrator and the rabbi try to mend this wounded relationship through a joint prayer for the narrator's family, to which the narrator adds a silent prayer for the 'amour de tn' (Latiri, 2013: 107). This symbolic gesture allows the narrator to conjure up the cosmopolitanism of her childhood and to bring it into the present.

The narrator walks the streets of La Goulette in search for this 'amour de tn' in encounters with strangers. This, too, is at odds with the traditional conceptualization of *flânerie* in which the *flâneur* simply observes the characters of his city. The narrator's street encounters are mostly very taciturn and very guarded. It is she who always initiates the conversation and pushes to know more about her interlocutor, but she is always met with resistance. She counts among the rejections a number of women who found her camera threatening and did not permit her to take pictures of their Italian-style apartment building (Latiri, 2013: 59), a taxi driver who did not want to talk politics (97) and a street vendor who accepted to be photographed but refused to make small talk (91).

Like Khlifi, Latiri expresses considerable interest in the figure of the street vendor. She dedicates a whole chapter to honouring this class of impoverished Tunisians and names it after Mohamed Bouazizi, the instigator of the Tunisian uprising. She observes the 'invasion' of the streets by fruit merchants, notes the customers' satisfaction with the low prices and recognizes the taxi drivers' anger over their loss of space (Latiri, 2013: 87). She even laments that the vendors do not know the value of their merchandise and their time (Latiri, 2013: 90). By positioning herself on the side of the street vendors, the narrator frames this urban scene of unregulated trade as a normal and legitimate pursuit of economic justice. It is necessary to mention, however, that after the uprising it became unclear who had inherited control of the parallel economy from Ben Ali's family. The Tunisian media has been talking about the emergence of new 'barons' whose relationship with the state and with the country's capitalist class remains unclear. We cannot really make any claims that these street vendors are building a counter-economy, at least not yet.

The narrator's pursuit of La Goulette's cosmopolitan past and her quest to showcase Tunisia's modern-day diversity stem from her belief in the fluidity of identity. The narrator knows that questioning the myth of the homogeneity of Tunisian society, a myth perpetrated by the post-independence nation state, makes her an easy target for Islamists and nationalists, especially in the transitional period in which Latiri was writing. To shield herself from any possible ideological attacks, the narrator builds a textual alliance with two widely respected Palestinian intellectuals: Mahmoud Darwish and Edward Said. Both Darwish and Said sought to dismantle the myth of fixed identities, while also being engaged in efforts of political resistance to colonialism and imperialism. Latiri uses their legacy to dismantle the widespread belief that fluid identities are necessarily an imperialist construct. She dedicates a chapter to each author and begins her book with two epigraphs gleaned from two of Darwish's poems. The first epigraph is from the poem 'Ṭibāq' [Antithesis], written in honour of Edward Said; the second is from a patriotic poem entitled 'Ana min Hunak' [I am From Over There]. The epigraphs celebrate the power of memory and multiple belongings in anticipation of their unfolding in the rest of the life narrative.

In her chapter 'Said سعيد', which is also the last chapter of this life narrative, Latiri quotes a sentence from his memoir, *Out of Place*, and translates it into Arabic and French, for a full multilingual experience. The quote reads, 'I occasionally experience myself as a cluster of flowing currents. I prefer this to the idea of a solid self, the identity to which so many attach so much significance' (Latiri, 2013: 113). Neither Said's name nor the title from which the quote is taken are mentioned beneath the quote, which shows the narrator's desire to assimilate Said's words. In classic Proustian fashion, the image of currents used by Said soon awakens a memory of a family gathering on the beach in La Goulette. The closing statement from the scene is pronounced by the narrator's mother: 'el mouja ma3adish ta5lit[5] la vague n'y arrive plus' (Latiri, 2013: 114). This statement marks the end of the book and hints at a certain failure. The reader is left wondering whether the narrator, with all the powerful currents flowing within her, has given up on her quest for the *amour de tn*.

The Francophone Question

Both Khlifi and Latiri were educated in French institutions. Khlifi studied in a Pères Blancs school, and Latiri considers French to be her 'first language' (2015: n. pag.). A French education in Tunisia is indicative not only of a considerable degree of financial ease, but also of a possible linguistic and cultural alienation from the rest of society. It is true that the rest of society, or the less privileged classes, continue to attend bilingual public schools, but this bilingualism has become increasingly criticized as a sham. Hatem Bourial, a francophone Tunisian journalist states that 'Jusqu'aux années 80, les Tunisiens étaient clairement bilingues. A condition bien-sûr qu'ils soient passés par l'école. Aujourd'hui, ils sont nombreux à être devenus bibègues tout en se targuant d'être de véritables arabophones' (2013: n. pag.). The late eighties marked Ben Ali's assent to power and the beginning of the process of 'structural adjustment' demanded by transnational monetary funds. The state's neglect of public services, especially in the non-coastal areas, took its toll on Tunisian public education. It led to the loss of French and the weakening even of Modern Standard Arabic (MSA). If you add this to the diglossia that characterizes Tunisian speech patterns, it becomes clear that Tunisian society is very much fragmented along class, regional and linguistic lines.

5 This statement is in the Tunisian vernacular and is transcribed in Chatspeak.

For Khlifi, her bourgeois and francophone upbringing is an endless source of guilt and confusion. She is extremely self-conscious about the way people perceive her *francophonie* and about the class privileges it connotes. Latiri, on the other hand, is more comfortable with her *francophonie* and more assertive of it, despite the identity problems that it caused her as a young woman. This comfort comes first from the fact that she no longer resides in Tunis and is therefore not subject to the same ideological demands as Khlifi. It also stems from her ability to manipulate her three languages for her own political and psychological benefit. Instead of battling or silencing the languages and dialects teeming within her (MSA, the vernacular and English), Latiri lets them invigorate her French text. The outcome is a translingual life narrative, marked with constant code-switching and punctuated with translations.

The French Language and Bourgeois Guilt in *Ce que Tunis ne m'a pas dit*

The narrator's internal tension is frequently exacerbated by her lover, who is from a forgotten village in the western part of Tunisia. The narrator describes her lover's native village as 'un de ces villages dont on n'entend pas trop parler, pas très loin des rares neiges que le journal télévisé traqué par des hivers exceptionnellement froids. Puis il faudra encore attendre longtemps avant que l'attention nationale ne se tourne de nouveau de ce côté-là' (Khlifi, 2008: 95). The lover himself is the son of a modest baker, or, as the narrator provocatively puts it, he is 'un petit-fils de Zola', who carries within him 'des restes de quelque nationalisme, de quelque panarabisme' (Khlifi, 2008: 98–90). The narrator looks at her lover with French literary eyes. He returns a nationalist and pan-Arabist gaze. The result is a very tense relationship that could easily be read as an allegory of the economic tension between coastal Tunisia and the interior of the country, and also between the francophone elite and the rest of society. It should not come as a surprise, then, when we see the narrator repeatedly comparing her interactions with her lover to boxing matches.

The two lovers often argue about Middle Eastern politics without either of them succeeding in understanding the other's position. Following the fall of Baghdad in 2003, and to the narrator's complete outrage, the lover began lamenting the fate of the Arabs and the former president Saddam Hussein (Khlifi, 2008: 88). The narrator remembers him screaming, 'Ils nous ont décapités' over the phone and tells us that her only answer to that was a gentle reminder that not so long ago, in a country much closer than Iraq, Muslims were beheading each other to little outrage (Khlifi, 2008: 87).[6] The narrator knows that it is a risky endeavour to engage in the 'deconstruction' of symbols and icons in times of war, but she finds self-victimization and hero-worship extremely revolting (Khlifi, 2008: 86). While she agrees with her lover about the arrogance of the United States in the Middle East, she refuses to wallow in what she considers the excessive 'sentimentality' of the Arab world (Khlifi, 2008: 89, 86). For the lover, this lack of sympathy with pan-Arabist causes can only be attributed to the narrator's francophone upbringing. He responds to her outrage with a hurtful accusation: 'J'ai le fardeau de Mohamed, moi, j'ai le fardeau de l'histoire. Toi, tu as peut-être celui de la géographie. Tu bouges dans l'espace, mais moi dans le temps. Honte à moi de t'aimer, fille de "Jeanne d'Arc" et des "Pères Blancs"' (Khlifi, 2008: 91).

Curiously, the lover uses Christian imagery (the prophet's burden/ cross) to express the personal responsibility he feels towards the 'Islamic nation'. We do not know if he does so on purpose to further ostracize the narrator, or if his rhetoric has been 'contaminated' by the very narrative with which he wants to imprison her. Later in the text, we see that the narrator has interiorized her lover's accusation. She draws a parallel between her suburbs and herself: 'Ma cité me ressemble. Elle n'a pas le fardeau de l'histoire. Elle ne bouge pas dans le temps. Elle n'a pas l'odeur de ces ancêtres et ne connait pas l'accent de ses grands-parents' (Khlifi, 2008: 130). This self-flagellation makes it clear that the narrator chooses to punish herself for her *francophonie* and for her economic privilege by being with this pan-Arabist man.

The lover fails to see that the narrator's *flâneries* testify to an acute awareness of the historical and geographical dimensions in which she circulates. These *flâneries* are motivated by the uneasy modernization and suburbanization of her *cité*. She flees the *cité* and heads to downtown Tunis to reconnect with the world in its diversity. Her world and her narrative of it are not populated by warlords like his, but by strangers, drunkards, actors, painters, thieves and herself. The narrator might feel burdened by her bourgeois guilt and defeated in her verbal sparring with this man, but her *flâneries* in Tunis and even in the suburbs demonstrate that, unlike him, she is on a serious quest to reconstruct her world and escape the dullness of suburban life.

---

6 This is in reference to the *décennie noire* in Algeria. The narrator never mentions Algeria by name.

Code-switching and Cosmopolitanism in *Un amour de tn*

Latiri considers herself to be part of a 'minority' in Tunisia for having French as her first language (2015: n. pag.). She speaks the Tunisian vernacular and can speak, read and write in MSA. Having lived in Lebanon and other Middle Eastern countries for a while, the author has also perfected 'le dialecte oriental' (Latiri, 2013: 15). Today, she lives in Great Britain, where she teaches cross-cultural literature at the University of Brighton. In *Un amour de tn*, the author writes in French, the only language in which she feels she can be creative (Latiri, 2015: n. pag.). Embedded within the French text are fragments in MSA, the vernacular and English. Sometimes, the Arabic fragments are transliterated and other times they are written in Arabic script. All English and Arabic fragments are 'reiterated' in French.

According to Gardner-Chloros and Weston (2015: 184), the technique of code-switching in written texts existed in the ancient world and in the Middle Ages. The birth of the nation state, however, seems to have imposed many obstacles on this free shuttling back and forth between languages. While code-switching continued to feature prominently in speech patterns, its use in literature and written texts became restricted for political and economic reasons. Modernist authors like Ezra Pound or James Joyce revived code-switching in order to achieve an effect of defamiliarization. Their use of this technique rarely mirrored real-life situations, however, and rarely came with a translation. As argued by Gardner-Chloros and Weston, the textual code-switching of Pound and Joyce cannot be said to emanate from a 'multicultural upbringing' since both of them 'only learned foreign languages later in life' (2015: 187).

For authors who bear the postcolonial burden and who 'come to writing' from an immigrant or cosmopolitan experience, code-switching is born out of very different political and aesthetic motivations. In their survey of postcolonial writers, Garner-Chloros and Weston note that postcolonial authors may use code-switching 'to get round the dilemma of either exclusively using the language of the former oppressor or using local languages, where [they] would risk limiting their readership and not being commercially viable' (2015: 187). This is not the case for Latiri, who considers French to be her first language and has explicitly stated that she is unable to write creatively in the local language. Latiri's class status and multicultural upbringing make her linguistic situation much more complex than that of the authors described by Gardner-Chloros and Weston.

Latiri chooses to get around this dilemma by questioning the relationship between French and France. Quoting Jacques Derrida's statement that 'languages don't belong', Latiri (2015: n. pag.) explains that code-switching is her way of proving that language is a living entity that transcends the nation state. Opponents of this Derridean view on language might say that such a perspective dehistoricizes the colonial spread of French, but this is definitely not the perspective that Latiri offers us in this narrative. The author is very self-conscious about her status and about her linguistic use. Her celebration of Arabic literature through extensive use of intertextuality and her appeal to Arabic script to fertilize her French text demonstrate her desire to disturb the supposed purity of the French language.

Latiri's code-switching also serves as a means to fight back against the exclusionary arabophone identity propagated by many politicians in post-uprising Tunisia. The debate over Tunisia's linguistic identity began after the 1956 post-independence Constitution declared Arabic the only official language of the country. It would resurface over the following decades in times of political crisis. According to Sayahi (2014: 52), up until 1999 the full Arabization of the public administration had been achieved only in the ministries of the interior and justice, but after a diplomatic crisis with France,[7] Ben Ali ordered the acceleration of Arabization in the other ministries. Sayahi (2014: 53) predicted that with the overthrow of the Ben Ali regime, the language issue would reappear again. Latiri (2015: n. pag.) confirms that 'it came back with a vengeance' after the uprising, especially during the drafting of the second Constitution and in the months leading up to the first democratic elections. Expressions like 'al-ḥuthāla al-frānkūfūniyya' [francophone trash] and ''aytām frānsā' [orphans of France] became widespread in the media. The targets were of course leftist-leaning bilingual Tunisian intellectuals, like Latiri. At the NeMLA conference, Latiri (2015: n. pag.) expressed her concern over the spread of such rhetoric:

> The three parties leading the Assembly[8] either through their leaders or through their representatives have all made strong statements on the linguistic usages of Tunisians, explicitly demonizing linguistic usages defined as 'alien' or 'impure,' stigmatizing both the Tunisian vernacular and French to enforce the construction of an Arabo-Islamic identity represented as the only 'real' Tunisian one.

7 France 2, a French state television channel, reported incriminating news about some members of Ben Ali's family (Sayahi, 2014: 52).
8 The Tunisian Constituent Assembly (2011–14).

Preserving code-switching in the written text allows Latiri to dismantle the myth of language purity and to call attention to the gap that exists between the reality of language use in Tunisia and the fantasy that some politicians want to impose. By asserting the coexistence of all these varieties in her text, Latiri fulfils an important component of her intellectual struggle, which is to highlight the fluidity of identity and to retrieve the cosmopolitan urbanism of her childhood.

Aesthetically speaking, the cohabitation of French, Arabic and English creates an effect of authenticity that fits the traditional generic requirements for autobiography. This effect of authenticity can be seen in the narrator's rendition of dialogues, but also, and perhaps more interestingly, in her rendition of her own thought processes. The following excerpt from the chapter 'Little Flower *Petite Fleur*' illustrates the narrator's use of code-switching perfectly:

> Je regarde la photo, les détails, l'expression, le beau visage. Je vois *flower* décliné trois fois sur le tee-shirt, je vois les fleurs sur les tongs, les orteils *bilhenna à la henna*, les orteils à droite se crispent un peu et répètent le mouvement des doigts dans le poing serré. *Flower* en anglais, *little flower*, le nom affectueux de sainte Thérèse de Lisieux dont une relique est conservée à l'église de la Goulette. C'est Sister Joan qui m'avait dit pray to little flower, *priez la petite fleur de Lisieux*, j'errais un peu, attendant E. qui tardait à venir, mon fils me dictait des lettres, papa quand est-ce-que tu viens, la mère n'y croyait pas trop, espérait même qu'il ne viendrait pas, trop compliqué tout ça à tn, les gens. (Latiri, 2013: 66–67)

The narrator uses English to transcribe a conversation she had with a Catholic nun in England, Tunisian Arabic to mimic the way her inner thoughts slip into different languages based on context (here the use of henna) and finally Chatspeak (the shortening of *Tunisie* to *tn*), which also figures in the title of the book. Her memories migrate between languages and dialects thus giving the reader a sense of what it is like to have multiple geographic and linguistic affiliations. Code-switching here also goes hand in hand with the content of the memories being disclosed. Just as the languages slip into each other, the narrator's memories generate each other.

The excerpt is sandwiched between two photographs taken by the narrator. The first is of a young Tunisian girl wearing a 'Flower' t-shirt and leaning against a white wall, and the second is of a church wall dedicated to Little Flower (Saint Therese de Lisieux). Associative Proustian memory connects the innocence of the young Tunisian girl and the French saint by way of photography. The two memories then conjure up scenes of family discord over the narrator's transgressive marriage to a British man, or her 'exogamy', as she calls it elsewhere in the narrative (Latiri, 2013: 21). The final effect is that of a swinging back and forth between multiple times, languages, cultures and religions—a mirroring of the narrator's life in La Goulette.

This chapter has studied the production of spatiality and subjectivity in the life writing of Kaouthar Khlifi and Dora Latiri. It focused on the conceptualization of Tunis from the point of view of francophone women intellectuals who are privileged enough to walk around the city as *flâneuses* and/or photographers. The Tunis produced in these narratives is fraught with contradictions, divided along class and regional lines, but still inspiring, diverse and constantly changing. *Ce que Tunis ne m'a pas dit* and *Un amour de tn* usher in a new trend of urban literature in the Tunisian literary scene. Highly focused on making the city visible and on stressing its cosmopolitan nature, these texts offer a fresh literary perspective on Tunis.

Bibliography

Abu-Lughod, Janet. 1987. The Islamic city—historic myth, Islamic essence, and contemporary relevance. *International Journal of Middle East Studies* 19(2): 155–76. http://www.jstor.org/stable/163352.

Bourial, Hatem. 2013. Notre perte du français a fait le lit de l'intégrisme. *Webdo*, 17 December. http://www.webdo.tn/2013/12/17/le-billet-de-hatem-bourial-notre-perte-du-francais-a-fait-le-lit-de-lintegrisme.

Carrera Suarez, Isabella. 2015. The stranger *flâneuse* and the aesthetics of pedestrianism. *Interventions: International Journal of Postcolonial Studies* 17(6): 853–65. http://www.tandfonline.com/doi/full/10.1080/1369801X.2014.998259.

Dana, Joseph. 2013. D.I.Y. urbanism and Cairo's public space revolution: Cairo is changing from the ground up. *Next City*, 11 February. https://nextcity.org/features/view/cairo-urbanist-revolution-tahrir.

D'Souza, Aruna and Tom McDonough. 2006. *The invisible flâneuse? Gender, public space, and visual culture in nineteenth-century Paris*. Manchester: Manchester University Press.

Elsheshtawy, Yasser. 2004. *Planning the Middle Eastern city: An urban kaleidoscope in a globalizing world*. London: Routledge.

Gardner-Chloros, Penelope and Daniel Weston. 2015. Code-switching and multilingualism in literature. *Language and Literature* 24(3): 182–93. doi:10.1177/0963947015585065.

Hartwiger, Alexander Greer. 2016. The postcolonial flâneur: *Open City* and the urban palimpsest. *Postcolonial Text* 11(1). https://www.postcolonial.org/index.php/pct/article/download/1970/1938.
Khlifi, Kaouthar. 2008. *Ce que Tunis ne m'a pas dit*. Tunis: Elyzad.
Latiri, Dora. 2013. *Un amour de tn: carnet photographique d'un retour au pays natal*. Tunis: Elyzad.
———. 2015. Post-revolution Tunisia: A travel narrative. Paper presented at the Northeast Modern Language Association Annual Meeting, Toronto, 30 April–3 May.
Minnaard, Liesbeth. 2013. The postcolonial flâneur: Ramsey Nasr's 'Antwerpse Stadsgedichten'. *Dutch Crossing* 37(1): 79–92.
Pollock, Griselda. 1988. Modernity and the spaces of femininity. In *Vision and difference: Femininity, feminism and the histories of art*, 50–90. New York: Routledge.
Rodaway, Paul. 1994. *Sensuous geographies: Body, sense, and place*. London: Routledge.
Sayahi, Lotfi. 2014. *Diglossia and language contact: Language variation and change in North Africa*. Cambridge: Cambridge University Press.
Simmel, Georg. 1969. The metropolis and mental life. In Richard Sennett, ed., *Classic essays on the culture of cities*, 47–60. New York: Appleton-Century-Crofts.
Westphal, Bertrand. 2007. *La Géocritique: réel, fiction, espace*. Paris: Minuit.
Wilson, Elisabeth. 1992. The invisible flâneur. *New Left Review* 1(191): 90–110. http://newleftreview.org/I/191/elizabeth-wilson-the-invisible-flaneur.
Wolff, Janet. 1985. The invisible flâneuse: Women and the literature of modernity. *Theory, Culture & Society* 2(3): 37–46.

2

City Speak

Nice through the Eyes of Jean Vigo, Jacques Demy and Emmanuel Roblès

Christa Jones

This chapter examines cinematographic and literary depictions of the Mediterranean city of Nice in Jean Vigo's classic documentary *A propos de Nice* (1930), Jacques Demy's *La Baie des anges* (1962) and Emmanuel Roblès's crime novel *La Remontée du fleuve* (1964). All three works depict Nice as capital-driven, cosmopolitan, glamorous, luxurious and full of life with its iconic Promenade des Anglais, its pebble beaches, Belle Époque palaces and bombastic hotels, such as the emblematic Negresco, the Hotel Régina (where Queen Victoria used to reside), the Majestic Eden Roc and the Westminster. Also known as Niça, Nissa and Nizza, Nice only became a part of France in 1860. Given its historical, geographical and cultural proximity to Italy, France's second largest Mediterranean city has always been at a crossroads of cultures and migrations. An international meeting point for wealthy jetsetters who took advantage of its proximity to Monaco and its famous casino, Nice became a symbol of a new international urbanism during the Belle Époque. In the late nineteenth and early twentieth century, Nice thrived on winter wellness tourism *avant la lettre*, mainly British and Russian aristocrats, until wealthy Americans made Nice one of their favourite destinations in the 1960s. The city continues to attract tourists and to inspire artists from all over the world. Over the years, it has been visited and immortalized by painters (Raoul Dufy, Henri Matisse, Marc Chagall, Max Beckmann, Yves Klein, Claude Gilli, Claude Pascal, Arman, Keith Sonnier, Cédric Teisseir, Jonathon Brown), photographers (Charles Nègre, Stéphane Steiner), sculptors (Niki de Saint Phalle, Frédéric Lanovsky and Jedrzei Cichosz) and performance artists (Élisabeth Morcellet, Ben, Pierre Pinoncelli and Jean Mas).

In this chapter, I will compare and contrast twentieth-century cinematographic and literary representations of Nice in selected works by Jean Vigo, Jacques Demy and Emmanuel Roblès.

A propos de Nice: A Social Cinema

Chronologically, Jean Vigo (1905–34) and film-makers of his generation, such as René Bresson, René Clair, Jean Cocteau, Jean Renoir and Jacques Tati, preceded Jacques Demy (1931–90) and other new wave film-makers of Demy's generation.[1] Vigo's silent black-and-white documentary *A propos de Nice* (co-directed with Boris Kaufman and shot on location in late 1929 through March 1930), was very well received and is considered a classic today. Its subtitle, 'point de vue documenté', underlines the directors' personal vision of Nice, a city that Vigo had never visited before starting work on his documentary. The director's vision of Nice appears somewhat outlandish, if not surrealist, in particular his caricatured portrayal of sunbathers that borders on the grotesque (Gomes, 1971: 209). Even though Vigo was not part of the surrealist movement, his films have been linked to surrealism (see Gomes, 1971; Grossman, 1973). In the 1920s and 1930s, Nice was a very cosmopolitan city that attracted many wealthy European aristocrats who came to enjoy the mild and sunny winter days. When Vigo presented his film on 14 June 1931 to an audience at the Vieux-Colombier theatre in Paris, he explained the meaning of the subtitle 'point de vue documenté', stressing the significance of this new, thought-provoking social cinema:

> Mais je désirerais vous entretenir d'un cinéma social plus défini, et dont je suis plus près: du documentaire social ou plus exactement du point de vue documenté [...] Ce documentaire exige que l'on prenne position [...]

---

1   Such film-makers include Claude Chabrol, Jean-Luc Godard, Louis Malle, Jacques Rivette, François Truffaut and Agnès Varda. Jean Vigo belongs to a generation of documentary film-makers that includes Luis Buñuel (whose *Chien andalou* he admired), Joris Ivens, Ester Shub and Mikhail Vertov. Tragically, Vigo died on 6 October 1935 at the age of 29 from septicemia, limiting his cinematic output to only four films: his very first short documentary, *A propos de Nice* (1930), *Taris ou la natation* (1931), *Zéro de conduite* (1933) and *L'Atalante* (1934). Regardless, Vigo's popularity and recognition as a key French film-maker remains intact in France today, as evidenced by the prestigious Prix Jean Vigo, created in his honour in 1951.

Dans ce film, par le truchement d'une ville dont les manifestations sont significatives, on assiste au procès d'un certain monde [...] les derniers soubresauts d'une société qui s'oublie jusqu'à vous donner la nausée et vous faire le complice d'une solution révolutionnaire. (Lherminier, 1985: 65–67)

And, indeed, Nice is the main protagonist in this 24-minute documentary that reveals the daily spectacle, reminiscent of the Commedia dell'arte, that the city has to offer both the mundane visitor and the *niçois*. Boris Kaufman explains the *point de vue documenté* technique as follows: 'The method was to take by surprise facts, actions, attitudes, expressions, and to stop shooting as soon as the subjects became conscious of being photographed' (1979: 78). In their scathingly satirical portrait of Nice, Vigo and Kaufman masterfully critique and unravel the hierarchical make-up of the individuals who pace up and down its legendary promenade, providing 'documentary evidence of the contrast between rich and poor' (Buss, 1988: 73) in the 1920s. Indeed, the camerawork highlights the discrepancy between obscenely rich vacationers, and the very poor inhabitants of Vieux-Nice (mostly Italian immigrants), the refined champagne or coffee-sipping foreign aristocrats and the working class (shoeshine boys, street sweepers, waiters). With his camerawork, Vigo uses satire to unmask and mock the idle aristocrats who indulge in sunbathing, strolling on the Prom', dancing, gambling, playing sports, wining and dining. He shows the busy working class who struggle to make ends meet and, finally, the poor who live in misery just a few metres away from the Prom' in Vieux-Nice. Vigo's technique of low-angle shots, close-ups (of faces, legs and other body parts) and constant juxtaposition, or 'segmented quotidian urban life, as it has been called (Trippe, 2011: 123), brilliantly reveals the city's contradictions: the hectic quotidian lifestyle of the working class continuously on the move and the leisurely, paced demeanour of the wealthy, who enjoy a thoroughly relaxing time at the beach, or are slumped in their chairs on the Prom' soaking in the Mediterranean sun.

Motion is a major theme of the film. While the disenfranchised are forced to run around incessantly to make a living, the rich and famous lead a decadent, 'm'as-tu vu?' lifestyle. They engage in a wide variety of sports activities, not because they must, but because they do not have to work. Vigo films moving pedestrians mainly, but also machines, athletes and animals, including trains, cars (limousines and race cars), water airplanes, regattas, tennis players, *pétanque* players and flocks of seagulls swooping over the Mediterranean seas, mimicking the moving crowd on the Prom'. The sequences of recreational sports suggest that this is a 'fun' city, but only for those with a lot of capital and who want to see and foremost *be seen*. Nice is a social meeting point for the rich and wealthy, both old and young, or the ill, the *poitrinaires*, who are there to indulge in hygienic baths and breathe the fresh sea air.

Vigo's documented point of view, or 'cinematic poem', as it has been called (Hooker, 1976: 252), that combines realist and surrealist imagery with *cinéma vérité*, presents a panorama, an authentic slice of life of Nice in the 1930s. The film opens with a series of fades, or *fondus*: an aerial view of the old port and of Nice, the Mediterranean Sea and the Promenade des Anglais, where we can see miniature people and cars moving. Interestingly, the first indoor sequence anticipates Jacques Demy's theme of gambling and combines travelling and speed. The camera shows a miniature train rolling followed by a close-up of a roulette table with miniature figurines—losers at the roulette table—that are swept away by the croupier's rake, suggesting the ephemeral nature of capital that can be reclaimed at any point. This is followed by alternating shots of the pebble beach, waves breaking on shore and palm trees, underlining the stunning beauty of the place. Vigo's nature sequence, which is accompanied by a more slowly paced musical tune, echoes with the peaceful and relaxing break taken by Demy's protagonists (Jean and Jackie) at the beach between their gambling sessions. Looking at the sunbathers, Demy's female protagonist Jackie expresses her contempt: 'Cet étalage de chair molle me soulève le cœur', as she struggles to walk straight on the pebbles in her high heels. That said, the combination of sea, sun and blue skies appear to somewhat soothe the pain of losing at the roulette table. In Vigo's short, the hellish madness at the casino parallels the frenzy outside through a series of alternating shots featuring artists painting their gigantic papier-mâché clown figures for the upcoming famous carnival, followed by an army of waiters hectically cleaning bistro tables, carrying bundles of beach umbrellas, preparing for yet another busy workday in the sun servicing the European aristocracy. Even the palm trees get a makeover for the rich and famous. These early-morning sequences of the working class are followed by sequences showing the great palaces: the Negresco and the Westminster. Finally, a hectic shot down at the pavement and then up at the people shows hordes of people busily walking up and down the Promenade to see and be seen. Then, we get to take a close look at those people. They are aristocrats, men and women, wearing hats and/or umbrellas, but also street cleaners and newspaper boys, sunglass vendors and beggars that are seen pestering the rich and famous. This is followed by another aerial shot of the Promenade des Anglais, which brilliantly shows the daily spectacle that unfolds here: a double row of seated vacationers who are watching pedestrians leisurely stroll up and down the Promenade, followed by bathers running into the water and sunbathers enjoying their own private spectacle. The spectacle continues with sequences of a regatta, a game of tennis that is watched with great interest, and a game of boules. Subsequent sequences of car races are followed by shots of limousines pulling up in front of the glitzy ritzy palaces, where they discharge their wealthy customers. Vigo's documentary point of view hints at the decadence of a certain milieu and the perverseness of a situation and a social milieu in which a beautiful place is occupied, used and fully invested and enjoyed by complete strangers, while the *niçois* appear reduced to servant status with only the annual carnival celebration providing temporary relief.

Apéritif time affords the vacationers (seated at the tables that were prepared for them earlier) the opportunity to take a closer look at their fellow vacationers. Some of the tourists appear ludicrous, such as one lady glaring particularly sternly into the eye of the camera, as she walks by, firmly clutching her umbrella, followed by a shot of a dog wrapped in a giant bow. Vigo uses anthropomorphism and animal metaphors to mock the individuals he shows: thus, a tall woman is compared to an ostrich and a sunbathing sailor's face suddenly turns black. Vigo's unflattering camerawork underlines the sluggishness of the rich and famous, mostly middle-aged vacationers slumped in their bistro chairs on the Promenade chit-chatting with one another, reading the newspaper, falling asleep while reading the paper, in one case pretending to read with the newspaper upside down—not even able to overcome their inertia to pay attention to the street musicians. The identical dress code of these wealthy vacationers suggest that they are interchangeable. These petty people, we are to conclude, are ultimately tediously unimportant—if only we could see them in the nude to detect a sign of individuality! Vigo's merciless camerawork highlights that the rich are mere mortals, imperfect human beings. Of course, the most famous shot in Vigo's film is that of a young and pretty, evidently very well-to-do woman sitting on the Promenade wearing different dresses until the camera suddenly shows her nude. The subsequent carnival sequences are interrupted by a funeral procession, suggesting that people can party all they want (and Vigo himself can be seen dancing on a parade float surrounded by pretty girls), one day they will have to die, too (including Vigo, who was ill and knew that his days were numbered).

The midpoint of the movie shows the afternoon with sunbathers and children playing ball in the water and yes—crocodiles on the beach, a surrealist scene hinting at the mad, carnival aspect of the city and the voracious, greedy animality of the vacationers. The general sense of disequilibrium is reinforced by a series of low-angle shots of buildings in the historic old town. After focusing mostly on the rich in the first half, Vigo shifts his focus to the working-class people, showing clotheslines hanging across narrow alleys in the old town and laundrywomen at work, men gambling and restaurant workers delivering *pissaladière* and *socca*, the street food specialties of Vieux-Nice. After showing some poor areas in the old town, refuse-filled gutters and a frightened alley cat staring at the camera, he makes a cut to show the rich and famous dining and dancing, before devoting the last third of his documentary to the carnival. The carnival, with its floats of oversized, made-up thick-lipped puppets and group of frantically dancing girls throwing flowers—the Battle of Flowers—is interrupted by shots of a funeral procession and the cemetery, again hinting at the futility of all this capital-driven, short-lived insanity. In Vigo's film, capital is symbolized by a panoramic view of the Promenade des Anglais, the casino, the aristocrats, their various leisure and sports activities, their food and drink, and the Palaces they occupy, while smoking factory towers reveal the exploitation of the working class who suffer to create an opulent lifestyle for the happy few. In Vigo's documentary, Nice and in particular the microcosm of the Prom' is a site of cultural and linguistic exchange that encourages transcultural dialogue, a space of mass exchanges of people and capital, mainly with Russia and Great Britain. Jacques Demy's film, on the other hand, centres on two individuals who aspire to be rich but have not yet succeeded. In his film, money (and the improved social status that comes with the acquisition of substantial capital) is the main incentive that inexorably draws Jacques Demy's protagonists to the roulette tables of the seaside towns of Enghien-les-Bains, Nice and Monaco.

The Addictive Allure of Gambling: Demy's *Bay of Angels*

While Vigo's documentary presents a fragmented view (or *tranche(s) de vie*, to borrow André Gide's terminology) of what could be considered a typical winter day in 1930s Nice, Demy's film takes us to 1960s France. *La Baie des anges* stars the handsome Claude Mann (playing Jean Fournier) and the beautiful Jeanne Moreau (Jacqueline Demaistre), who meet at the roulette table (they share a fascination with gambling) and gradually become lovers. Demy wrote the script in a fortnight, inspired by a visit to the casino in Cannes with Mag Bodard.[2] The film highlights the dangers of compulsive gambling, which are hammered home by the visual and musical theme of a spinning roulette wheel to the tune of the 'obsessively repeated' dramatic soundtrack of Michel Legrand (Jousse, 1989: 24). The dangerous allure of gambling is paralleled by the powerful sexual allure of a platinum blond bombshell, Jacqueline, who insists on being called 'Jackie'. During his casino visit, Demy had a strange feeling:

> L'idée du film *La Baie des Anges* est née d'une impression de casino où j'ai découvert une singulière collectivité, une foule absente, hagarde, possédée, et dont l'expression traduisait bien l'angoisse et la déchéance morale. Déchéance qui peut être rachetée par l'amour comme j'ai tenté de le montrer à travers un couple de joueurs qui cherche à s'entraider pour 'remonter à la surface. (2008: n. pag.)

The iconic Promenade des Anglais, which opens the film, provides an emblematic, decadent backdrop that sets the tone for the entire film. In the opening sequence, Jackie walks down the deserted promenade very early in the morning, starting on the Quai des Etats-Unis, near Vieux-Nice and the port area, and makes her way towards the casino, as the camera travels back along the famous seaside walk. A cut takes us back to the beginning of the story and introduces the other main character, Jean, as well as his co-worker Caron (Paul Guers), both of whom work diligently at a Parisian bank. A wall calendar in the office informs us that it is 6 August, a period when most French employees have left for summer vacation.

---

2 Demy related his frustration at being unable to secure funding to produce *Les Parapluies de Cherbourg* at the Cannes film festival: 'Pour produire "Les Parapluies," j'avais trouvé Mag Bodard, mais nous n'avions pas d'argent [...] Comme une blague, elle avait dit à Cannes "je vais vous emmener au casino, on va gagner de l'argent pour faire le film". C'était une boutade bien sûr, mais pour la première fois, j'ai mis les pieds dans un casino. Et ça m'a donné l'idée de "La Baie des Anges". Si bien qu'en rentrant à Paris, quand j'ai vu qu'on ne pouvait pas tourner "Les Parapluies de Cherbourg," j'ai écrit "La Baie des Anges," en quinze jours. Sur le souvenir de gens qui jouaient, des gens passionnés par les choses, embrigadés. Ça m'a plu et le film s'est fait très vite. Ce qui m'a permis de ne pas devenir fou en attendant de faire "Les Parapluies." Cela nous a permis aussi de réfléchir un peu plus, de travailler encore, et nous avons fait "Les Parapluies" l'année d'après, en 1963' (Ould Khelifa, 2008: 5–6).

The storyline is simple: Caron, a married man in his mid-thirties, introduces his younger, single co-worker Jean Fournier to gambling. Burned out by his job at the bank and frustrated that he barely makes enough money to make ends meet, Jean is astonished to learn that his co-worker Caron has been able to acquire a brand-new Citroën DS, a highly popular car in 1960s France. Caron explains that he purchased this gem after winning at a casino in Enghien-les-Bains, a spa resort north of Paris. Jean's decision to gamble is triggered by jealousy and greed. After some initial resistance, he agrees to accompany Caron to Enghien to try his luck at the roulette table. Jean quickly takes a liking to gambling after winning 500,000 francs, the equivalent of six months' salary, in less than an hour. As Caron and Jean leave the casino in Enghien, Jean notices Jackie for the first time. It becomes clear to all that Jackie, who is acting hysterically, has been evicted from the casino for cheating. Caron then tries to convince Jean to vacation on the Côte d'Azur, the French Riviera, because, he says, it boasts much more profitable casinos.

Paralleling Jackie's eviction from the casino, Jean is kicked out by his father, an honest and hardworking clockmaker, who considers gambling to be immoral and does not want to be held responsible for any debt contracted by his son. Jean decides to follow Caron's advice and heads south on the train to vacation in Nice. As soon as he arrives, Jean rents a room for two weeks in an inexpensive hotel located in Vieux-Nice and immediately asks the receptionist for directions to the Promenade and its casino. Like Vigo's documentary, much of Demy's footage was shot on the Promenade des Anglais (as well as at the casino, in Jean's hotel room and Monaco). The film depicts the juxtaposition of rich and poor—the crumbling, laundry-lined houses of Vieux-Nice, just a stone's throw away from the glitzy Promenade and the mundane world of gambling. The 'big question' that keeps the spectator watching is whether or not Jean will succeed in winning a fortune and earn a permanent place on the Prom'. It is at the casino in Nice that Jean finally has a chance to meet and talk to Jackie. After establishing eye contact and choosing the same numbers, they win big at the roulette table. Jackie tells him that she is a divorcee and has lost custody of her son. They become acquainted and Jean invites Jackie to a luxurious dinner on a terrace with champagne and a band:

[On the Promenade des Anglais]
Jean: Mais je vous invite.
Jackie: J'ai envie, enfin, si vous êtes d'accord avec moi, je voudrais, j'ai

envie de tout ce qu'il y a de mieux, avec une terrasse, un orchestre et du champagne.
[At the restaurant]
Jean: C'est une drôle d'idée.
Jackie: Voyons, ça ne vous arrive jamais?
Jean: A vrai dire tout ça est très nouveau pour moi. *Et je vais vous paraitre naif, mais je croyais même que cette existence n'existait plus* [...] *Que cette existence n'existait plus, vous m'avez compris, je veux dire, qui n'existait plus qu'au cinéma, par exemple, ou dans certains livres américains.*
Jackie: Quelle existence?
Jean: Celle que nous vivons, cet hôtel, cette terrasse, cet orchestre [...] Richesse comme on dit, et vous aussi.
Jackie: Moi? Moi je ressemble à un livre américain?
Jean: Un personnage de roman.
Jackie: C'est drôle ce que vous dites. J'avais jamais pensé à ça.

Both Vigo's and Demy's films expose and critique a decadent, capital-driven lifestyle that is accessible only to the happy few, the rich and famous, a lifestyle that appears so outlandish and blatantly antiquated that it must indeed be fictional—a character in a novel or a thing of the past, such as the Russian and British aristocrats vacationing in Nice in Vigo's documentary. In Demy's film, two worlds collide: Jean, the lower middle-class character who meets the former wife of a very wealthy manufacturer and mother of a three-year-old nicknamed Michou. Jackie repeatedly asks 'vous comprenez', because Jean really is very confused and in need of explanation. He does not understand this luxury, this world that Jackie inhabits; he needs her support and encouragement to make up for his lack of worldliness and he needs to be able to blend in to make her love him. Jean was never meant to vacation in Nice, nor should he have met and fallen head over heels in love with a 'loose' and immoral woman like Jackie, a character who comes across as shockingly emancipated for a pre-1968 film. The promising allure of beauty, capital and sex is the glue that holds this unlikely couple together, because both Jean and Jackie are drawn to luxury, money and sex. Even though Jackie purports not to care about money—'Le gain, l'argent ne signifient rien pour moi'—she is elated every time they win big at the roulette table. As suggested by the symbolism of their similar names (J and J), this is a symbiotic couple: Jean offers Jackie his intelligence and the expertise in probability theory she needs to select the right numbers and win, while Jackie provides the beauty, sexual allure and promise of love that Jean needs to motivate him to gamble and win. He knows that he can only win her if he is able to offer her the luxurious lifestyle and social standing she craves. Jackie's strength stems from her independence and from her ability to slip seamlessly between the world of the rich and the dispossessed. She tells Jean that she has repeatedly lost every penny she owned, but that she keeps on gambling all the same. Demy's female character mirrors the extremes that characterize Vieux-Nice and its nearby glorious Promenade: 'She's light and dark, glorious and abject, a charismatic mess of contradictions' (Rafferty, 2014: 16). Jean and Jackie's rollercoaster love affair is symbolized by their roulette addiction with its constant ups and downs of alternating wins and losses. After winning big in Nice, they go shopping in luxury boutiques, buy a convertible and drive to Monaco, where they check into one of the big palaces. When they gamble at the famous casino in Monaco, their luck turns and they lose everything. Reluctantly, Jean sells his convertible and they take the train back to Nice, since, as Jean puts it, it is the bay of angels that brings them luck. Jean writes a letter to his father asking for forgiveness and his father bails him out by sending him a money order. The ending suggests that Jean has learned an important life lesson and is about to resume his former lacklustre life. He intends to head back to Paris and earn an honest living at the bank. The inveterate gambler Jackie leaves Jean but he runs after her and wins her back: 'The film's happy ending springs up so suddenly that the roulette wheel is left spinning: significantly we never know whether Jackie wins or loses. Happiness too seems regulated by the enigmatic logic of mathematical probability, and can achieve only a transient status' (Henderson, 2002: n. pag.). The unexpected departure of Jean and Jackie, an unlikely and somewhat disappointing happy ending, suggests that Nice is but a misleading façade, a transitory mirage of opulence and sunshine that is incompatible with responsibility, irreproachable morals and honesty, the very qualities required by a bank clerk, and certainly for a clerk who might marry a divorcee with questionable values. The city of Nice as the epitome of a city through which capital flows lavishly, is only surpassed by its Mediterranean sister city Monaco. While redemption appears possible in Nice, Monaco is presented as an utterly ruthless capital machine that invites but also easily expels voyagers who lack the capital to earn a place in the principality.

The Return of Spirituality: Emmanuel Roblès's *La Remontée du fleuve*

Emmanuel Roblès's *La Remontée du fleuve* combines a whodunit with a romance built on a love triangle and a spiritual debate.[3] The novel recounts the story of a 28-year-old German teacher called André Gersaint, who arrives in Nice just after the carnival, following a chaotic journey that takes him through Stuttgart, Geneva and Marseille. Once he arrives in Nice, he starts working as a night guard in a paper warehouse, a job that is well below his qualifications. He occasionally meets up with old friends from college, Christiane Herbillon (an artist who has always been infatuated with him but is too shy to express her feelings) and Marc Josserand. Apart from his landlady and co-worker Arrighi, these are the only people he knows in Nice. Like Vigo's documentary, the novel is set in March, yet the city appears still wintery and gloomy. Rainy and inhospitable, it becomes synonymous with death and hopelessness:

> Il resterait à Nice puisque Nice était la ville-sépulcre, la ville-mausolée, conçue spécialement pour ceux qui n'espéraient plus rien. A moins de trente ans il [Gersaint] appartenait déjà à cette confrérie de larves, de spectres qui attendaient à Nice, dans le frileux soleil d'hiver, l'effacement définitif [...] l'engloutissement discret, solitaire, l'adieu-de-bon-ton avec le parapluie au poing ou la couverture écossaise sur les cuisses! (Roblès, 1966 [1964]: 84–85)

The cold, windiness and darkness reflect the inner turmoil of Gersaint, who suffers a crisis of faith after witnessing the death of a teenager following a tragic motorcycle accident in the French Alps.[4] The

---

3   Emmanuel Roblès (1914–95), the son of a mason and a dry-cleaner, friend of Mouloud Feraoun and Albert Camus, was born and raised in Oran, French Algeria, where he grew up speaking French and Spanish. A member of the Académie Goncourt since 1973, Roblès was a prolific novelist, playwright and poet. He is mostly known for his novels *Les Hauteurs de la ville* (Prix Fémina 1948), *Le Vésuve* (1961, set in Naples), *Saison violente* (1974), his play *Montserrat* (1954) and his poetry. Before becoming a writer, he was a schoolteacher, a journalist and translator. He also worked as a war correspondent during the Second World War, a profession that took him around the world and, later, he directed the literary series 'Méditerranée' at the prestigious Editions du Seuil (Pélégri, 1982: 13).

4   In an interview, Roblès explained that he carefully chose Nice for its authenticity as a location of his novel, in order to underline the contrast between the city of freedom and fun, and Gersaint's inner turmoil. Even Holberg's house exists and can be visited: 'Puisqu'il a fallu choisir un lieu précis, j'ai préféré Nice, non sans

gratuitous death of the student shakes Gersaint's faith in God to the core, as it casts a doubt over the possibility of redemption and an afterlife. Gersaint is an intelligent but also a hot-tempered young man. In an act of rebellion against his own religious upbringing, he decides to steal a gun from the warehouse. In the middle of the night, he shoots at a random person just off the Quai des Etats-Unis, near the port area in Nice, a notoriously bad corner ('sale coin', Roblès, 1966 [1964]: 115). After this senseless act, he ruminates that his deed has no importance whatsoever, given the nothingness that defines human existence: 'Duperie! La mort était vraiment la mort! [...] Quelle aurore? Quand tout en vérité n'était que—oui—ténèbres, tâtonnements, dans une horreur gluante ou pétaradaient d'assourdissants moteurs' (Roblès, 1966 [1964]: 56, 67). Still, he feels very guilty and cannot stop thinking about his crime. Gersaint becomes ill and is unable to leave his room for days. His passion is tempered by his rationality, the potential consequences of the shooting and the awareness of his own weakness and mortality. Nature reflects his state of mental instability: 'un vent de folie' hits the louvered shutters, and even when he walks outside, the ceiling of the sky becomes menacingly low (Roblès, 1966 [1964]: 64, 65). As he obsessively peruses the newspaper for an obituary, Gersaint discovers that the man he aimed at, a 45-year-old Dutch stockbroker called Carl Holberg, did not die but was merely wounded in the hip. Paranoid that everybody suspects that he is the criminal, Gersaint starts hallucinating and the Promenade des Anglais becomes particularly threatening to him:

> Il s'engagea sur la promenade et vit que sans erreur possible, c'était lui-même qui était couché sur toutes les chaises longues, sur tous les fauteuils, face à la mer, dans le tremblant soleil de midi, et tous ces Gersaint grotesques—plumes, foulards, boas, chapeaux tyroliens!—avaient les yeux vides, les yeux sans rayons de ceux qui ont perdu leur âme, perdue par inadvertance, insouciance, lâcheté! (Roblès, 1966 [1964]: 82–83)

After getting a grip on himself, Gersaint quits his night guard job to be closer to his victim. His new secretarial job takes him to the

avoir longuement pesé ce choix. J'y ai même passe—exprès—quelques semaines, juste avant de commencer à rédiger mon livre, pour me convaincre—entre autres choses—que ce décor convenait à mon thème, de préférence à Paris, New York ou Amsterdam. *C'est que Nice est en effet un lieu de vacances et de liberté, dont le seul nom est évocateur de fêtes scolaires, d'insouciance heureuse, de plaisir facile. Cela me procurait le contraste violent que je souhaitais avec l'obsession dans laquelle s'était enfermé Gersaint*' (Roblès, 1966 [1964]: 10; emphasis added).

wealthy residential area of Cimiez, to the very man he tried to kill. Gersaint's loss of faith eventually also leads him to a young woman called Françoise Dewoëvre (his employer's mistress), with whom he falls in love. Nice is the city of fate, as in Demy's film, where the two protagonists meet and make off together. As Françoise informs Gersaint, she quit her secretarial job in Paris to follow Holberg to Nice, not because of Holberg but because she anticipated the imminence of a life-changing encounter: 'J'étais certaine qu'à Nice m'attendait un événement inconnu, un grand bonheur ou un grand malheur' (Roblès, 1966 [1964]: 200). Holberg, s symbol of capital and power (and a member of a private gambling club where he had played poker right before the shooting), is but a means to obtain happiness and bliss for both Gersaint and Françoise, who start a secret love affair. Thus Holberg is victimized twice: first shot and then betrayed by his young mistress. The unlikely storyline and Holberg-Françoise-Gersaint love triangle have been criticized as 'du Dostoïevsky accéléré' (Estang, 1964: 5). On the other hand, Gersaint's mental turmoil, his impetuous conduct and passion for Françoise appear credible given his young age. According to Roblès, his novel is quintessentially 'Mediterranean' in spirit:

> Quant à *La Remontée du fleuve*, je crois en effet qu'il s'agit là d'un livre essentiellement méditerranéen si vous tenez compte de ce portrait de l'homme que je viens d'esquisser et cette dualité en lui: la passion et la mesure, le goût de la vie et l'obsession de la mort, l'adhésion au monde et le renoncement, ce flux et ce reflux que connaissent tous les hommes de soleil. (Depierris, 1967: 166)

Just as in *La Baie des anges*, where Jean's loss of innocence—that is, his magnetic pull to lust (Jackie) and luxuriousness (gambling)— can be seen as a 'metaphorical descent into hell', as Demy stated in an interview (Hill, 2008: 390–91), Gersaint's *ascent* to Holberg's mansion in Cimiez, a wealthy residential area situated in the hills overlooking Nice, can be interpreted as a spiritual ascent that promises the possibility of redemption, if not salvation. The mansion, with its large bay windows, is suffused with light and odours, translucent, full of precious glass bowls and filigreed objects. By now it is April, and trees and flowers are beginning to bloom everywhere. In May and June it is already summer. Holberg's yard has become a garden of Eden with its lush vegetation (myoporum shrubs, carnations, fuchsias, irises, walls covered with bougainvillea) and a swimming pool. The ethereal atmosphere is graced by the angelic Françoise and her luminous presence, as she emerges from the water, watched by Gersaint, who cannot but help thinking that she is *'belle comme la première femme au premier matin du monde!'* (Roblès, 1966 [1964]: 206). Gersaint's daily interactions with Holberg allow him to witness his employer's slow but steady recovery and unburdens him of some of his guilt. He even comes dangerously close to confessing his crime to Holberg on several occasions, and the visit of a police inspector puts him on edge. Finally, Gersaint resigns from his position and leaves Françoise to Holberg. However, Françoise confesses her love for Gersaint to Holberg and leaves to be with Gersaint. Gersaint and Françoise make love in his crummy apartment in the old town and plan to elope to southern Italy, now that there is no reason for them to stay in Nice. Before leaving town, Gersaint wants to see Holberg one more time, presumably to confess his crime. When they arrive at the mansion, they are greeted by the inspector and crying servants. Holberg's suicide note, which refers to a wound that is not healing (thus hinting at both his breakup with Françoise and his physical wound) implies that he suspected Gersaint all along. Ironically, it is Pietri, the inspector who interrogates him and declares Gersaint to be innocent, who summarizes the young man's lifelong dilemma: 'Vous êtes un homme sensible. Cette fois encore, vous avez été bouleversé. Et vous allez à présent vous torturer avec l'idée qu'on peut tuer un homme en lui tirant dessus, mais qu'on peut tout aussi sûrement le tuer en lui ôtant ce qui donne un sens à sa vie' (Roblès, 1966 [1964]: 245). Having finished off Holberg twice—physically and emotionally—Gersaint is now convinced that he has lost his soul and he finally confesses his crime to Françoise, who forgives him. As we have seen, *La Remontée du fleuve* at once opens and shuts the door to a metaphysical dimension, as Gersaint's gratuitous crime expresses his denial of the existence of a divine order.

To conclude, in all three works Nice is depicted as a city through which an abundance of capital flows, most evidently in the films of Demy and Vigo but also in Roblès's novel (via Holberg). The city functions as a pathway to a better life, a bridge to human fulfilment in the form of wealth and or love. The bridging aspect in all three works is symbolically conveyed by the emblematic Promenade des Anglais, a runway to human monetary success, human passion and moral depravity. This promise of wealth as well as happiness either rules out (in Demy's and Vigo's films) or clashes with a human need for redemption through spirituality (in Roblès's novel). In Demy's film, God and religion are never mentioned explicitly, yet the religious undercurrent—the sacred—is mimicked through the highly ceremonial, organized etiquette that surrounds gambling (Jousse, 1989: 25). In essence, the casino is Jackie's church. The casino, Vieux-Nice and its glamorous Promenade des Anglais take centre stage in Jacques Demy's *La Baie des anges*, which depicts the dangers of compulsive gambling. The tormented characters of both Demy's film and Roblès's novel hope to attain happiness through love and, in doing so, they downplay the spiritual dimension of human existence. As Roblès's Françoise admits in a conversation with Gersaint, 'Pour tout dire, je me moque bien que Dieu existe ou non depuis que je suis amoureuse!' (1966 [1964]: 201). Vigo's documentary also alludes to the problem of mortality and the afterlife, but quickly dismisses their importance, focusing instead of the city's party spirit, using the powerful imagery of the famous *carnaval* de Nice. All three works uncover different aspects of the city's tumultuous life, the worries, but foremost the *joie de vivre* of those who live in it. The carnival with its excessive character, its uncontrollable madness, recalls the riveting nature of gambling and the momentary insanity of Gersaint, who shoots a complete stranger in the street. Vigo's message is the same: everyone must die but that does not keep them from living their lives to the fullest.

Bibliography

Buss, Robin. 1988. *The French through their films*. New York: Ungar.
Demy, Jacques. 2008. *Jacques Demy [un album inédit de photos et de textes]*. Paris: Arte France Développement.
Depierris, Jean-Louis. 1967. *Entretiens avec Emmanuel Roblès*. Paris: Editions du Seuil.
Estang Luc. 1964. *La Remontée du fleuve* d'Emmanuel Roblès. *Le Figaro Littéraire* 935, 19 March: 5.
Gomes, Paulo Emílio Salles. 1971. *Jean Vigo*. Berkeley: University of California Press.
Grossman, Manuel L. 1973. Jean Vigo and the development of surrealist cinema. *Symposium: A Quarterly Journal in Modern Literatures* 27(2): 111–25. http://dx.doi.org/10.1080/00397709.1973.10733198.
Henderson, Lindsay. 2002. Demy, Jacques (1931–1990): La Baie des anges (1963). *Senses of Cinema: An Online Journal Devoted to the Serious and Eclectic Discussion of Cinema* 21. https://www.sensesofcinema.com/2018/cteq/bay-of-angels/.
Hill, Rodney. 2008. Demy monde: The new-wave films of Jacques Demy. *Quarterly Review of Film and Video* 25: 382–94. http://dx.doi.org/10.1080/10509200601093256.

Hooker, Charlotte S. 1976. Jean Vigo's *A propos de Nice*: Documentary film and cinematic poem. *Literary Film Quarterly* 4(3): 251–58.
Jousse, Thierry. 1989. Du côté de Nice: *La Baie des anges* de Jacques Demy. *Cahiers du Cinéma* 415: 24–25.
Kaufman, Boris. 1979. Jean Vigo's *A propos de Nice* by Boris Kaufman. In Lewis Jacob, ed., *The documentary tradition*, 77–79. New York: W.W. Norton and Company.
Lherminier, Pierre, ed. 1985. *Jean Vigo: œuvre de cinéma*. Paris: Editions Pierre Lherminier.
Ould Khelifa, Saïd. 2008. Rencontre avec Jacques Demy: propos recueillis par Saïd Ould Khelifa en novembre 1986. In *Jacques Demy [un album inédit de photos et de textes]*, 3–11. Paris: Arte France Développement.
Pélégri, Jean. 1982. Le Voyageur immobile. *Revue CELFAN: Emmanuel Roblès* 1(3): 12–14.
Rafferty, Terrence. 2014. Walking on sand. In *The essential Jacques Demy*, 16–21. Irvington: The Criterion Collection.
Roblès, Emmanuel. 1948. *Les Hauteurs de la ville*. Paris: Charlot.
———. 1954. *Montserrat*. Paris: Editions du Seuil.
———. 1961. *Le Vésuve*. Paris: Editions du Seuil.
———. 1966 [1964]. *La Remontée du fleuve*. Paris: Brodart et Taupin.
———. 1974. *Saison violente*. Paris: Editions du Seuil.
Trippe, Micah. 2011. The segmented quotidian made visible: Jean Vigo's *A propos de Nice*. In Camilla Perrone and Gabriele Manella, eds., *Everyday life in the segmented city*, 121–41. Bingley: Emerald.

Filmography

A propos de Nice. 1930. Dir. Jean Vigo. France: Pathé-Natan.
La Baie des anges. 1963. Dir. Jacques Demy. France/Monaco: Sud-Pacifique Films.

3

Moroccan Narratives of Dystopia

Representations of Tangier in Leïla Kilani's film *Sur la planche*

Marzia Caporale

In the course of the 12 centuries of its documented history, Morocco has been alternately subject to a series of foreign invasions (Romans, Vandals, Muslims), decades of colonial domination (France from 1912 to 1956), and internal political instability, which have routinely hampered the country's potential leadership in the area of the southern Mediterranean. After the years of unrest that followed independence from France in 1956, Morocco today is a constitutional monarchy striving to foster modernization through economic policies that will attract foreign investors to North African shores. A fluid society still seeking an equilibrium, contemporary Moroccan culture oscillates between adherence to its strong Arab/Muslim cultural heritage and a growing determination to embrace the Western world and its values. The dialectic tension between the local and the global and its effects on society are echoed in the intellectual discourse currently taking place in the country. In the case of cinema as an artistic representation of such a discourse, recent film trends have demonstrated the need to articulate a narrative of reflection on the important social and cultural changes that the country has undergone, particularly in the time frame spanning the death of King Hassan II (1999) to the present day.

The overwhelming majority of films produced in Morocco since the year 2000 have painted a portrait of a culture still struggling to define its identity as a modern nation. As Sandra Gayle Carter remarks in *What Moroccan Cinema? A Historical and Critical Study, 1956–2006*, 'once colonized, now negotiating the tightrope of tradition and modernity, Morocco remains the site of a rich traditional culture and history while simultaneously embracing modern Europe and a significant rule in power relations' (2009: 13). Similarly, critic Valérie Orlando observes that most contemporary Moroccan cities are 'ripe with contradictions that arise when modernity clashes with traditionalism, and the colonial past is molded into the globalized present' (2011: 73), a condition which provides fertile grounds for cinematic representation and aesthetic investigation. While the ongoing tension between nationalism and globalization is a phenomenon affecting most major urban centres in Morocco, the northern port city of Tangier, located on the Strait of Gibraltar and historically considered as a principal gateway to the Mediterranean, is particularly exemplary of the dualities that lie beneath the surface of Moroccan society. This ancient city, founded by the Phoenicians around 1450 BC, reproduces within its microstructure the struggles of the country as a whole and duplicates within its perimeter the larger scale tension created by the cohabitation of Arab and Western Culture. In this sense, Tangier can be viewed as a *mise-en-abîme* of Morocco itself, its sociocultural and economic foundation inlaid with multifaceted realities that juxtapose paralysis and economic opportunity, inhibition of freedom of expression and sexual liberation.

A populous urban centre of almost a million people, Tangier boasts a particularly rich and diverse heritage by virtue of the many conquests that have distinguished its past.[1] Its multifaceted history and cosmopolitan make-up have excited the artistic imagination of many Western intellectuals, particularly in the twentieth century. Tennessee Williams, Paul Bowles, Roland Barthes, Jean Genet and other francophone and anglophone writers sojourned in the city and found artistic inspiration in Tangier's cultural vibrancy and openness. Additionally, in the course of the century, the city's long history of legitimate and illegitimate international trafficking supplied Western film-makers with a backdrop

---

1 Over the centuries, Tangier has been subject to several occupiers with political and commercial interests in the Mediterranean. A trading post for the Carthaginians, Tangier was later allied with the Romans and, after the fall of the empire, was abandoned to predators of different origins (Vandals, Byzantines, Arabs). Portuguese occupation of the town in 1471 gave Tangier a more European character, further enhanced by the subsequent British occupation. During the First and Second World Wars, all the major European powers, Great Britain, France, Spain and Germany, fought for control of the city, a source of worry for the remainder of the country which considered Tangier and its International Zone in particular a land of sin, infested by infidels. For an in-depth account of the city's history, see Landau (1953) and Graham (1931).

for successful spy films, from the 1948 American crime story *The Woman from Tangier* to the 1987 James Bond instalment *The Living Daylights*.[2] Conversely, recent cinematic production by Moroccan-born film-makers has set aside the mythical lure of the city, privileging a social realist approach to cinema and focusing on social issues such as economic inequalities, gender disparities, emigration and other controversial subjects.[3]

In 1995 director Jilali Ferhati wrote and directed *Chevaux de fortune* [Make-believe Horses], a film that recounts the stories of a group of Moroccans in Tangier who share the aspiration of crossing the Mediterranean to reach Europe, a geographically close yet hard-to-access land for most migrants. Tangier as the hypotext for a socially relevant filmic narrative resurfaces just a few years later in 2002, in the award winning documentary *Tanger, le rêve des brûleurs* by Moroccan director Leïla Kilani.[4] The film chronicles the hopes and dreams of the many Africans (*les brûleurs*) who reach the port of Tangier to await their chance at a better life on the European continent. In a video interview given at 'La quinzaine des réalisateurs' at the Cannes Film Festival in 2011, Kilani retraces the genesis of the documentary and explains that, while she was filming *Les brûleurs* at night near the seaport in Tangier, she was struck by the image of hordes of women routinely coming and going to and from their shift work in the same area. The visual impact of this large group of individuals, whom she describes as 'une armée en marche', provided her with the inspiration for her first feature film, *Sur la planche* [On the Edge], which was

2   The city's reputation as a site for criminal activities of different kinds was already widespread in the Middle Ages, when Tangier was considered to be 'a city of madness and illusory vanities, liable to seduce the stoutest virtues and mislead the firmest foot measuring its steps through the alleys of depravity'. See Finlayson (1992: 25).

3   Roy Armes notes that the dominant trend in Moroccan and in Maghrebi cinema has been 'realist drama treating some important social issue or other, punctuated in each decade by a handful of films that adopt a more experimental approach' (2009: 7). He further observes that despite censorship constraints, 'filmmakers have shown an admirable willingness to explore previously taboo subjects whenever the opportunity has arisen'.

4   Kilani was born in Casablanca in 1970. She studied economics in Paris, where she received a Master's degree in Mediterranean history and civilization. After preparing her thesis at the École des hautes études en sciences sociales, Kilani worked as a journalist before embarking on her activity as a documentary and film director.

selected for the Cannes Film Festival in 2011 (in the Un certain regard section) (Kilani, 2015: n. pag.).[5]

The film, shot in Moroccan Arabic and distributed in the European and American markets with subtitles, features Badia, a restless 20-year-old who, along with her friend Imane, moves north to Tangier from the province of Casablanca in search of a better life in a cosmopolitan city where employment opportunities seem to abound. Her disillusionment and the dystopic nature of life in Tangier, however, are revealed from the opening scenes of the film, which portray Badia hard at work as 'fille crevette', one of hundreds of female 'shrimp peelers' who spend their days in slave-like conditions for only a few dirhams. Due to her disadvantaged socio-economic status and her presumed lack of education, which prevent her from attaining a more profitable and socially accepted job, Badia routinely resorts to seducing wealthy men and stealing from them in order to survive. A chance encounter with Nawal and Asma, two local higher-class 'filles textiles', alerts Badia and Imane to the possibility of joining the more respected and better-paid workforce of Tangier's seaport Free Zone, where European and other Western companies have established their factories.[6]

Kilani chose Tangier as a paradigmatic representation of an urban space regulated by an inflexible hegemonic structure that relegates weaker social subjects (particularly impoverished and less educated women) to a subaltern role. The aporia between the promising presence of foreign investors on Tangier's soil and the harsh everyday reality that limits access to better employment sites, creates misleading expectations of success particularly for newcomers who flock to the city in search of the Promised Land. As the events narrated in the film denote, Moroccan society is structured according to the principles of a new exploitative capitalist economy which privileges profit over social justice. The almost inevitable unhappy ending, where Badia is arrested after she and Imane burgle an empty house to steal boxes of iPhones, confirms the illusory nature of the protagonist's dreams of achieving wealth and economic stability in the city. Through the skilful opposition of rapid movement and still scenes, darkness and

---

5 All translations from the French are mine.

6 Kilani again explains that there exists a distinct hierarchy at the seaport between 'les ouvrières textiles et les ouvrières crevettes' [textile workers and shrimp workers]. In her film, she intertwines their story with that of a local girl gang of robbers: 'A partir de là, j'ai imaginé un film noir qui partait d'une matrice [... à] coloration naturaliste' (Kilani, 2015: n. pag.).

light, intense close-ups and panoramic views of the characters running tirelessly through the streets of Tangier, Kilani suggests that these bodies in motion are ultimately destined to fail in their endeavours to become part of a utopic space they had initially envisioned as attainable. Tangier, a potential economic paradise for young people who see in this port city a concrete prospect for social advancement and easy money-making, reveals itself as an impermeable and impenetrable site still plagued by injustice and corruption, where access to wealth and upward movement in the social hierarchy are still the privilege of a lucky few. Despite its strong social undertones, Kilani claims that *Sur la planche* is primarily a work of fiction which imagines the attempted rise and fall of two young women whose dream is to make fast money and live life to the fullest:

> L'esprit du film est ici résumé: à la fois très documenté, constamment irrigué par le réel—ces filles qui quittent leur famille et leur région pour venir tenter leur chance à Tanger—et pourtant très stylisé, voire anti-naturaliste. Je ne prétends pas du tout à l'objectivité : *Sur la planche* n'est pas une fresque social. (2016: n. pag.)

> [The spirit of the film is summarized as follows: both well documented, constantly permeated by reality—young girls who leave their families and their region to come and try their luck in Tangier—and yet very minimalistic and even anti-naturalist. I do not claim at objectivity at all: *Sur la planche* is not a social fresco]

Indeed, the diegetic focus in the film is almost entirely centred on the main female character, Badia, and on her desire to experience 'le vertige', the head-spinning, adrenaline-infused sensation created by a fast-moving city, which ultimately causes her to embark on a downward spiral. *Sur la planche* opens on a close-up of Badia dressed in a white coat, later revealed to be her work attire. The scene frames her upper body with a frontal shot as she runs towards the camera and jumps rhythmically as if attempting to climb a wall, her face fading out of focus as she approaches. Simultaneously, the commentary of her own voice-off, provides a contextual explanations of her views on life. For Badia, the number one survival rule in a society that has no mercy on young women is lying. By distorting the truth, she justifies all her shady dealings, from stealing to prostitution:

> L'orgueil ment. Et a bien raison de le faire. Pourquoi? Mieux vaut être debout, tenu par son mensonge, qu'allongé, écrasé par la vérité des autres. Je ne vole pas: je me rembourse. Je cambriole pas, je récupère, [...] je ne me prostitue pas, je m'invite.

[Pride is a liar. And so he should be. Why? Better to stand up through lies than to be crushed down by the truth of others. I don't steal: I take my fair share. I don't burgle: I get even [...] I'm not a prostitute. I invite myself]

Following this short yet revealing preamble, the narrative begins by proleptically unveiling the end of the story. In a fast-moving and visually fragmented scene that depicts the dark interior of a home, the spectator witnesses Badia scrubbing herself in a shower prior to being arrested and taken into custody by the local police. The segment is constructed through a series of confused visual fragments which leave the spectator unable to decode and contextualize the events taking place. The camera is positioned uncomfortably close to the body parts Badia is attempting to clean, then follows her down the dark hallway and into the police van that takes her into custody, eventually providing the spectator with a wider-angle frame, filmed from inside the van, to include partial shots of a small group of bystanders which include Badia's accomplices, Imane, Nawal and Asma.

The remainder of the film's storyline is a flashback reconstructing the events leading up to the pivotal moment of the arrest. The sequence following the opening scene rewinds the diegesis to a few weeks earlier, capturing Badia and Imane mechanically performing the task of peeling shrimp in one of the many factories located in the port of Tangier. The camera, situated high above the peeling stations, frames the multiple rows of seemingly identical working girls performing the same action under a centrally positioned blinding neon light. The scene paints a disturbingly real picture of a shapeless mass of chain workers whose individuality has been erased by the identical bright white uniforms (coat, cap, mask) they are obliged to wear. The gaze of the camera then zooms in on Badia and on her nervous mechanical movements, her body representing just an insignificantly small piece in the wide-scale mechanism of shrimp peeling and production. The bright artificial lights which nullify any distinction between night and day, along with the girls' all-white attire, evokes the sterility and unwelcoming nature of such an environment, where people are disposable members of a work force with no dignity and no identity, the human correlative of the shrimp they are diligently peeling.[7]

[7] Director of photography Eric Devin explains that they wanted to faithfully recreate the working conditions of the *filles crevettes* forced to spend countless hours in freezing temperatures, the pungent odour of fish and ammonia seeping into their skin. Since the actual factories did not allow the film crew to shoot inside

In this all-female universe where a person's worth is measured by how many kilos of shrimp she can peel in a set amount of time, the young workers dream of bigger and better prospects. Badia's reality inside and outside the factory, however, is that of a *fille crevette* who, at the end of her shift, returns to a gloomily shabby apartment with dirty walls and barely any running water. The camera's intrusive gaze forces the spectator to sit by Badia's side as she consumes a more than modest meal in her spartan room, tormented by the building's unfriendly landlady, who regularly threatens to evict her for coming and going at all hours of the day and night. Kilani's camera, which alternates powerful still portraits to fast-paced scenes of rapid movement, reinforces the image of Badia as a precarious body in a series of transitional spaces—the shrimp factory, her temporary living quarters, or the dark streets of Tangier at night where daily chance encounters provide her with opportunities to experience the thrill of making quick cash.

The metamorphosis from poor yet respectable working girl to daring *criminelle* who can shrewdly navigate Tangier's perilous nocturnal space is depicted in a poignant transitional scene which takes place in Badia's apartment. Impregnated with the putrid smell of fish and ammonia from her all-day shift at the shrimp factory, Badia must first scrub the offensive odour off her body in order to turn into a potential seductress. The director's camera frames the character's rhythmic and anxiety-ridden movements through a series of extreme close-ups capturing details of body parts such as arms, neck, legs. No dialogue or voice-off commentary elucidates the actions in the scene, which is marked only by a frantic panting accompanied by the sound of the vegetable-soapy mixture rubbed violently against the skin. While Badia is attempting to transform her body into a sexual object that can seduce potential targets and enable her robberies, the camera's gaze undercuts such a stance by desexualizing the scene and removing any voyeuristic perspective from the narrative. Kilani's representation of the female body does not advocate the aesthetic theory connecting pleasure with the gaze elaborated by Laura Mulvey in her famed 1975 essay

---

their facilities, they duplicated the set in an empty hangar: 'Paradoxalement, ce décor gigantesque exigeait un travail de précision: avec la costumière et le chef décorateur, nous avons tout passé en revue des centaines de fois, de la blancheur des blouses à celle, clinique, des néons électriques' [Paradoxically, this gigantic décor demanded precision work: with the costume designer and interior designer, we reviewed everything hundreds of times, from the whiteness of the blouses to the clinical white of the electric neon lights] (Kilani, 2015: n. pag.).

'Visual Pleasure and narrative Cinema'. In enunciating her theory of the pleasure of looking in cinematic representation, Mulvey argues that what she defines as scopophilia 'arises from pleasure in using another person as an object of sexual stimulation through sight'. Mulvey further involves the spectator in such dynamics and adds:

> Pleasure, developed through narcissism and the constitution of the ego, comes from identification with the image seen. Thus, in film terms, one implies a separation of the erotic identity of the subject from the object on the screen (active scopophilia), the other demands identification of the ego with the object on the screen through the spectator's fascination with and recognition of his like. (1999: 836–37)

In Kilani's aesthetic vision, the female body is purposely void of any sexual fascination for the spectator. Badia's body in the bath scene is curled up in a ball, almost in a foetal position, largely hidden from sight and only offered to the spectator in pieces, a metaphorical representation of the character's fragmented life and her multiple identities—*fille crevette*, thief, prostitute or, simply, as she declares, a 'petite bricoleuse de l'urgence' [a grab-all-you-can enthusiast] who takes what she needs when she needs it. The desexualization of the body is further confirmed by the ensuing filmic sequence, where Badia and Imane play 'hooker' with a group of men they encounter at a local café. While it is contextually clear that Badia has sexual relations with one of the men, explicit sex scenes are purposely elided. The camera only registers the aftermath of the sexual act, filming Badia (always in the dark) as she leaves the bed and sneaks into the bathroom to clean her private parts before returning to the streets, her loot hidden in her bag.

Dressed in sober and rather boy-like attire (pants, man's shirt, leather jacket) with little or no make-up, Badia's character resists identification with the gender stereotype of the seductress as typically portrayed on the big screen. In this cinematic narrative, the director's camera shifts its focus from the body as a sexual object to the body as a social subject within the city space. Badia bounces obstinately from one location to another, not unlike the ball in a pinball machine, while she and Imane pursue their unlikely race towards affluence. Building on the illusion that she will soon become a textile worker in the Free Zone despite having no inside contact and no recommendation, Badia promises her friend more than she can deliver: 'une fois à la zone, je te fais entrer et je t'apprends le métier [...] En janvier, on y est. Plus rien à glander au vieux port' [Once I'm in the zone, I will get you in, I will teach you the trade. In January, it will be done. No more wasting our time at the old port].

Representations of Tangier

Through Badia's idiosyncratic perception of the space she inhabits, Kilani's visual discourse contrasts two conflictive images of the city of Tangier: the subjective, utopic space that exists in the protagonist's mind and the objective, dystopic reality represented by the constant setbacks that the character actually experiences in the city.

In an essay titled 'Of Other Spaces: Utopias and Heterotopias', Michel Foucault articulates a theory of space as a relational concept which can help elucidate the association between the social subject and the urban environment as articulated in Kilani's filmic discourse. In Foucault's words, human beings do not live inside a void, but rather inhabit 'a set of relations that delineates sites which are irreducible to one another and absolutely not superimposable to one another'. Following Foucault's argument, within this system of spaces lie utopias which he defines as a 'sites with no real place. They are sites that have a general relation of direct or inverted analogy with the real space of society. They present society itself in a perfected form or else society turned upside down, but in any case these utopias are fundamentally unreal spaces' (1984 [1967]: 46–49). In *Sur la planche*, this illusory yet concrete site which lies within the city's borders but is inaccessible to unqualified labour force is a European microcosm run, in Badia's words, by 'the Spanish', 'the English' and 'the Germans', among others. In the character's mind, these Western investors have created countless employment opportunities for locals and will soon be granting her and Imane a free pass to this bountiful land. As in many utopic spaces, the partaking of such abundance is limited by physical walls and gates with access monitored closely by local powers. A well-orchestrated security system makes the Free Zone physically unreachable and ensures that opportunities inside this protected area continue to be the privilege of only a few selected individuals. As in a foreign territory, entrance to the zone can only be granted to those who carry a passport and a badge which determines affiliation with a specific company.

A modern-day utopia, the Free Zone is a commercial venture developed in recent years by the local government in partnership with foreign investors, its structure mirroring a former utopic site of a similar name, the International Zone. After the Second World War, Tangier was divided into three sections for administrative and economic purposes: the French, the Spanish and the International Zone, each with its own rules regulating access. The latter was designed as an area which enjoyed special status and where investments could flow freely with very few limitations. Due to its policy of unrestricted commercial exchange, the Zone created a substantial outpouring of capital and provided a much-needed boost for the local economy.[8] Managed simultaneously by multiple European powers, including France, Britain, Spain, Portugal, and later even by the USA, the International Zone clearly represented a type of limbo, a non-space geographically located within the Moroccan territory but thriving on its own multinational identity, commercial profit and political neutrality. Throughout the nearly thirty years of its existence, the Zone flourished especially as a commercial model, leading the city of Tangier to regain a prominent role in the economy of the Mediterranean region.

After the period of great poverty which followed the abrogation of Tangier's special status as a free money market in 1952, in recent years the new Free Zone has encouraged foreign entrepreneurs to renew investment through regulations which grant companies a favourable taxation system and a low-cost labour force. A press release titled 'Tangier, the new Dubai' provides a clear definition of what the new Zone means for the local community today:

> The Tangier Exportation Free Zone is a protected free-trade environment where companies from around the world can operate tax-free. It's literally a massive project covering 345 hectares of land. It incorporates a vast container port at the junction of the biggest maritime routes in the world with the capacity to handle both cargo and passenger ships. (Direct Morocco, 2015: n. pag.)[9]

In *Sur la planche*, Kilani suggests that, while the new Free Zone is in itself a tangible space which provides numerous jobs to locals, its

---

8 The document regarding the status of the Tangier International Zone was signed in Paris on 18 December 1923. The articles of the statute outlined the neutrality of the Tangier Zone, which was not to be treated as a military establishment and was not to engage in or be the target of any act of war. The agreement further indicated the joint administration of all matters (legal, economic, military) within the Zone by the powers signatory of the act. The International Zone ceased to exist in its juridical form in 1952. For a copy of the Tangier Statute, see Graham (1931: 239–316).

9 The goals and strategies of this commercial endeavour are further explained by the website www.zonefranchetanger.com. As the site reports, 'Tanger Free Zone has several different activities: Automotive, aviation, textile, food, electronics, logistics, IT engineering and training industries… more than 500 companies of all sizes generated from foreign investment from Asia, the European Union, the United States, North Africa and the Middle East […]. Alongside companies established since its foundation, the industrial zone regularly welcomes new businesses attracted by its dynamics, its positioning and the opportunities it offers'.

strict internal organizational system has simultaneously transformed it into an unreachable utopia. Like the characters in the film, many potential workers are excluded from its grounds and therefore remain on the sidelines of the city's most profitable production enterprise. As French philosopher and space theorist Henri Lefebvre contends, 'social space is produced and reproduced with the forces of production (and with the relations of production'. Lefebvre further adds that 'Space is never produced in a way that a kilogram of sugar or a yard of cloth is produced [...] It is at once a precondition and a result of social superstructures' (1991: 85). This theory closely associates social space with the concept of production. The appropriation of space is inextricably linked to the assumption that a subject's role in society will be validated only when he/she becomes a legitimate part of the aforementioned mechanism and engages in viable productivity. Being outside production within the Zone in particular leads the subject (Badia) to be relegated to a marginal position in society, immobilized and forever trapped in the role of other. In this sense, Badia's constant movement throughout the city is a paradoxical representation of her otherness and social immobility, a visual sign that she is excluded from the one site she longs to access in order to be socially accepted.

The scene in which Badia enters the Zone clandestinely to meet her new accomplices Nawal and Asma is indicative of her condition of alienation in relation to a space to which she clearly does not belong. The segment is one of very few filmed in broad daylight. The natural soft white light of the clear skies creates a bold visual contrast with the blinding artificial light of Badia's working environment at the shrimp factory, and generates an even sharper opposition when juxtaposed to the darkness of the streets of Tangier at night. The camera follows the protagonist closely as she nervously enters the perimeter of the Zone and sneaks among the vans designed to take the textile workers to their individual factories. Representation of Badia's body in space indicates her condition of otherness. Despite her 'disguise', visually marked by a somewhat stylish black-and-white chequered jacket, Badia is clearly not a *fille textile*, as indicated by her orange sweater, the same one she typically wears under her white coat at the shrimp factory. On the verge of being unmasked by security personnel, Badia begins to run, frantically searching for a landmark that may direct her to the meeting point with the two girls with whom she had previously struck a money deal. The handheld camera constantly changes its filming angle from the back to the side to the front, to wider-angle shots that frame Badia's petite body within the vastness of the space in the Zone. While Badia ultimately manages to reach the location of her appointment without being caught, this experience proves to her that this utopic space is indeed out of her reach. The lies she tells Nawal and Asma (that she is indeed a textile girl and works nearby) are undercut by the visual portrayal of a lost and scared Badia who cannot find her bearings within the confines of this alien environment.

The progression of Tangier and of its Free Zone from utopic spaces to sites of disillusionment and dystopia advances the narrative towards a denouement which is inevitably tragic. Badia is ultimately unable to find her place inside the city space and become a fully functioning social body. Like her friend Imane, Badia cannot overcome her marginalization. Under such adverse conditions, the only viable solutions for survival are to be found on the streets of Tangier, where illegal prospects of earning fast money abound. When Nawal and Asma inform her of the opportunity to burglarize an empty villa and steal a large number of iPhones, Badia, after an initial refusal, decides to accept, swearing to a worried Imane that this will be their last illicit deal. The scene of Badia's final robbery, which diegetically reconnects the narrative to the opening of the film, is built on a crescendo of anxiety. While Nawal and Asma are safely on the lookout, ready to run away unscathed if things go amiss, Badia and Imane enter the premises. The camera shifts its focus from Badia, intent on transferring iPhones from their boxes to her bags, to Imane's paralysed face, as she becomes progressively aware that their enterprise is hopeless and that their fantasy of rising above their innate condition of poverty will never come to fruition. While Badia continues to steal and count, chanting that she will not bow down and that she is not a shrimp girl ('Moi je fais pas de courbettes, je suis pas une fille crevette'), Imane makes the drastic decision to pour gasoline on the floor and set the villa on fire. This act, previously agreed upon to erase their traces in case the mission needed to be aborted, also marks the end of their friendship and partnership. In a long silent scene shot in the bathroom, with Badia in the shower washing off the traces of gasoline from her clothes, the camera frames Imane's face, silently staring at her friend, tears streaming down her cheeks as she prepares to abandon her partner before the police arrive. Left alone in a burning building, Badia is rescued by the authorities only to be placed in the city's dystopic site and closed space *par excellence*—prison.

As the final sequences of the film confirm, Tangier and its Free Zone remain a utopic space for Badia and other women like her who do not possess the prerequisites to be a *fille textile*. A rough and unconventional beauty, poor and uneducated, with no prior experience in the field and no connection in Tangier, Badia is predestined to remain a subordinate social subject. The film demonstrates through the freefall of its protagonist that Tangier, a *mise-en-abîme* of Morocco itself, is still plagued by social immobility and a lack of economic growth, despite the flow of Western capital. The harsh portrayal of the city today, tormented by gross inequalities and few possibilities of advancement, contrasts sharply with its long history as a hegemonic power in the Mediterranean. While the presence of the new Free Zone indicates that a process of modernization and globalization is underway, the personal story of Badia and Imane's failure in *Sur la planche* suggests that this society is still regulated by inflexible vertical power structures that hamper true progress. Kilani's aesthetics of representation combine social awareness with her own artistic vision as an innovative auteure who draws upon multiple cinematic traditions ranging from documentary to social drama to crime fiction. The director uses her filmic narrative to weave a discourse which Touria Khannous defines as a 'site for subverting oppressive relationships' (2001: 48), where the city's unjust social hierarchies are scrutinized and exposed. At the same time, *Sur la planche* is the result of an original artistic endeavour in which reality and imagination interlace to explore the hopes and dreams of a new 'fast and furious' generation intent on living dangerously on the edge.

Bibliography

Armes, Roy. 2009. Cinemas of the Maghreb. *Black Camera* 1(1): 5–29.
Carter, Sandra Gayle. 2009. *What Moroccan cinema? A historical and critical study, 1956–2006*. Lanham: Lexington Books.
Finlayson, Iain. 1992. *Tangier: City of the dream*. London: Harper Collins.
Foucault, Michel. 1984 [1967]. Des espaces autres. Translated by Jay Miskoviec. *Architecture/Movement/Continuité* 5: 46–49.
Graham, Stuart. 1931. *The international city of Tangier*. Stanford: Stanford University Press.
Khannous, Touria. 2001. Realms of memory: Strategies of representation and postcolonial identity in North African women's cinema. *Journal X: A Journal of Culture and Criticism* 6(1): 47–61.
Kilani, Leïla. 2015. Portrait Leila Kilani 'Sur la Planche' (On the Edge) Quinzaine des Réalisateurs Directors fortnight Cannes 2011, 22 December. https://vimeo.com/35166924.
——. 2016. Extraits commentés: 'Sur la planche', par sa réalisatrice Leïla Kilani. *Télérama*, 5 January. http://www.telerama.fr/cinema/extraits-commentes-sur-la-planche-par-sa-realisatrice-leila-kilani,77632.php.

Landau, Rom. 1953. *Portrait of Tangier*. London: Robert Hale.
Lefebvre, Henri. 1991. *The production of space*. Translated by Donald Nicholson-Smith. Oxford: Blackwell.
Mulvey, Laura. 1999. Visual pleasure and narrative cinema. In Leo Braudy and Marshall Cohen, eds., *Film theory and criticism: Introductory readings*, 833–44. New York: Oxford University Press.
Orlando, Valérie. 2011. *Screening Morocco: Contemporary film in a changing society*. Athens: Ohio University Press.
Tangier, the new Dubai. 2015. *Webwire*, 20 December. http://www.webwire.com/ViewPressRel.asp?aId=23641.

Filmography

Sur la planche. 2011. Dir. Leïla Kilani. France: Epicentre Films.

4

Cultural Capitals in Crisis

Meditating on the Mediterranean and Memory between Paris and Athens in *La clarinette* by Vassilis Alexakis

Alison Rice

> Comment une identité culturelle peut-elle répondre, et de façon responsable—de soi, de l'autre et devant l'autre—à la double question du capital et de la capitale?
>
> Jacques Derrida, *L'Autre cap*

Building Bridges: *Paris–Athènes*

In his 2015 novel *La clarinette*, Greek-born francophone writer Vassilis Alexakis returns to his homeland to examine the economic crisis in detail.[1] He is concerned not only to understand the current climate in the Greek capital city, but also to create comparisons with the French metropolis where he has resided since the 1960s. In *La clarinette*,

---

1 The question of genre is complicated when it comes to Vassilis Alexakis's literary works. While his publications usually carry the designation of 'novel', they do not follow many of the conventions for this categorization. In *La clarinette*, the author reflects on this ambiguity in his work: 'J'ai toujours pensé que les récits autobiographiques comportaient autant de mensonges que les œuvres de fiction. C'est vrai des miens, en tout cas, que j'intitule romans pour la bonne raison que je mens tout le temps, comme dans la vie. Un mensonge transposé dans un livre n'est peut-être qu'à moitié faux puisqu'on l'a vraiment dit' (2015: 48). Due to the fact that his written work is composed of a great deal of autobiographical reflection, the proper name Alexakis, and the terms 'author' and 'narrator' overlap and in many cases can be employed interchangeably.

the award-winning author establishes convincing connections between Paris and Athens, demonstrating that both of these major European cities are at present characterized by considerable economic challenges, as well as by remarkably xenophobic attitudes.

This recent text is not the first in Alexakis's prolific corpus to focus on the two major cities that have marked the writer's itinerary. He unites these locations in the very title of *Paris-Athènes*, a novel containing rich reflections on the respective roles these places have played in his formation: 'J'avais décidée d'assumer mes deux identités, d'utiliser à tour de rôle les deux langues, de partager ma vie entre Paris et Athènes' (Alexakis, 1989: 263). As the first-person narrative voice affirms, the capitals are not as far from each other as one might think: 'Parfois j'ai l'impression qu'il n'y a aucune distance entre Athènes et Paris' (Alexakis, 1989: 284). Despite this professed proximity, the two urban centres have represented very different things for the author, particularly when he was just beginning to write: 'Mon principal objectif était bien entendu d'écrire un roman. Je ne savais pas si j'en étais capable, je n'avais aucune idée de roman en tête, mais j'avais hâte d'essayer. Paris me donnait la possibilité de le faire en toute liberté' (Alexakis, 1989: 231). Alexakis maintains that the environment he was becoming accustomed to as a young journalist in Paris allowed him the freedom he needed to write a novel. It was not only *the place* that spurred his creative energies, but also *the language*, for this idiom provided another means of expression: 'Le grec m'attendrissait, me rappelait qui j'étais. Le français me permettait de prendre plus facilement congé de la réalité, de m'égarer' (Alexakis, 1989: 263). As the narrative voice relates in a text composed over a dozen years later, *Les mots étrangers*, Alexakis never could have written in French if the language itself hadn't been welcoming: 'Je n'aurais pas pu écrire en français si la langue ne m'avait pas accepté tel que je suis' (2002: 295). According to this account, the only tongue in which the writer envisaged writing a novel was French, thanks to a certain acceptance that he found within it, thanks to an openness that Jacques Derrida evokes in his reflections on hospitality.

Despite the positive tenor of Alexakis's comments on Paris as a pad from which to launch a literary career, his works abound with serious critiques of the city, and *La clarinette* is no exception. In this recent publication, the narrator admits that he has grown tired of the French capital, and he entertains the possibility of leaving for good. He laments the fact that it has never been a very warm location, even in his early years when he was nonetheless inspired by his surroundings: 'Même à l'époque où j'étais heureux à Paris, je ne me faisais guère d'illusions sur la bienveillance de la ville' (Alexakis, 2015: 329). One of his interlocutors reminds him that Paris is different from the rest of France when it comes to friendly exchanges: 'J'ai posé la question à François, qui m'a fait remarquer que l'isolement des individus n'est aussi flagrant qu'à Paris: —En province en se parle davantage. Si tu vivais en Corse, tu tutoierais tout le monde' (Alexakis, 2015: 329). The intense solitude experienced by those who inhabit Paris is in no way simply analogous to that typically known in bustling urban centres; it is unique to this city and the attitude that reigns there: 'la capacité d'indifférence des Parisiens est incomparable' (Alexakis, 2015: 34). The text confirms that you cannot count on compassion when you find yourself in need in Paris, and indicates that this is why there are so many institutions that are designed to provide help:

> Quand on a besoin de réconfort à Paris, il vaut mieux s'adresser aux institutions plutôt qu'aux individus, aux hôpitaux, aux mairies, aux pompiers, au Secours catholique, à Emmaüs. Je connais des assistantes sociales très attentionnées et des infirmières absolument charmantes. Si nous disposons de tant d'associations humanitaires, c'est peut-être pour compenser l'indifférence des particuliers. (Alexakis, 2015: 329)

Alexakis recalls the prejudicial attitudes he encountered when he was first seeking a place to live in the French capital city. He relates that he was interested in an apartment near the Seine, but that the owner told him that he should head instead towards the outskirts of the city, or at least aim for the outer *arrondissements*. He indicates that this person was probably right to push him in that direction, for he has always lived at the city's periphery: 'c'est dire qu'en quarante ans de vie parisienne je n'ai pas réussi à me rapprocher vraiment du centre' (Alexakis, 2015: 11). The fact that this has not changed in the 40 years he has been in the capital does not mean that other things haven't. In fact, sentiments against foreigners have become noticeably worse, and Alexakis has observed first-hand the rise of the far right: 'La naissance du Front national en 1972 est passée à peu près inaperçue. J'ai noté toutefois que son slogan, "La France aux Français", semblait faire écho au mot d'ordre de la junte d'Athènes, "La Grèce aux Grecs chrétiens"' (2015: 200). The fact that anti-immigrant sentiment has escalated in recent years, and that foreign-born individuals and their offspring have been the victims of prejudicial treatment in ever-increasing numbers means that the author is curious and cautionary when he sees a younger traveller on a plane heading from Athens to Paris:

> Au premier rang, côté hublot, j'ai remarqué un jeune homme qui regardait le ciel d'un air songeur, préoccupé même. Allait-il chercher du travail à Paris? Était-il au courant des multiples garanties qu'il fallait présenter aux propriétaires pour obtenir un logement? Savait-il que le chômage était en augmentation constante en France aussi? Que les thèses de l'extrême droite se répandaient dans l'opinion? Que les groupes fascistes n'étaient pas moins résolus à Paris qu'à Athènes, qu'ils avaient notamment à leur actif le meurtre d'un étudiant du nom de Clément Méric? (2015: 182–83)

The author assumes that the young man hopes to improve his prospects by leaving Athens for Paris, but he is not convinced that this move will prove profitable, in any sense of the term.

Alexakis knows from observation the many challenges homeless individuals face in Paris, and in *La clarinette*, this theme comes back with urgency in Athens, as this metatextual reflection indicates: 'Étais-je en train d'établir la version grecque de ma vie parisienne? J'avais fréquenté à une époque La Moquette, je m'étais entretenu avec son public. Le fait est qu'il m'a paru indispensable d'aller à la rencontre des SDF athéniens' (2015: 288). This reference to a French text recalls the author's devotion to composing some of his books in French and others in Greek, and his concomitant commitment to translating these texts himself into the other tongue; this practice plays into a conscious desire to unite the two locations: 'Je me traduisais donc. Les mots grecs rendaient le paysage parisien plus familier, rapprochaient le Luxembourg du Jardin national d'Athènes. En me traduisant je gommais une frontière' (2015: 122). Illustrating the continuities between the cities is an important element of Alexakis's life and work, and part of this movement entails highlighting what is Greek in Paris, as well as what is French in Athens.

The strong French presence in the Greek capital city is underscored in the following passage, in which a trajectory on foot takes the first-person narrator past places that matter to him:

> La rue Didot que je prends d'habitude pour rentrer chez moi d'Exarkheia est en réalité un pont qui relie les deux parties de mon histoire: elle porte un nom français, mais c'est celui du célèbre imprimeur parisien qui publia le *Trésor de la langue grecque*. La maison de Magda se trouve dans cette rue, et aussi l'École française d'Athènes où j'ai puisé l'essentiel de la documentation dont j'avais besoin pour écrire en grec un roman sur l'epsilon de Delphes. (Alexakis, 2015: 118–19)

The bridge that Alexakis establishes here between the two parts of his personal history finds a parallel in the bridges that he regularly constructs in his texts between Paris and Athens, as well as between French and Greek culture, language, and people. The treasure that figures in the title cited above refers to a linguistic heritage that Alexakis is continually contemplating in his written work. Incorporating Greek words into his French publications is a crucial component of his idiosyncratic contributions to the Parisian literary scene. The narrator regularly calls attention to this in questions such as the following: '"Médusé" est un mot grec, bien sûr, comme "épopée" d'ailleurs. Aurais-je tendance à emprunter davantage un vocabulaire grec que ne le font en général mes confrères parisiens?' (Alexakis, 2015: 10). If Alexakis is motivated to comment on the presence of the Greek language in his French-language text, it is in part because of an awareness that he must not leave this part of himself behind: 'Les mots grecs me remettent en mémoire que le français n'est pas ma langue maternelle, ils me rappellent à l'ordre en quelque sorte' (2015: 10–11). His choice to move to France was not made on a personal whim, but was politically motivated, precipitated in 1968 by the need to escape the Greek military dictatorship: 'J'ai expliqué pourquoi je considérais comme un avantage le fait d'écrire en deux langues, pourquoi mes rapports avec le français avaient toujours été plus détendus qu'avec le grec, je me suis souvenu que ma machine à écrire croupissait sous ma table à l'époque de la dictature des colonels' (Alexakis, 2015: 146). Given this past, words in French do not carry the same weight as do words in Greek. But both languages serve as vehicles to communicate histories and stories at a time when they are desperately needed, in both European capital cities. Indeed, it becomes evident in *La clarinette* that the economic crisis that is by no means exclusive to Greece may likely stem from a larger crisis of cultural capital.

Cultural Capital: Repetition, Memory and Responsibility

Jacques Derrida turns his attention to cultural capital when he explores the work of Paul Valéry, this 'Européen de la Méditerranée gréco-romaine', in *L'autre cap*. Derrida insists that what endangers cultural capital is the vanishing ability to read, to listen and to hear, and, more importantly, to reread, to listen once more and to hear again; what is essential in our age is to be open to repetition and memory:

> Ce qui met le capital culturel en crise, c'est la disparition de ces hommes qui 'savaient lire: vertu qui est perdue', ces hommes qui 'savaient entendre et même écouter', qui 'savaient voir', 'relire', 'ré-entendre'

et 'revoir'—en un mot, ces hommes capables aussi de répétition et de mémoire, de répondre de et à ce qu'ils avaient une première fois entendu, vu, lu, su. (1991: 70)

It is not an accident that *La clarinette*, this timely text by Alexakis that homes in on the growing Greek economic crisis, begins with a personal account of a memory lapse. The title of the novel is precisely the word that slipped the author's mind for a period of time. While he was able to picture the instrument in question, the term escaped him in both his mother tongue and his adopted idiom. This occurrence provides an entry point for a novel that reconsiders how memory functions on a deeply personal level, as well as on other terrains that are at once national, European, francophone and Mediterranean.

La clarinette is in many respects an epistolary text; written in the second person, it is a missive destined for Alexakis's long-time friend and publisher, Jean-Marc Roberts. The printed words give off the impression that the author is saying them aloud to this dear acquaintance, this beloved being whose illness and death coincide with the creation of the work. A certain memory is effaced with this loss of life: 'Tu connaissais mes livres bien mieux que moi: tu me rappelais parfois que j'avais déjà raconté dans un autre de mes textes telle anecdote, telle scène' (Alexakis, 2015: 20). Roberts was more than a companion; he was also the writer's most faithful reader, and his insights into Alexakis's work—as well as his recollection of what has already appeared in print—will be missed after his passing. Alexakis nonetheless has no trouble admitting that he doesn't remember if he has already written about certain topics, for the memory that is of interest to him in his current projects is one that is much more long-term, and that concerns entities that extend far beyond himself and his œuvre.

His desire to learn about the history of a word of Greek origin that is unfortunately preponderant at present inspires the narrator of *La clarinette* to plunge into the larger history of Greece: 'j'ai songé au mot "xénophobie": de quand datait-il au juste? Figurait-il dans les textes classiques? Avait-il été forgé plus récemment? Je savais que le vocabulaire du grec ancien avait servi à la fabrication d'innombrables néologismes, imposés notamment par le progrès scientifique' (Alexakis, 2015: 116). It turns out that the term that translates into a 'fear of foreigners' was only added to the Greek dictionary relatively recently, a fact that indicates that such an attitude was foreign to his native country for centuries:

[I]l y a bien eu une époque où les étrangers étaient reçus avec des égards, où on leur offrait des cadeaux, où ils jouissaient de la plus haute des protections, celle de Zeus, le père des dieux, qui était surnommé l'Hospitalier. C'est le mot *xénos*, l'étranger, toujours en vigueur dans la langue d'aujourd'hui, et qui signifiait à l'origine 'l'hôte', qui m'a servi de guide dans cette recherche. *Xénophobie* n'est pas un mot ancien: il date selon le *Robert* de 1903, selon le dictionnaire grec de 1887. Les Athéniens accueillaient d'autant plus chaleureusement leurs hôtes qu'ils parlaient le grec et venaient d'une cité amie. Ils leur accordaient parfois le droit d'épouser une Athénienne, mais rarement la citoyenneté. (Alexakis, 2015: 119–20)

Alexakis's desire to discover if there is a precedent for inhospitable treatment of foreigners in his homeland is reminiscent of Derrida's attention to classical Greek reception of those from elsewhere in *De l'hospitalité*. In this text, Derrida draws from Émile Benveniste's study to emphasize the ways Socrates's words point to the rights that foreigners must have known in the Athenian legal system:

À Athènes, l'étranger avait des droits. Il se voyait reconnaître le droit d'avoir accès aux tribunaux, puisque Socrate en fait l'hypothèse [...] Il y a donc un droit des étrangers, un droit d'hospitalité pour les étrangers à Athènes. (1997: 25)

It is no accident that in Derrida's contemplation of this history of hospitality in Greece, he demonstrates special sensitivity to the linguistic challenges foreigners inevitably face, underscoring the complex relationship that exists between individuals from elsewhere and the language they encounter in formal settings such as the court system: '[l'étranger] doit demander l'hospitalité dans une langue qui par définition n'est pas la sienne' (1997: 21). Alexakis is equally attuned to the role language has played in determining the treatment of foreigners in Greece, observing that those of other origins have received differing welcomes according to their proficiency in the Greek tongue:

Les non-hellénophones, les barbares en somme, des gens modestes en général, étaient perçus non sans quelque réserve: on les interrogeait sur leurs projets, on examinait leurs papiers, des parchemins où figurait, en guise de photo, la description de leur personne. Au bout d'un mois, ils obtenaient le titre de métèque en s'acquittant d'une taxe, et pouvaient rester. C'est dire qu'ils jouissaient tout de même d'une certaine considération. (2015: 120)

The narrative voice insists here on the consideration that was habitually accorded even to those foreigners who hailed from humbler backgrounds. These precisions indicate that the path to acceptance for foreign-born individuals in ancient Athens wasn't easy, but that it wasn't overwhelmingly difficult either. In this respect, Athens was different from other Greek locations, and this openness set the city apart:

> L'attitude envers les étrangers variait cependant d'une cité à l'autre [...] Périclès oppose le libéralisme d'Athènes, 'ville ouverte à tous', à la sauvagerie de la cité lacédémonienne, qui procède à des expulsions d'étrangers. Si le mot *xénophobie* ne figure pas dans les vieux dictionnaires, le terme *xénilassia*, le bannissement des étrangers, est bien présent. (Alexakis, 2015: 120)

These contrasting historical mindsets with respect to the proper treatment of foreigners are especially pertinent at present, in light of the ever-growing number of migrants from a variety of origins who are arriving in Greece.

Those who possess Greek citizenship and reside in Greece today have conflicting views about the strangers in their midst. Many see foreigners as a burden: 'À côté de moi, Lazare et Daphné, une pianiste au chômage, discutaient vivement de l'impact de l'immigration sur l'économie grecque. Daphné soutenait le point de vue des gens de droite que les étrangers sont une charge' (Alexakis, 2015: 164). It may not be merely anecdotal that the Greek pianist who argues that immigrants represent an undue expense for her society is out of work and experiencing financial challenges on a personal level. *La clarinette* is a book that is deeply concerned with the current state of Greece, on all levels. Things are indeed grave, given this summary of the situation: 'Nous détenons tous les tristes records: nous sommes le pays de la zone euro le plus endetté, celui où la récession est la plus forte, où les salaires ont le plus baissé, où le chômage est le plus élevé et où le système de santé est le moins fiable' (Alexakis, 2015: 77). In other terms, people are suffering from widespread poverty in Greece and nobody outside of the country appears to be taking notice in a serious, thoughtful way:

> Le tiers de la population, trois millions et demi de personnes, vit en dessous du seuil de pauvreté. Il existe bien sûr des pays encore plus miséreux: le cas de la Grèce est cependant particulier dans la mesure où on la tient pour responsable de sa détresse. Elle est le seul pays pauvre que personne ne plaint. On l'accuse au contraire dans toutes les langues d'avoir eu la folie des grandeurs, d'avoir abusé des fonds européens, d'avoir trafiqué ses statistiques pour accéder à la zone euro. La Grèce n'a plus qu'un seul visage, celui de ses fautes. C'est un pays sans qualités, sans passé. L'opprobre international tend à persuader mes compatriotes qu'ils ont bien mérité les mesures d'austérité qui leur sont imposées par un gouvernement aux ordres des créanciers du pays. Le fait est qu'ils les

acceptent assez docilement. Il ne se passe rien en Grèce en ce moment. (Alexakis, 2015: 201–02)

It seems ironic that the land whose history is so often lauded should be critiqued with such intensity at present, and with such little attention to context. Focusing only on the faults of Greece, considering Greece to be uniquely at fault, goes hand in hand with a forgetting of many of its pasts, distant and more recent.

La clarinette reconsiders the history—and the heritage—of Greece through research and interviews conducted in Athens, as well as in Paris. The text relates a conversation between the author and an historian named Guy Burgel, whom he meets at the Hôtel de Ville in the heart of the French capital. In Burgel's opinion, Greece may be suffering from special treatment it received over the years from other members of the European Union:

> Il est persuadé que la Grèce a bénéficié d'un régime de faveur de la part de l'Union européenne en raison de son histoire et de sa position géographique: jusqu'à la chute du mur de Berlin, elle a été un avant-poste de l'Occident face au bloc communiste. Elle avait été acceptée au sein de l'Union en 1979, peu de temps après la chute des colonels, malgré les insuffisances de son développement, parce qu'il fallait bien consolider sa démocratie, et aussi parce que c'était la Grèce. (Alexakis, 2015: 331)

If it is helpful for most people to be reminded of these more recent events with respect to Greece and its evolving position within Europe, it practically goes without saying that what took place long ago needs to be revisited often: 'Le long passé de la Grèce oblige à un effort de mémoire constant. Les lieux sont chargés de souvenirs' (Alexakis, 2015: 179). When the narrator devotes himself to reflecting on his own temporary loss of memory at the outset of the book, wondering what exactly has happened when a specific term eludes him, when a word he knows well slips his mind, and in both of his languages, he plunges into contemplations of the ways memories work for those who reside far from their homelands: 'Les temps anciens occupent la même place dans l'esprit de mes compatriotes que le pays d'origine dans la mémoire des immigrés. La nostalgie fait partie de la culture nationale' (Alexakis, 2015: 179). In these evocative sentences, Alexakis likens the contemporary Greeks' relationship to ancient Greece to that of many of today's migrants to the native country they have had to leave behind: for those who are far from them, both places are familiar, but out of reach, and are frequently recalled and longed for by those who now inhabit another reality. When Derrida emphasizes the need to reread, listen once more, and to hear again, when he delineates the importance of remaining open to repetition and memory in *L'autre cap*, he also insists on what must follow such acts: an appropriate *response*. We must be prepared to *respond to* what we have heard, read, seen, and known, and we must *be responsible for* this as well. Derrida creates the expression 'responsible memory' (1992: 70) to refer to a form of remembering the past that has effects on the ways we behave and the values we embrace in the present. This is a form of memory that is attentive to 'human rights and international law' (1992: 52) at a time when many people are deprived of these rights and unable to defend themselves in the face of terrible injustice.

Harking back to the tradition of showing respect, generosity, and protection to foreigners who made their way to Greece in the ancient past, and especially to the practice of extending them hospitality, is a textual gesture in *La clarinette* that serves to underscore the contrasting horrors of present-day treatment of individuals from elsewhere in Alexakis's homeland. The text details the unlawful imprisonment of two dozen people in Athens in the following terms:

> Au commissariat de Kypséli, vingt-quatre personnes sont enfermées dans une cave qui est une sorte de tombeau, puisqu'il leur est défendu de sortir à l'extérieur, ne serait-ce que pour faire quelques pas, et que le local ne possède aucune fenêtre. La Grèce les a plongés dans une nuit perpétuelle. Il y a parmi eux trois Syriens qui ont droit théoriquement au statut de réfugiés politiques et un jeune Albanais qui a fait sa scolarité en Grèce et qui, bizarrement, est en instance d'expulsion. (Alexakis, 2015: 132)

These individuals are locked up without the slightest concern for their welfare. They are incarcerated without a chance to seek legal guidance or to defend themselves in any way. They are not even given an opportunity to tell their stories. And they are kept in the dark in more ways than one, since their windowless prison is one that they have no information about whatsoever, and their detainment stretches on indefinitely: 'On interne les étrangers sans la moindre décision de justice, sans chercher à connaître leur histoire, sans les informer de leurs droits, sans leur dire combien de temps durera leur calvaire, ni même s'il prendra fin un jour' (Alexakis, 2015: 132). Their rights are elided altogether; the responsible memory evoked by Derrida could not be further removed from this scenario: 'Ils sont enfermés pour dix-huit mois d'abord, mais ce délai peut être prolongé à l'infini. C'est dire que l'État grec se donne le temps d'oublier qu'ils existent' (Alexakis, 2015: 132). This deliberate forgetting finds an echo elsewhere:

Les pays d'accueil étant forcément ceux du Sud, on peut s'étonner que l'Europe ait confié aux moins fortunés de ses membres le soin de faire face à la misère du monde. Bruxelles n'ignore pas que les droits des immigrés sont bafoués en Grèce, mais elle fait comme si elle ne le savait pas, puisqu'elle finance ces casernes. (Alexakis, 2015: 132)

If Europe has failed to pay attention to this instance of injustice, that doesn't mean it has not taken a look at other human rights violations in Greece in recent years. The author's investigations and conversations lead him to learn of official condemnations for similar abuses:

J'ai vu Zoé, l'avocate, mais rapidement: elle m'a fourni un paquet de photocopies d'arrêts de la Cour européenne des droits de l'homme condamnant l'État grec pour les traitements dégradants infligés aux étrangers. Celui daté de 31 juillet 2012 concerne une famille d'Afghans, comprenant une mère enceinte de neuf mois et trois enfants en bas âge, qui fut arrêtée sur une embarcation de fortune en pleine mer Égée et conduite à Lesbos dans un camp 'insalubre au-delà de toute description', note l'arrêt. Il fournit néanmoins quelques renseignements sur ce lieu, où il n'y a qu'une latrine pour vingt personnes, une douche pour cinquante, où le droit de se promener dans la cour n'est accordé qu'aux mineurs et ne dure qu'un quart d'heure par jour, où sont enfermées mille deux cents personnes alors qu'il n'y a de place que pour six cents. La femme enceinte a pu accoucher à l'hôpital de l'île, mais les autorités grecques ont refusé d'enregistrer cette naissance, comme pour décliner toute responsabilité sur le sort de cet enfant. (Alexakis, 2015: 309)

The refusal to accept any responsibility in the case of this birth on Greek soil reflects a larger strategy that seeks to strongly dissuade the arrival of foreigners: 'La solution grecque pour décourager d'autres étrangers à passer la frontière consiste en somme à terroriser ceux qui l'ont déjà franchie' (Alexakis, 2015: 309). This stark declaration makes waves in a text that is clearly invested in promoting diversity and upholding fruitful interactions among various peoples whose Mediterranean crossings have led them to land on Greek shores.

Musical Mixings: Actively Tuning *La clarinette*

In *La clarinette*, the author describes a book signing in Athens during which a young woman came up to meet him. He noticed that she wore a sapphire around her neck and asked her about this piece of jewellery. She replied that she had purchased it in Egypt, where this particular stone is considered to be an attribute of truth. This information sparks the writer to think of a discussion he had with his editor about the Greek word for truth and the linguistic revelation it had brought about: 'Je venais de découvrir que le mot grec *alétheia,* vérité, est composé du *a* privatif et du *léthé,* l'oubli' (Alexakis, 2015: 49). The truth is what emerges when we remember.[2] In his analysis, the Greek word itself assures that the truth is impossible to forget. And, in his assessment, it is truth's memorability that makes it similar to music: 'La vérité est une musique, ai-je pensé. Elle se soustrait à l'usure du temps par sa légèreté' (Alexakis, 2015: 147).

The Athenian bookstore event at which the author met this unforgettable young intellectual with the sapphire necklace featured a variety of his books that were available for purchase, but the one that sold the best was the 2012 novel recounting the author's apprenticeship of Sango, a language of the Central African Republic. The narrator explains his reaction to this preference among his readers: 'J'ai trouvé bien réconfortant l'intérêt qu'il a suscité auprès de ces jeunes gens: je l'ai interprété comme une manifestation de sympathie à l'égard des populations africaines fraîchement installées en Grèce' (Alexakis, 2015: 147). The comfort he takes in the interest of young people for the new arrivals from Africa in their midst seems somewhat incongruous, given Alexakis's answer to a question posed during an earlier discussion: 'j'ai pu dire tout le mal que je pensais du roman engagé, j'ai même eu l'aplomb d'affirmer que je n'écrivais jamais si bien que quand je n'avais rien à dire' (Alexakis, 2015: 146–47). While the author may consider that his best literary creations don't contain messages and he may not believe in promoting an agenda through his written works, Alexakis's very interpretation of the reason behind the success of *Les mots étrangers* points towards the ways in which his texts communicate important truths through their insights into the experiences of others.[3]

This is one of the greatest strengths of *La clarinette,* as it paints the portraits of a range of individuals with whom Alexakis connects

---

2 The textual ruminations in *La clarinette* reveal that forgetting is not considered a fault, according to this construct: 'L'oubli suggère un égarement, une méconnaissance de ce qui est vrai, de ce qui s'est réellement passé. En grec c'est la chose oubliée qui prend l'initiative de disparaître, de se soustraire à notre vigilance. Nous n'avons pas à nous sentir honteux de nos oublis puisque les choses elles-mêmes s'amusent à se cacher' (Alexakis, 2015: 51).

3 The book that sold especially well at the bookstore event, *Les mots étrangers,* was not devoid of comments with particular pertinence to a crowd from Athens, for Alexakis was already reflecting on the economic crisis in Greece in this 2012 publication.

in Athens. One is aptly named Athéna, who was born in Greece but doesn't have Greek nationality: 'bien qu'elle parle beaucoup mieux le grec que l'idiome de ses parents, la Grèce la considère toujours comme une étrangère. Elle n'a droit qu'à une carte de séjour renouvelable tous les cinq ans' (Alexakis, 2015: 160). Her parents, originally from Nigeria, used to make their living by reselling leather bags and shoes but have met with tremendous difficulty since the Minister of the Interior has taken away the right of all foreigners to sell goods at stands in markets or special events. Since Athéna's parents can no longer afford to contribute to the fund for artisans and traders, their family has lost their health insurance. They are not alone in this conundrum; this is not only the lot of foreigners on Greek land, it is also the fate of many Greeks.

There is a musical tradition that began in underprivileged areas of Athens in the 1930s that is designated by a word of foreign origin, *rébétiko*. Alexakis reveals his etymological proclivities, as he is wont to do, when he states that the word comes from the Turkish term for 'thug', or *voyou* in French, and refers to tunes of 'oriental inspiration' that the Greek bourgeois dislike, but that have nonetheless touched a number of young people in Greece. Even though it initially developed during a period of intense censorship, this music has managed to survive and continues to thrive because of the message it communicates as well as its form of communication (Alexakis, 2015: 165). The lyrics of this 'disenchanted' music tell of poverty, despair and the nostalgia of the immigrant who is far from his mother. While the hero of this genre is a penniless individual who is rejected by society and even by his friends, the narrative voice explains, since this is the perceived lot of so many in Athens today, there are nightclubs devoted solely to these strains, and a concert allows people to come together and feel a sense of a shared destiny, at least for the evening. Athéna takes advantage of the opportunity to 'dance superbly', with 'charming rigor', and to thunderous applause (Alexakis, 2015: 167). In a time when so much of what truly matters seems to be forgotten, this musical moment carves out a space of solidarity, reminding people of other values, far from economic concerns: 'Le rébétiko véhicule la conviction que la musique vaut toutes les richesses du monde' (Alexakis, 2015: 165).

The author brings up a number of francophone friends, demonstrating that his path has often crossed other French speakers whose meanderings across the Mediterranean and among the capitals of Europe have brought them to Athens. For instance, there is a man who calls out to him in a café: 'il était marocain et avait longtemps vécu à Paris' (Alexakis, 2015: 196). And there is another individual from Senegal who settled down in the capital after serving in the Greek merchant marine: 'À force de nous croiser nous avions fini par faire connaissance. Il me parlait tantôt en grec, tantôt en français' (Alexakis, 2015: 114). But the most striking acquaintance the author depicts is a woman named Lilie who learned the French language when she was very young, in Constantinople (Alexakis, 2015: 108). Lilie is actively involved in making a difference, in whatever way she can. She knits sweaters for children in need, for example, giving the garments to the Church to assure their distribution. Lilie is not the only member of her family to devote herself to noble causes. Her son is a lawyer who defends the rights of foreigners arrested in Greece before the European Court of Human Rights; her daughter-in-law is also a lawyer, whose engagement Lilie describes as follows: 'Elle s'occupe, elle, des enfants qui n'ont plus leurs parents, ou dont les parents ne sont plus en mesure de veiller sur eux' (Alexakis, 2015: 350). When boats carrying migrants from Syria and Egypt capsize, this lawyer is quick to focus on the children who survive. Lilie's own humanitarian activities date back to the Second World War, and she carries within her profoundly painful memories of torture and execution in that context. She asserts that the most painful scene of irrevocable loss is one that she will never be able to get out of her mind: 'C'est probablement ce que nous aimerions oublier que notre mémoire retient le mieux' (Alexakis, 2015: 352). When Lilie told him the details of that particular scene, the narrator couldn't restrain his emotion: 'Cette fois je l'ai embrassée. J'ai eu un bref instant l'illusion que je tenais la Grèce dans mes bras' (Alexakis, 2015: 352). Lilie, a francophone woman originally from Constantinople, is the embodiment of Alexakis's homeland. She and those dear to her understand what it means to be at the meeting point of Europe and the Mediterranean, devoting their lives to working towards welcoming others.

La clarinette unveils the efforts of engaged individuals and associations to come to the aid of migrants arriving from all directions, often from across the Mediterranean, to capitals that are ill-equipped to receive them. Aware of the many tragedies that have plagued inhabitants of Paris and Athens alike, the narrative responds to Derrida's exhortation in *L'autre cap* to respect difference, minority, singularity, and to support translation instead of adhering to nationalism or racism. Alexakis provides the *déshérités*, the homeless and the disheartened of both Paris and Athens, with a textual abode in an inclusive gesture of hospitality, which, in Derrida's understanding, is not a culture among others, but rather is culture in itself.

Bibliography

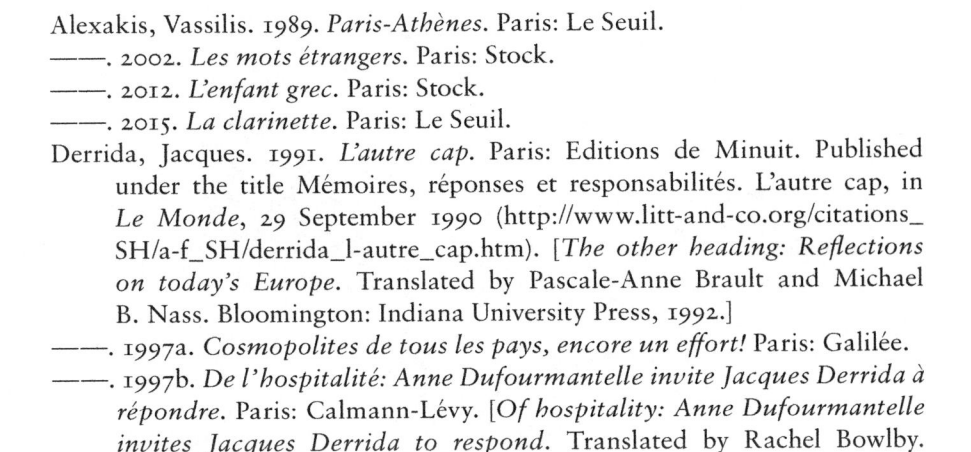

Alexakis, Vassilis. 1989. *Paris-Athènes*. Paris: Le Seuil.
———. 2002. *Les mots étrangers*. Paris: Stock.
———. 2012. *L'enfant grec*. Paris: Stock.
———. 2015. *La clarinette*. Paris: Le Seuil.
Derrida, Jacques. 1991. *L'autre cap*. Paris: Editions de Minuit. Published under the title Mémoires, réponses et responsabilités. L'autre cap, in *Le Monde*, 29 September 1990 (http://www.litt-and-co.org/citations_SH/a-f_SH/derrida_l-autre_cap.htm). [*The other heading: Reflections on today's Europe*. Translated by Pascale-Anne Brault and Michael B. Nass. Bloomington: Indiana University Press, 1992.]
———. 1997a. *Cosmopolites de tous les pays, encore un effort!* Paris: Galilée.
———. 1997b. *De l'hospitalité: Anne Dufourmantelle invite Jacques Derrida à répondre*. Paris: Calmann-Lévy. [*Of hospitality: Anne Dufourmantelle invites Jacques Derrida to respond*. Translated by Rachel Bowlby. Stanford: Stanford University Press, 2000.]

PART II

Marseille *Multiples*:
Capital of Culture

PART II

Marseille Multiples: Capital of Culture

5

Screening Cosmopolitan and Mediterranean Marseille

Ipek Çelik Rappas

Marseille was one of the two European Capitals of Culture in 2013. Billions of Euros were invested to dispel the city's bad reputation as a centre of gang and drug-related violence and rehabilitate its appearance. At the centre of the renovation project was the creation of a Mediterranean cultural site at Marseille's post-industrial port, a site that includes two major constructions—the first museum dedicated to Mediterranean history and culture (the Musée des civilisations de l'Europe et de la Méditerranées, MUCEM) and a dialogue space that brings together researchers and policymakers from the Mediterranean countries (Villa Méditerranée)—along with several smaller museums (such as the Musée Regards de Provence showcasing fine arts from the Provence region) and exhibition spaces. The creation of museums and the hosting of hundreds of Mediterranean-themed cultural events and exhibitions of works by artists from the northern and southern shores of the Middle Sea all promoted a cosmopolitan Mediterranean identity of the city, which was a significant element of the Capital of Culture project. This article explores the ways in which moving images including fiction films, video installations and documentaries formulated a cosmopolitan and Mediterranean Marseille in the years leading up to and during 2013. It examines the role of such dual identity in the renovation of the city as well as the images of resistance against an elitist understanding and top-down application of cosmopolitanism and Mediterranean-ness.

The exhibition *Méditerranées, des grandes cités d'hier aux hommes d'aujourd'hui* was on display at J1 (a former warehouse converted into an exhibition space in the port area) from January to May 2013. In the exhibit a contemporary Odysseus travels through 12 Mediterranean cities, each meant to capture a specific epoch in the Middle Sea's history. The exhibition starts with a section on ancient Troy, and continues with a historical exploration of Tyre/Beirut, Athens, Alexandria, Rome, Cordoba, Venice, Genoa, Istanbul, Algiers, Tunis in different periods of history and ends in late nineteenth-century Marseille. Therefore, this spatial history of the Mediterranean, presented through a combination of archaeological artefacts and historical documentaries, stops at the height of the Marseille's (and France's) maritime imperial and industrial power. The exhibit is not only historical, it also presents the contemporary life of these Mediterranean cities through a series of short videos titled *Ulysse le brûleur de frontières et la mer blanche du milieu* by Algerian-French director Malek Bensmaïl. In the documentary shorts the Odysseus character interviews the residents of these 12 cities to evoke the social and political issues that shape their lives today. In Athens, for instance, a middle-aged unemployed man explains how severely he has been affected by the economic crisis, while in Alexandria a family of four discuss their political involvement during the Arab Spring in a video shot in the library of Alexandria.

While the videos of all other Mediterranean cities show political issues that concern these cities' residents—from economic crisis to memories of violence during civil war and experiences of illegal migration—the video on Marseille depicts the city as a distant utopia detached from earthly worries. The video shows the fictional Odysseus sailing to Marseille, on his return home, talking to the other passengers. In close-ups the interviewees who happen to be residents of the city praise Marseille as 'the most beautiful city in the world' or a 'city of love' as they watch it from a distance. In contrast to the videos that depict the other cities, the one on Marseille remains literally and figuratively distant from the social and political concerns of its residents (Figure 5.1). The city is imagined and seen from afar, from a boat floating on the Mediterranean. The boat approaches the safety of the renovated port area—now housing the restored Fort Saint-Jean and the glorious MUCEM, the museum that showcases European *and* Mediterranean history and culture, its name suggesting a closer connection to the northern shores of the Middle Sea than the southern ones.

The video constructs Marseille as a well-connected transnational city (the boat symbolizing the city itself) with its Mediterranean charms—sunny, bright and beautiful, a 'city of love' devoid of the problems experienced in the other Mediterranean cities exhibited. The

Figure 5.1. Odysseus approaching the port of Marseille.
Courtesy of © Les Films d'ici, *Ulysse le brûleur de frontières et la mer blanche du milieu*, Malek Bensmaïl.

older residents of Marseille interviewed on the boat declare the city's Greek or Italian (i.e. European) roots, not mentioning its strong North African heritage. Indeed, the main character Odysseus assumes that the Algerian-French residents he interviews are first-time visitors to Marseille.

As such the video and the exhibition itself are representative of a certain visual construction of cosmopolitan Marseille for and through the Capital of Culture year. Far from representations in the media as a chaotic product of multiculturalism and migration, Marseille is constructed as the site of an orderly cosmopolitanism inherited from cross-cultural experiences with other Mediterranean cities. Such visual representation, while portraying Marseille as the final stop on a trip through the Mediterranean, and hence as a space where all cultures meet and mingle, does not delve into the city's local history of multiculturalism, especially its non-European and postcolonial elements.

The reconstruction of a cosmopolitan Mediterranean Marseille by urban planners started long before its year as Capital of Culture, when the French government introduced Euroméditerranée, a top-down urban renovation project that allocated over 50 million Euros of investment to Marseille between 1995 and 2012 to transform the urban landscape, and especially the port area (L'Euroméditerranée, 2014). Similar to the fate of other post-industrial port cities such as London or Liverpool, Marseille has been reconstructed by turning defunct dock areas into art galleries and museums and renovating housing in the port area which led to evictions of lower-income residents (Andres, 2011; Megerle, 2008). These events went hand in hand with the cultural promotion of cosmopolitan Mediterranean Marseille in the 1990s and the 2000s.

The film industry and the visual representation of cities in films and TV series have been an increasingly important part of the post-industrial city's economic revival through the promotion of culture and heritage tourism. As Paul Swann observes, films and the film industry have been crucial for establishing 'a postmodern inexorability in valuing cities as images rather than as sites of production' (2001: 96). During and after Marseille's year as the Capital of Culture the municipality's official website intended to draw film-makers to Marseille by showcasing the recently built Belle de Mai multimedia centre as an affordable facility for film-makers, and to attract film tourists by mentioning the construction of La Maison des Cinématographies de la Méditerranée at Marcel Pagnol's family home, and through the visual appeal of the city as revealed in the popular French TV series *Plus belle la vie*, screened every night on France 3 since 2004. The website declares in English: 'Marseille loves the movies and cinema, something that becomes it well. It is the most filmed city in France after Paris. Its warm light, blue sea, its rich and varied heritage, and the simplicity of its inhabitants have long attracted filmmakers and inspired scenarists' (Ville de Marseille, 2014: n. pag.). These lines portray Marseille as a visually marketable Mediterranean city, with an attractive landscape and history, and with residents who are 'simple' and accommodating. The influence of images in the city's Mediterranean branding and marketing for tourists may be best observed through *Plus belle la vie*, which takes place in a fictional neighbourhood of Marseille, Le Mistral, modelled on the Le Panier neighbourhood:

> The show has encouraged tourists to flock to Le Panier, where a shop dedicated to merchandise relating to the series recently opened. The *quartier*'s old bars have been turned into ice-cream parlours, its facades repainted in bright colours. The cardboard neighbourhood of the soap has begun to obscure the real neighbourhood it was supposed to portray. (Dell'Umbria, 2012: 85)

While the series promotes nostalgia for a simple and accommodating communal life, its fictional neighbourhood imposes itself on and shapes a real neighbourhood in order to attract tourists.

Despite the promotion of image tourism in Marseille, when Marseille-based organization Aflam offered to organize a festival of Arab cinema, which was initially accepted, the organizers later faced opposition by the municipality, which vetoed the festival on the grounds that its title would lead to intercommunity problems and 'stigmatize' a community. The municipality proposed instead that it should be reframed as a Mediterranean film festival, which took place on a smaller scale than originally foreseen (Bullen, 2010).

Such insistence on erasing allusions to the city's Maghrebi ethnic heritage and transposing it into a Mediterranean one gives a hint of the kind of cosmopolitanism imagined for the city in the years that led up to 2013. The emphasis on the cosmopolitan-ness of Marseille is not a strategy without precedent in city branding and marketing. The promotion of the cosmopolitanism or multiculturalism of a European city has often been used as an ideological strategy by urban planners in the transition of cities from industrial to creative economies. Yet the promotion of cosmopolitanism in terms of ideology and culture often goes hand in hand with a contradictory lack of social policies that stimulate the existing local diversity in cities. Kira Kosnick (2008) explains that since the late 1990s, Berlin has been flourishing with multicultural projects that are part of the effort to present the city as Europe's cosmopolitan capital. Ironically though, behind this foreground of cultural prosperity, the city, and particularly its non-European minority populations, have been hit by economic recession and neoliberal policies that have produced high rates of unemployment. Hence, Kosnick points out that multiculturalism and cosmopolitanism is often mobilized by certain institutions and policymakers to promote their own interests, rather than those of the city's multicultural residents. Cosmopolitanism becomes a strategy on which urban policymakers capitalize 'to transform, to govern, and to successfully market the city', and one that opens the city to creative classes, along with tourists and investors (Kosnick, 2009: 165).

Only in recent decades have cosmopolitan and multicultural become desired and marketable aspects of cities. In the 1920s and 1930s, Marseille's port was described condescendingly as an area gathering North African migrants: 'Voulez-vous voir l'Algérie, le Maroc, la Tunisie? Je vous conduis rue des Chapeliers. Voici les gourbis, les Bicots, les mouquères ...' (Albert Londres, qtd. in Gastaut, 2003: 3). As Stephen Heath suggests, what made cosmopolitan Marseille a 'respectable' Mediterranean port was Marcel Pagnol's trilogy. Pagnol's trilogy—*Marius* (Alexander Korda, 1931), *Fanny* (Marc Allégret, 1932) and

César (Marcel Pagnol, 1936)—showcased for the first time the singing southern accent, the charms of the Vieux-Port and its community spirit coloured with traditional games such as *belote* and *pétanque*. Recently, there has been interest in reviving the Marseille imagined in this trilogy. Channel France 2's adaptation of the trilogy in 2000, Daniel Auteuil's remakes of *Marius* (2013) and *Fanny* (2013), which came out simultaneously in the Capital of Culture year with the financial support of the Région Provence-Alpes-Côte d'Azur and, finally, the restoration of the original trilogy by La Cinémathèque Française for screening at Cannes 2015 reveal the resurgent nostalgia for Pagnol's image of Marseille. In order to understand the reasons behind the revival of Pagnol's trilogy in the 2010s, one needs to explore the parallels between the Marseille that the trilogy depicts and today's Marseille under urban renovation, imagined as a Mediterranean Capital of Culture.

Pagnol's trilogy revolves around the Vieux-Port area. Anything outside the port (especially the Middle Sea) signifies adventure but also the risk and danger that the rebellious soul of young Marius craves. Hence, Mediterranean-ness is grounded and established within the white, middle-class Vieux-Port community and is distinguished in opposition to Parisian identity, since the only identitarian difference emphasized in the film is that between Paris and Marseille. Within the Marseillais community, as Stephen Heath points out, class and especially ethnic differences are erased, which is striking when one considers that 20 per cent of the city's population were immigrants at the time, predominantly living around the Vieux-Port area where the film is set. Another significant point that Heath emphasizes is that while time clearly passes in the trilogy (the clearest indicator being the growth of Fanny and Marius's child Césariot), the world of the series gives the sense of being 'historically static […] a time out of time, of a world set apart in which characters move along without much interaction with outside reality' (2004: 38).[1] In Pagnol's trilogy the social and

---

[1] Such romanticization of Mediterranean temporality as stagnant, peaceful and idyllic is a cliché that dates back to nineteenth-century European travel writing. This is further reinforced by images of the Mediterranean as a 'timeless' terrain, defined by stagnant structures that determine a human geography resistant to change (such as in Fernand Braudel's *The Mediterranean and the Mediterranean world in the age of Philip II* (1949)), and most recently marked by the Academy Award winning film *Mediterraneo* (1991), probably the most optimistic Second World War movie to date with its call for unity in common humanity. For more on such stagnant representation of the Mediterranean, see Çelik (2011).

political realities of Marseille in the 1930s—such as economic crisis, the approaching war and the city's multicultural composition—are sidelined. Possibly as a result of the stagnant temporality of the trilogy, it is described as a universal, timeless piece: 'humanist, realistic [...] with a universal message and a South of France feel' (Cannes Press Pack, 2015: 4).

I do not suggest here that events organized around the Capital of Culture year and L'Euroméditerranée urban renovation project imagine a similarly stagnant temporality for Marseille or the Mediterranean. On the contrary, the city's dynamism is often underlined, especially concerning its economic revival. However, such dynamism stands side by side with a claim on the collection and protection of a certain cultural heritage for and of the Mediterranean. The centrepiece of the renovation is a museum that claims itself to be 'the first museum in the world devoted to Mediterranean cultures' (Bonnefoy, 2013: 9). This is similar to Pagnol's original goal in writing the theatrical plays upon which the film trilogy is based: 'a local work, which was profoundly sincere and authentic, [that] could [...] find a place in the literary heritage of a country and be popular the world over' (Pagnol, qtd. in Cannes Press Pack, 2015: 1).

The cultural promotion of the city is not only accomplished through the images of local Mediterranean charms and community spirit that Pagnol's trilogy proposes. Counterculture images of seedy parts of the city and the marginal characters proposed in other films are equally attractive for a different group of spectator-tourists, as they perpetuate the image of the edgy, cool and alternative city (Stehle, 2012). Settings such as derelict factories, former industrial spaces, harbours and 'shady' neighbourhoods (stereotypically *banlieues* in French cities) are recycled in crime and action films for marketing the counterculture image of the city. Most recently, in Netflix-produced series *Marseille* (2016–), the city is depicted as on its way to becoming a Mediterranean capital through fighting against the crime and corruption dragging it down. Released on the internet in May 2016 featuring celebrity names such as Gerard Depardieu and Benoît Magimel, the TV series portrays the mayor's office, the political manoeuvres to win power in the city and the relations between politicians and the mafia. While the *cités* of Marseille are associated with drug-dealing and a spiral of violence, the major source of power struggles and corruption in Marseille is the development of the Vieux-Port, which the mayor (played by Depardieu and depicted as a selfless protector of the city), promotes as the mafia fights against urban change.

The series' association of the city with crime and corruption is not unprecedented. Crime and the action genres are frequently linked to the city and often promote another kind of cosmopolitanism for Marseille: rather than focusing on its local Mediterranean colours, the wealth of crime and action films that use Marseille as a background situate the city as a transnational capital of crime where the harbour and the docks are hotbeds of criminal activity. Around the same time Pagnol's trilogy came out, *Justin de Marseille* (Maurice Tournier, 1935), influenced by Albert Londres's investigative journalism, opened up a different trajectory for the city's and the harbour's representation (Ungar, 2013). The city is represented as a dark centre of the international drug trade, a location for gangsters and crime-related noir films, most famously *The French Connection* (William Friedkin, 1971), a film inspired by real events, and its sequel *French Connection II* (John Frankenheimer, 1975). In the latter two films the drug trade connects Marseille to New York and also gives it transnational legibility as city of noir. Marseille as a city of crime is revisited and established further in the 2000s with thrillers such as *The Transporter* (Louis Leterrier and Corey Yuen, 2002), *The Transporter 3* (Olivier Megaton, 2008), *MR 73* [*The Last Deadly Mission*] (Olivier Marchal, 2008) and *La French* [*The Connection*] (Cédric Jimenez, 2014), the former two produced by Luc Besson's production company EuropaCorp. All of these films reflect an urgent drive to formulate Marseille as a Mediterranean capital with transnational (albeit shady) connections.

Among popular French productions, the most successful franchise in imagining a cosmopolitan Marseille as the capital of international crime has been the *Taxi* series, five films shot between the years of 1998 and 2018. This Luc Besson production reflects the urgency to formulate the city as a flexible neoliberal urban space (with a Mediterranean twist, emphatic on the strong sense of local community and unruliness) and to refashion an always already diverse city into a site of safe cosmopolitanism. The city in these films is a transnational attraction for crime tourism with heists organized by German or Belgian gangs and operations run by the Japanese and Chinese mafia. These crisis situations (always exported from abroad) bring together the police officer Émilien and the taxi driver Daniel Morales played by Samy Naceri, a French-Algerian actor whose ethnicity remains a 'taboo' in the film (McGonagle, 2017). This is not to say that Naceri needs to play his minority ethnicity; yet opting for almost complete invisibility of any ethnicity in a film shot in Marseille—except for extreme clichés of black characters who smoke pot and listen to Bob Marley—reveals how the multicultural make-up of the city is effaced for another kind of cosmopolitanism. Marseille is portrayed as on its way to gentrification with sanitized streets and docks, and clean roads that enable Daniel's car to move smoothly, faster even than the high-speed train. The analogy between Daniel's taxi and the high-speed train, which is often voiced in the film, is telling since at the time a TGV line was being built to connect Marseille to Paris. In the first film of the series Daniel traps a German gang on top of an unfinished highway bridge, a construction site that will give new mobility and accessibility to Marseille. *Taxi* put Marseille on the international map of genre film locations, and opened it up for spectators as a Mediterranean city blending easy mobility with a whitewashed community spirit just as the Euroméditerranée urban renewal project was starting to take shape.[2]

In recent crime thrillers the local multiculturalism of Marseille is not always evaded or whitewashed as in the *Taxi* series, but when it is represented it often works through stereotypes and is, mainly as a consequence of genre conventions, associated with conflict and violence. In another action/crime/thriller set in the city, *L'Immortel* (22 Bullets, Richard Berry, 2010), again produced by EuropaCorp, the main character Charly Mattei (Jean Reno) is a retired mafia member of Italian heritage. Mattei survives 22 bullets after an assassination attempt and is drawn into a fight with a mafia boss after he refuses to get involved in the drug trade, as he desires a peaceful life. The film opens and ends with family scenes in sun-filled Marseillais houses or beaches and brings together the sense of community with an action-filled crime thriller. The multicultural community spirit is revered with stereotypical symbols throughout the film, such as the star of David representing the Jewish police officer, the Italian opera that calms the repentant Mattei, North African family meals, and the lavish marriage ceremonies of both the new mafia boss and his primary victim. The film shows Marseille as cosmopolitan, cool and increasingly hospitable and secure as the elements of violence are eliminated and Italian heritage dominates with its protective guardianship.

Through the 1990s and 2000s, along with the nostalgic revival of Pagnol's trilogy and the resurgence of crime thrillers that promote a cosmopolitan sense of Marseille that tends to disregard its local diversity

2 For a longer discussion of urban change in Marseille in the 1990s and the 2000s and its representation in the *Taxi* series, see my article Çelik Rappas (2016). I would like to thank *French Cultural Studies* for allowing me to use some excerpts from this article here.

or reduce it to stereotypes, there have been filmic representations of a more inclusive cosmopolitanism, as well as critiques of the urban changes that the city is going through. Robert Guédiguian's *Marius et Jeannette* (1997—a clear reference to Pagnol in the film's title), for instance, promotes Marseille as a city with a colourful community spirit similar to Pagnol's trilogy, but with a more class-conscious approach. In *Marius et Jeanette* we see a crumbling industrial space as one of the main filming locations. Through the central place taken by a closed down cement factory in ruins (it brings together the two protagonists: it is the setting where Marius works as the night watchman and where Jeannette's father died on the job), we see nostalgia for the loss of 'real labour'. Along with this nostalgia, the film reflects on the dominance and precarity of service economy work. Jeannette is quickly fired from her job as a cashier for criticizing her boss (soon to be fired himself), and finds herself part of the large market of unemployed represented by the long queue for a job application. As Mazierska and Rascaroli emphasize, while the film conveys 'the experience of displacement and loss of identity' as a result of Marseille's changing urban landscape and economy, it also sustains an element of 'belligerent spirit', humour and political consciousness (2003: 85). Hence, Marseillais diversity is represented through the screening of its most precarious groups in strong solidarity under the duress of urban change and impoverishment.

Compared to *Marius and Jeannette*, Karim Dridi's *Bye-Bye* (1995) draws a more multicultural picture of community, and Marseille is defined as a zone of transition between Africa and Europe. The film begins with the arrival of two brothers, Ismael and Mouloud, from Paris and ends with their departure towards an unknown distant horizon in the south, possibly Spain. Similar to *Marius et Jeannette*, Dridi's characters are part of the underclass of Marseille and the city is represented as an industrial and working-class city of great ethnic diversity—portrayed through the friendship between Ismael and Jacky, who both work in the docks, and through scenes such as an interracial wedding party. Dridi is far from idealizing interethnic relations though, since both the *blanc-beur* friendship and the wedding party are spoiled in part by the intervention of a group of racist dockworkers. Neither does the film idealize the connections between the two shores of the Mediterranean. Even though Ismael often turns his gaze towards the sea, neither he nor his brother has any interest in going *au bled*, here Tunisia. Marseille becomes a Mediterranean opening, a gate through which one leaves behind painful personal histories and connections to roots. As Mazierska and Rascaroli point out, the frequent shots of the Mediterranean in the film symbolize the fluidity of identity between shores and ports: 'Marseille in *Bye-Bye* is represented as a crossroads of cultures, peoples, migrations and epochs' (2003: 80). The city is portrayed as a diverse place of passage, with a rich local underclass diversity that is at times conflictual, other times harmonious, cosmopolitan and Mediterranean with advantages and drawbacks.

Conclusion

During research conducted in Marseille in 2011, anthropologist Claire Bullen asked residents if Marseille is a Mediterranean city. While the mayor of one of its districts described Marseille as having 'an absolutely unique geographical position in the Mediterranean', for one elderly female resident, despite being born in Tunisia, having Italian parents and living in a neighbourhood whose residents are predominantly of North African origin, it did not make sense to describe the city as Mediterranean (Bullen, 2012). Responding to another survey, 24-year-old Mounir Benaziza, who had been unemployed for a year, interprets the Euroméditerranée investments in Marseille as follows: 'Avec tout cet argent, on aurait pu rassembler les gens mais là, on nous divise. Ce sont nous les habitants qui, les premiers, nous sentons comme des touristes. Pour redorer l'image de Marseille, on éloigne les quartiers Nord de et nous ne profitons pas de ce qui se passe' (Cesar, 2103: n. pag.). While the Mediterranean-ness of Marseille becomes a marketable trait praised by bureaucrats, it lacks meaning for its residents as Marseille's stint as the Mediterranean capital seems to serve tourists rather than the city's own diverse populations.

In order to critique the problems of the cultural capital project, Marseillais hip-hop artist Keny Arkana composed the song 'Capitale de la rupture' and made a 20-minute documentary that carries the same title. In the documentary, Arkana combines interviews with various residents—including local artists, activists and owners of alternative cultural centres—with images of the city under construction, expulsions, protests against expulsions, promotional posters of the Capital of Culture, graffiti against it and the daily life in the neighbourhoods of Marseille undergoing renovation. 'Rupture', rhyming with and replacing 'culture', as Arkana's interviewees emphasize, is the split between the image that the organizers want to give of Marseille as a multicultural Mediterranean capital and the reality that the project has enthusiastically ignored the need for economic and cultural support to the city's diverse migrant and minority populations. The director of a social centre in a northern *banlieue* declares that 'l'Euromed c'est pour redéfinir le centre-ville de le nettoyer des milieux populaires des immigrations récentes', while another resident explains that the Capital of Culture puts a logo on the city: 'on mets ça sur Marseille et ça va faire venir du blanc, du cadre, du touriste, du promoteur, de l'investisseur'. Yet another interviewee, an artist, underlines that the culture mentioned here has nothing to do with the way people live, or with 'la culture de métissage' of Marseille; it is 'la production industrielle de la culture'. Among the issues discussed are the lack of involvement of local organizations and resident artists in the Capital of Culture process, and the lack of support for local artistic productivity. Arkana and her interviewees point out that there has been no integration of the city's rich local multicultural texture within the Capital of Culture activities. Instead of organizing a hip-hop festival that would showcase the strong and diverse hip-hop culture of Marseille, for instance, non-local figures of international reputation, such as David Guetta, were invited for a concert. Simply put, the desires of the inhabitants of Marseille were not taken into account in the creation of this imaginary cosmopolitan Mediterranean space, a project led by business and commercial circles, the perfect evidence of this (as the director of an alternative cultural centre declares in Arkana's documentary) being that the head of the organizing committee for the Capital of Culture was the president of the Marseille-Provence Chamber of Commerce and Industry.

In sum, the Capital of Culture project promoted an elitist and sterile sense of cosmopolitanism that ignores Marseille's local cultural diversity. The year as Capital of Culture, however, was the final part in the long process of Marseille's urban renovation, which, as is common in post-industrial cities, brought creative industries into play to transform former industrial spaces into sites of culture (in this case Mediterranean culture), a culture that is defined by and through grand institutions such as the MuCEM, rather than by local artists and residents. This chapter has traced how moving images of the city (from films to documentaries and video productions) from the 1990s on have at times reflected and contributed to, and at other times resisted, the urban transformation of Marseille and the redefinition of its always already cosmopolitan and Mediterranean identity. Certain films produced in and of Marseille— from nostalgic remakes and adaptations of Pagnol's trilogy to crime/ action films such as the *Taxi* series—distil the city's Mediterranean-ness into a sterile cosmopolitanism that is easily marketed to tourists. While other images such as *Bye-bye*, *Marius et Jeannette* and Keny Arkana's documentary reflect the ethnic diversity of the city, the urban changes that affect its most precarious residents and present insightful critiques of the Capital of Culture project. All these cases mark the increasing role of moving images of the city in the making of the city's image.

Bibliography

Andres, Lauren. 2011. Marseille 2013 or the final round of a long and complex regeneration strategy? *Town Planning Review* 82(1): 61–76.

Bonnefoy, Françoise. 2013. *MUCEM: Spirit of place*. Paris: Scala.

Braudel, Fernand. 1996. *The Mediterranean and the Mediterranean world in the age of Philip II*. Translated by Siân Reynolds. Berkeley: University of California Press.

Bullen, Claire. 2010. *European capitals of culture and everyday cultural diversity: A comparison of Liverpool (UK) and Marseille (France)*. European Cultural Foundation: Cultural Policy Award Winner. http://www.encatc.org/pages/fileadmin/user_upload/2011_CPRA/2010_CPRA_Winner_Publication_Claire_Bullen.pdf.

———. 2012. Marseille, ville méditerranéenne? Enjeux de pouvoir dans la construction des identités urbaines. *Rives méditerranéennes* 42: 157–71.

Cannes Press Pack. 2015. Classics official selection. http://www.festival-cannes.com/assets/Image/Direct/57a90508ad26b0eff3e2b1a877ccba51.pdf.

Çelik, Ipek A. 2011. New directions for studying the Mediterranean: Eventfulness in Rhea Galanaki's novel *The life of Ismail Ferik Pasha: Spina nel Cuore*. *Clio: Journal of Literature, History and the Philosophy of History* 41(1): 75–101.

Çelik Rappas, Ipek. 2016. The urban renovation of Marseille in Luc Besson's *Taxi* series. *French Cultural Studies* 27(4): 385–97.

Cesar, Journal. 2013. Marseille Provence 2013: enquête dans les quartiers 'créatifs'. *Mediapart*, 1 August. https://blogs.mediapart.fr/journal-cesar/blog/010813/marseille-provence-2013-enquete-dans-les-quartiers-creatifs.

Dell'Umbria, Alèssi. 2012. The sinking of Marseille. *New Left Review* 75: 69–87.

Gastaut, Yvan. 2003. Marseille cosmopolite après les décolonisations: un enjeu identitaire. *Cahiers de la Méditerranée* 67: 269–85.

Heath, Stephen. 2004. *César*. London: BFI Publishing.

Kosnick, Kira. 2008. Conflicting mobilities: Cultural diversity and city branding in Berlin. In Stephanie Hemelryk Donald, Eleonore Kofman and Catherine Kevin, eds., *Branding cities: Cosmopolitanism, parochialism, and social change*, 28–43. New York: Routledge.

———. 2009. Cosmopolitan capital or multicultural community? Reflections on the production and management of differential mobilities in Germany's capital city. In Magdalena Nowicka and Maria Rovisco, eds., *Cosmopolitanism in practice*, 161–80. Farnham: Ashgate.

L'Euroméditerranée. 2014. Les partenaires publics. http://www.euromediterranee.fr/who-are-we/public-partners.html?L=0.

McGonagle, Joseph. 2017. *Representing ethnicity in contemporary French visual culture*. Manchester: Manchester University Press.

Mazierska, Ewa and Laura Rascaroli. 2003. Marseille: Intersection, fragment, ruin. In *From Moscow to Madrid: Postmodern cities, european cinema*, 73–90. London: I.B. Tauris.

Megerle, Heidi Elisabeth. 2008. Present-day development processes in the inner city of Marseille: Tensions between upgrading and marginalisation. *Die Erde* 139(4): 357–78.

Stehle, Maria. 2012. Money, mobility, and commodified bodies: The politics of gentrification in German city films of the late 1990s. *The German Quarterly* 85(1): 40–54.

Swann, P. 2001. From workshop to backlot: The greater Philadelphia film office. In Mark Shiel and Tony Fitzmaurice, eds., *Cinema and the city: Film and urban societies in a global context*, 88–98. Oxford: Blackwell.

Ungar, Steven. 2013. Marseille: City of imagination. In Marcelline Block, ed., *World film locations: Marseille*, 6–8. London: Intellect.

Ville de Marseille. 2014. Marseille: A city open to the world. http://www.marseille.fr/sitevdm/versions-etrangeres/english--discover-marseille.

Filmography

Bye-Bye. 1995. Dir. Karim Dridi. France/Belgium/Switzerland: ADR, La Compagnie Méditerranéenne du Cinéma, La Sept Cinéma et al.

César. 1936. Dir. Marcel Pagnol. France: Les Films Marcel Pagnol.

Fanny. 1932. Dir. Marc Allégret. France: Les Films Marcel Pagnol, Braunberger-Richebé.

Fanny. 2013. Dir. Daniel Auteuil. France: Les Films Alain Sarde, Pathé, Zack Films.

La French. 2014. Dir. Cédric Jimenez. France: Gaumont, Légende Films, France 2 Cinéma.

The French Connection. 1971. Dir. William Friedkin. USA: D'Antoni Productions, Schine-Moore Prod.

The French Connection II. 1975. Dir. John Frankenheimer. USA: 20th Century Fox.

L'Immortel. 2010. Dir. Richard Berry. France: EuropaCorp, TF1 Films.

Justin de Marseille. 1935. Dir. Maurice Tournier. France: Pathé-Natan.

Marius. 1931. Dir. Alexander Korda. France: Paramount Pictures.

Marius. 2013. Dir. Daniel Auteuil. France: Les Films Alain Sarde, Pathé.

Marius et Jeannette. 1997. Dir. Robert Guédiguian. France: Agat Films & Cie, La Sept Cinéma, Canal+.
Marseille. 2006–. Dir. Florent Emilio-Siri. France: Netflix, Federation Entertainment.
Mediterraneo. 1991. Dir. Gabriele Salvatores. Italy: A.M.A. Film, Penta Film, Silvio Berlusconi Communications et al.
Mini-docu: Marseille capitale de la rupture. 2013. Dir. Keny Arkana. France. http://www.youtube.com/watch?v=CEg1jMeTIjQ& feature=youtu.be.
MR 73. 2008. Olivier Marchal. France: LGM Productions, Gaumont, TF1 Films Production.
Taxi. 1998. Dir. Gérard Pirès. France: ARP, TF1 Films Production, Studio Canal+ et al.
Taxi 2. 2000. Dir. Gérard Krawczyk. France: ARP Sélection, Canal+, Leeloo Productions et al.
Taxi 3. 2003. Dir. Gérard Krawczyk. France: EuropaCorp, ARP, Apipoulai, et al.
Taxi 4. 2007. Dir. Gérard Krawczyk. France: EuropaCorp, ARP, TF1 Films Production, et al.
The Transporter. 2002. Dir. Louis Leterrier and Corey Yuen. France/USA: EuropaCorp, TF1 Films Production, Current Entertainment et al.
The Transporter 3. 2008. Dir. Olivier Megaton. France/USA/Ukraine: EuropaCorp, TF1 Film Productions, Grive Productions et al.
Ulysse le brûleur de frontiers et la mer blanche du milieu. 2013. Dir. Malek Bensmaïl. France: Les Films d'ici, Marseille-Provence 2013.

6

Shaping Mediterranean Geographies

The Museum of European and Mediterranean Civilizations in Marseille and the Making of Identity

Angela Giovanangeli

Engaging with Local and Transnational Narratives

In 2013, the Musée des Civilisations de l'Europe et de la Méditerranée (MuCEM) opened in the southern French port city of Marseille. This museum is dedicated to exploring and shaping the narratives about countries in the Mediterranean. Work on the Mediterranean is not new. Indeed, this geographic zone has come to be described in various ways. Former diplomat Jacques Huntzinger refers to it as made up of 'peuples de la mer' and characterized by mobility, trade and migration (2010: 22, 24). Philosopher and sociologist Edgar Morin describes it as representing 'unité', 'diversité' and 'oppositions', referring to once-cosmopolitan societies in the Mediterranean that have increasingly been torn apart culturally and politically by ethnic differences and religious beliefs (1998–99: 34). The opening of a national museum on Mediterranean civilizations in Marseille contributes to the ongoing dialogue about the practices and peoples of this region.

As the name of the MuCEM suggests, the focus of the museum is on Mediterranean civilizations, but it also evokes the connection of the Mediterranean to Europe. According to museum practitioners, this is the first museum devoted to collections and programmes on Mediterranean cultures (Colardelle, 1999: 21; Colardelle, 2002: 19; Dossier de presse, 2012: 4). Described as a cultural space at the entrance of the old harbour, the MuCEM houses a permanent collection and presents temporary exhibitions, conferences, films and audiovisual material. It also has an outdoor garden, restaurant, research centre and lookouts.

The decision to open this museum, defined as a 'musée de société',[1] was made in the context of French policies that have traditionally recognized cultural institutions as 'powerful identity-defining machines' (Duncan, 1991: 101). Indeed, the MuCEM fits into a larger political plan conceived in the mid-1990s to enhance the ailing economy and rundown infrastructure of Marseille, by strategically playing on the Mediterranean characteristics of the city to regenerate its centre and port area (Vigouroux, 1994a).

Meanwhile, since the 1990s certain museums, particularly in Western Europe, have increasingly de-emphasized national differences, compiling rather narratives highlighting the social diversity and cultural pluralism that exist within societies and between countries (Krankenhagen, 2011; Mazé, 2014).[2] The emergence of European museums examining transnational narratives coincides with political, economic and social developments in the European Union (EU) that have sparked numerous debates on international relations and ethical responsibilities. For instance, over the last two decades, foreign and security policymakers in the EU have considered its global responsibilities, with responsibility beginning, 'wherever it may end' with those 'closest to the EU' (Bulley, 2009: 63). EU countries have been developing policies benefiting EU members while also emphasizing ethical responsibilities towards

1 The MuCEM describes itself as a *musée de société*, a term that appeared in France at the end of the 1980s following earlier changes to museum approaches in Europe and North America integrating narratives on social transformations and First Nations representations (Watremez, 2013). The *musée de société* is, as historian Denis Chevallier frames it, a place where museum-goers acquire the tools 'pour vivre entre autres' (2013: 17). What is implicit in this approach to the MuCEM is the concern for cultural diversity within plural and transnational social contexts as well as technological and demographic transformations (see also Watremez, 2013).

2 Anthropologist Camille Mazé's work highlights the growing number of museums focusing on the idea of Europe, such as the Musée de l'Europe in Belgium, the Museum Europäischer Kulturen in Berlin, the Musée Européen Schengen in Luxembourg and the future Maison de l'Histoire Européenne in Belgium. According to Mazé, some European countries are rethinking the way they present their national collections in ethnographic museums, stating that narratives presenting a national identity are looked upon negatively in some European countries and are therefore being re-examined or recycled into new museum spaces (2014: 8). Similarly, Kerstin Poehls's work on European museums discusses how traditionally museums were detached from contemporary political debates while today exhibitions can be closely linked to transnational discourses and concerns (2011: 350).

neighbouring countries in terms of human rights as well as the political implications of EU borders (Bulley, 2009: 64). While the nature and objectives of such responsibilities remain ambiguous (Bulley, 2009: 69, 76), these debates nevertheless highlight the blurred nature of the EU's relations with neighbouring non-EU countries.

Similarly, the MuCEM reflects evolving attitudes towards local concerns as well as European integration that have affected museum practices to a certain degree. The museum attempts to address local and national priorities by presenting a 'pluralist story of France' (Lebovics, 2014: 295) while emphasizing France's relation to the Mediterranean and to Europe (Mazé, 2014). The ambivalent nature of local and transnational perspectives is, however, evident in the varying attitudes towards the museum. A recent French government report titled *Le MuCEM: une gestation laborieuse, un avenir incertain*, criticizes the national leanings of the museum's collection:

> [L]e projet du MuCEM s'est heurté, et se heurte encore, à la difficulté originelle de faire coïncider une collection essentiellement française, centrée sur la société préindustrielle, avec un projet scientifique et culturel (PSC) désormais axé sur les civilisations de l'Europe et de la Méditerranée. (Cour des comptes, 2015: 103)

Yet in 2015 the MuCEM was awarded the Council of Europe museum of the year prize for making a 'significant contribution to the understanding of European cultural heritage' and exploring 'the Mediterranean as the birthplace of civilisations and a crossroads of both European and Arab cultures' (Council of Europe, 2015: n. pag.).

In the face of discussions that oppose the local to the transnational, this chapter builds on and contributes to work on local and transnational paradigms. It locates this work in the Mediterranean to argue that perspectives on this geographic area are grounded in the local and that the local shapes the transnational focus of the museum. In order to explore this, the chapter presents a case study of the MuCEM's permanent collection, curatorial production and geographic location. Although research to date on museums of society has identified that these institutions often fail to present transnational narratives about specific geographic areas constructing rather 'universal' perspectives (Poehls, 2011; Mazé, 2009, 2014), there has not been an extended study on the way local interests in cultural practices influence transnational discourses with regard to the understanding of a geographic area.

The opening of the MuCEM in 2013 coincided with Marseille as host of the year-long European Union-led initiative European Capitals of

Culture (ECOC) programme, when the city showcased Mediterranean themes interpreted by locally and internationally acclaimed artists. The relation between a national French museum (the first outside of the capital city Paris) and an EU-led cultural programme focuses attention on the MuCEM as a discursive construction of transnational narratives that are tied to 'parochial' conceptions of urban space (Lazarus, 2011). Indeed, a 'parochial outlook values the local, its culture and solidarities, as a moral starting point and locus of ecological concern and a site for the development of virtues including commitment, fidelity, civility and nurture' and is defined against and with global perspectives (Tomaney, 2013: 659). In the context of the Mediterranean, the global has resonance with Morin's description of this area at the close of the twentieth century and our understanding of the transnational. For Morin, the Mediterranean is: 'tout ce qui s'oppose dans la planète: Occident et Orient, Nord et Sud, islam et christianisme (avec l'interférence aggravante du judaïsme), laïcité et religion, fondamentalisme et modernisme. Richesse et pauvreté' (1998–99: 34). Furthermore, Morin reiterates that in order to face the challenges that exist in the Mediterranean, 'il faut des réponses à la fois mondiales, régionales et locales' (1998–99: 47). Similarly, the MuCEM is anchored in national history but its geographic location creates bridges that extend to other Mediterranean places, creating a dialogue between communities at both a local and global level.

This chapter is divided into three main sections. Firstly it outlines the historic and political context of the museum. Then it reviews the museum's physical positioning as a site for the pluralization of curatorial narratives. The final section explores some of the 'figures of a common history' (Rancière, 2007: 91) as they are presented through the eyes of a national institution. It does this by analysing discourse in institutional and media-produced documents on Marseille in the context of the MuCEM published between the mid-1990s and 2015 as well as personal observations of the museum conducted in Marseille in 2012, 2013 and 2015.

From French Vernacular to European and Mediterranean Civilizations

The current collection now housed in the MuCEM once sat in the national museum of popular arts and traditions in Paris—le Musée National d'Arts et Traditions Populaires (MNAPT). Its journey is one that is closely tied not only to political ideologies and social change in France, but also to the connection between local priorities and wider transnational relations.

While the present focus of the MuCEM is centred on Mediterranean civilizations, the history of the museum's collection tells another story. Indeed, when the collection was first housed at the MNAPT in Paris between 1937 and 2005, the museum was a legacy of le Front Populaire, the first left-wing coalition to come to power in France (1936–38). The MNAPT reflected the social ideology of le Front Populaire that sought to give France's working-class people a sense of themselves through everyday objects (Colardelle, 1999; Poirrier, 2000). The scope of this museum's collection was vast, with the media describing the objects and audiovisual material as a reflection of 'la "douce France", ses folklores, ses fêtes, sa magie, voire sa sorcellerie [...] Il raconte la vie des Français de l'an mil à aujourd'hui' (Jaeglé, 2013: n. pag.). In 2005, the MNAPT closed its doors. The last director of the MNAPT, also the MuCEM's first director (2005–09), Michel Colardelle, described the museum of popular traditions in its final years as a 'musée en crise'. Aspects such as French rural life, festival rituals, regional dress and so on no longer attracted visitors to the museum in its final decade (Colardelle, 2002: 15). The collection was viewed as historically and culturally valuable but in need of reinvention in consideration of contemporary political and social developments (Colardelle, 1999).

Following the deepening of European integration in the 1980s (German unification, Maastricht, the European single currency), the transnational potential of the MNAPT's collection was identified. Rather than the telling of national narratives, the collection could be enhanced and used to construct transnational stories. Colardelle's (1999) report on the MNAPT's future underscores the moral responsibilities of ethnographic museum practices in terms of the social and cultural change taking place in Europe at the time. Referring to the increase in extreme right-wing nationalism in Europe in the 1990s and the ongoing failure of transnational European business collaborations, Colardelle connects a 'méconnaissance des cultures européennes' with the need for a museum featuring a cosmopolitan view 'qui se voie par rapport à l'autre, par rapport à d'autres espaces et ouvert aux courants extérieurs' (1999: 22–23). Meanwhile, Colardelle is also conscious of the problem posed by a museum on Europe, relating that 'il ne faut pas que l'on construise une identité européenne qui soit génératrice d'un nouveau conflit avec l'autre' (in Mazé, 2014: 132). These two viewpoints evoke the dilemma inherent in the creation of a museum that, on the one hand, seeks to break down cultural barriers and misunderstandings within Europe while, on the other, running the risk of representing a 'repetition of the nationalization processes of the nineteenth century under post-national conditions' with regard to who is European and who is not (Krankenhagen, 2011: 270).

In the late 1990s, discussions on European integration did however raise awareness on the role of the Mediterranean and the EU's policies on neighbouring countries. Morin, for instance, argued for the reconceptualization of the Mediterranean and its relation to Europe. According to Morin, 'Les notions d'Europe et de Méditerranée sont deux notions en interférence: la seconde n'est pas la frontière de la première. On ne peut retrouver la Méditerranée qu'en cessant de la percevoir comme frontière et qu'en la considérant comme bien commun et grande communicatrice' (1998–99: 43). These statements underscore the challenges facing our understanding of the Mediterranean. The 'interference' referred to by Morin reminds us of the historic cultural, political and economic ties of non-EU countries with Europe. Similarly, philosopher Etienne Balibar's work on the borders of Europe refers to the blurred space between Europe and the Mediterranean when he refers to Europe's 'overlapping peripheries' that are influenced from 'all other parts of Europe and from the whole world' (2009: 200).

The choice of Marseille as a site for the new museum creates a palpable dialogue between the notion of the Mediterranean and its relation to Europe for numerous reasons. Over the last two centuries, Marseille's population has been defined by the settlement of political refugees from various parts of Europe and by migrants, predominantly from France's former colonies in Africa.[3] Representations of the city entail narratives of passage (ancient traders, crusaders, colonizers, migrants) and a north-south dichotomy (Europe/Africa, Europe/Middle East, France/colonies, Christianity/Islam).

Furthermore, the building of a museum of European and Mediterranean civilizations in Marseille coincided with a major local and national political plan initiated in the mid-1990s to counter the

---

3 According to historians Blanchard and Boëtsch's work on Marseille, the number of people with migrant origins in Marseille total around 52 per cent, with a large proportion from Algeria, Comoros and Armenia (2005: 217). Sociologists Peraldi, Dupont and Samson refer to the predominantly North African ethnic make-up of Marseille's migrant population in their sociological study *Sociologie de Marseille* (2015: 74).

city's perceived public image as poor, dirty and dangerous (Boura, 2001; Peraldi et al., 2015). Titled the Euroméditerranée project, local policy-makers in Marseille selected the concept of the Mediterranean as part of their strategy to increase tourism, encourage the development of the creative industries and attract foreign investment to the city, as well as to suggest that the EU orient its attention towards the Mediterranean. Throughout the 1990s, strategic papers and promotional brochures presented the national and local ambition of this project, describing it as 'l'ambition de la prééminence de la France au cœur de la politique méditerranéenne de l'Union Européenne et de sa position centrale et structurante sur l'axe méditerranéen' (Euroméditerranée à Marseille, 1996: 4; see also Vigouroux, 1994a; Euroméditerranée, n.d.: 2). The advantage of Marseille over other Mediterranean cities was that it could contribute 'au nécessaire rééquilibrage entre une Europe qui se construit au Nord et les pays du bassin méditerranéen' (Vigouroux, 1994b: 1; see also Conseil d'Etat, n.d.: 2). This strategy shifts the EU focus away from the north of Europe (and other political capitals such as Paris) and directs it towards the Mediterranean as a potential space for transnational dialogue.

This local ambition for a Mediterranean plan in Marseille received national attention. Under Nicolas Sarkozy, then president of France (2007–12), the MuCEM was seen to play a key political role in the relation between Europe and the Mediterranean. The museum would be the cultural face of Sarkozy's plan for a French-led Mediterranean Union.[4]

It is difficult, however, to separate the national scope of the museum from a broader international agenda as well as from local urban priorities. In 2009, the government directive was to create 'le grand musée des cultures de la Méditerranée' (Mazé, 2014: 61), despite the name of the museum referring to the civilizations of both Europe and the Mediterranean. One of Sarkozy's presidential speeches highlighted

---

4 A proposal to establish a 'Mediterranean Union', consisting mainly of countries around the Mediterranean, was part of Nicolas Sarkozy's campaign for the 2007 French presidential election. Sarkozy said that the Mediterranean Union could mirror the European Union with common institutions as well as offer a space for dialogue between Israel and its Arab neighbours. Some EU members, such as Germany, felt that this project ran the risk of dividing the EU. Subsequently, the plan for an autonomous Mediterranean Union was dropped and in its place the 'Union for the Mediterranean' was created in 2008 to enhance multilateral relations in Europe and the Mediterranean (see Lebovics, 2014).

Figure 6.1. A billboard-sized poster placed at the exit of Marseille's main train station Saint-Charles featuring information on the Euroméditerranée project. At the top a reference to 'the new Marseille' echoes the 'new' Mediterranean evoked in the objectives of the MuCEM. The poster's caption, 'Bienvenue dans le nouveau Marseille' [Welcome to the new Marseille], connects the Euroméditerranée project with urban development around the old port that included the MuCEM, visible on the lower left, and the historic port entrance on the right. October 2015.
Photo A. Giovanangeli © A. Giovanangeli.

the cultural role France could play in the dialogue amongst peoples of the Mediterranean:

> [I]l faut évoquer nos politiques culturelles aux abords de la Méditerranée, dont plus que jamais je crois impératif de rapprocher les peuples. La France a porté le projet de l'Union pour la Méditerranée. On voit bien aujourd'hui combien il est nécessaire que les peuples de la Méditerranée, juifs, arabes, européens, se rencontrent, dialoguent. Ils sont condamnés à vivre ensemble. (Discours de M. le Président, 2009: 2)

In the lead-up to the opening of the MuCEM, the theme of the Mediterranean both within Europe and beyond took on an increasingly significant importance. Colardelle's successor as director, Bruno Suzzarelli (2009–14), appointed during the Sarkozy presidency, focused specifically on the Mediterranean, stating in 2013 that the MuCEM's objective was to create 'une nouvelle vision de la Méditerranée, qui n'impose pas un point de vue européaniste' (Freschel, 2013: n. pag.). This statement implies not only a predominantly Mediterranean focus but a 'new' way of conceptualizing the Mediterranean (see also Figure 6.1). For Suzzarelli, the new Mediterranean is a space with its own distinct identity centred around 'des grandes questions qui agitent la Méditerranée: la mobilité, la religion, les guerres, l'environnement' (Freschel, 2013: n. pag.).

Ethical and political considerations of how to present the Mediterranean have therefore been a key feature of the MuCEM. For the first director, Colardelle, the museum was to inform visitors about the intercultural relations between Europe and the Mediterranean. For his successor, the approach shifted from a European perspective to a new way of presenting the Mediterranean as a geographical entity first and foremost, with contemporary concerns associated with European and non-European issues. Subsequently, Jean François Chougnet, the present director appointed in 2014, has maintained the focus on the Mediterranean but connecting it to local participation. In a media interview he related that 'Le musée doit mieux s'insérer dans la vie culturelle locale', while also taking on a position of moral responsibility with regard to presenting contemporary events in the Mediterranean (Rof, 2014: n. pag.).

Narratives of Geographic and Curatorial Space

The connection between the museum's engagement with the local and a concern for the transnational has been integrated into the architecture of the museum as well as its geographic location and curatorial production. The museum's location on the water's edge is significant. In cultural geographer Mike Crang's scheme of things, the landscape is part of a symbolic system 'shaped according to the beliefs of the inhabitants and the meanings invested in that landscape' (1998: 27). The MuCEM's positioning is emblematic of Marseille's evolving connection with the Mediterranean and the notion of passage alluded to earlier.[5]

---

5 Specifically, the notion of passage in Marseille can be seen through the legendary arrival of the Greek sailor Protis and the foundation of Massalia in 600BC and the city's role as the starting point for the exploration and colonization of Africa and more distant places; the first place of contact for the repatriation

The MuCEMS's architect Rudy Ricciotti defines the museum as:

> Une casbah verticale, un carré parfait de 72 mètres de côté, tenu par des structures arborescentes élancées, protégé par une enveloppe brise-soleil tel un moucharabieh. Minérale, tout en béton fibré, de couleur poussière mate, c'est une architecture de la maigreur, étirée comme les muscles tendus d'un coureur de fond, armée d'une délicatesse puissante et féminine. Elle renvoie à la métaphore de l'espace méditerranéen. (in Maliszewski, 2012: n. pag.)

What stands out in this statement are the references to North Africa, as if the MuCEM were throwing out a net from Marseille across the Mediterranean to embrace North African culture, rather than presenting itself as a museum in Marseille in isolation or an outpost of centralized Paris-based French culture. The main building is a large rectangular block of dark glass enveloped by dark grey concrete that from afar looks like lacework: this brings a sense of lightness to the enormous block shape. Behind this building, and itself a part of the museum, is the Fort Saint-Jean, the historic stone fortification dating back to 1660. There is an ambivalence with regard to how the new building can be read in the landscape. For instance, Ricciotti's reference to the space and architecture of the Arab world is taken further in the work of historian Herman Lebovics, who likens the MuCEM to the 'massive black stone of the Kaaba in Mecca, where pilgrims from all over the world come in peace and unity' (2014: 295). That it could be read as a place of prayer as Lebovics intimates is an idea that has resonance with Duncan's definition of museum spaces as places for contemplation and learning (1991: 91) similar to religious temples or shrines, however the fusion of Arab and Western features is also an acknowledgement of the European and African characteristics of Marseille as well as of the wider Mediterranean region. Furthermore, the MuCEM is located alongside other significant landmarks of the city: military fortifications, cargo and cruise ships, dockyards and the most iconic symbols of Marseille's port and the city's Catholic heritage: the basilica Notre-Dame de la Garde and the Cathédrale de la Major. Michel Peraldi and Michel Samson's 2006 sociological study of Marseille points out that the image of Notre-Dame de la Garde is intricately tied to a hierarchical representation of the city which favours its Catholic identity, but fails to acknowledge the migrant heritage of many of its residents (2006: 278). Since 2013, however, the

of the exiled from Algeria during decolonization; the gateway into Europe for numerous waves of migrants; and the chosen site for the Euro-Mediterranean project.

Shaping Mediterranean Geographies

Figure 6.2. The iconic presence of the Catholic Cathédrale de la Major (left) at the entrance of the historic port is now in dialogue with the MuCEM (centre) as a distinct architectural presence of Marseille's symbolic landscape. December 2012. Photo A. Giovanangeli © A. Giovanangeli.

juxtaposition of the MuCEM alongside other iconic Marseillais symbols not only grants the museum local status, it also adds a new reading of the city's cultural heritage as Ricciotti's desired 'metaphor of Mediterranean space' (Maliszewski, 2012: n. pag.) and ethnic diversity in Marseille (see Figure 6.2). Likewise, Lebovics points out that 'the concrete act of pluralism in locating France's first national museum [...] outside Paris in this diverse city' was done in the context of France's need to reinvent itself as a nation framed 'by its ties to Europe and its near neighbours around the Mediterranean' (2014: 295).

The relation between the local and the transnational is further reinforced architecturally and metaphorically by two long, narrow, dark bridges. One bridge links the block-shaped building to the historic fortifications, while the other connects the fortifications to the old quarters of the city (see Figures 6.3 and 6.4). If the depiction of the urban landscape expresses beliefs about society and life (Crang, 1998: 49), this design gives the viewer a sense of continuous flow between the historic, iconic features of Marseille and the new museum space that projects itself towards the sweeping blue horizon of the Mediterranean sea and

Figure 6.3. View of one of the bridges linking the MuCEM (right) to the historic fortifications of the Fort Saint-Jean (left). June 2013. Photo A. Giovanangeli © A. Giovanangeli.

sky. There exists a connection between the old stones of Marseille's port and the new Mediterranean narrative evoked by the glass and concrete of the museum. Furthermore, the bridges of the MuCEM can also be seen as connections and traverses, to borrow a notion from Deleuze and Guattari (1987), with regard to the routes (as opposed to static notions) of identity that flow in the Mediterranean space.

Inside the dark block building of the MuCEM, the architecture echoes the external features of the museum. Organic grey shapes reflect light through glass panelled walls (see Figure 6.5). In the exhibition spaces, grey transparent curtains prevent the intense Mediterranean light and glare reflecting off the water from damaging the displays inside, yet allow visitors to catch glimpses of the Mediterranean Sea outside. The permanent collection is housed on the ground floor extending around three sides of the building and is titled 'The Gallery of the Mediterranean'. Themes identified in the permanent collection explore the invention of farming, the ancient presence of gods, the birth of monotheism in Jerusalem, citizenship, human rights and sea exploration. The diverse themes are not divided by walls but rather by ceiling-to-floor partitions made out of sheer white fabric. While visitors

Shaping Mediterranean Geographies

Figure 6.4. View of the other bridge linking the fortifications (right) to the old quarters of Marseille (left). In the background one of the most iconic features of Marseille, the Catholic basilica Notre-Dame de la Garde can be seen at the top of the hill overlooking the port's entrance. June 2013.
Photo A. Giovanangeli © A. Giovanangeli.

can follow a themed route, there is no set direction and it is possible to zigzag through various sections of the exhibition (see Figure 6.6). Boundaries in the display spaces of this floor are not explicitly delineated. One cannot help but relate these curatorial features to Morin's vision of a Mediterranean that has no borders and is a space that acts as an agent of communication and shared knowledge (1998–99: 43), or to Balibar's Europe as 'overlapping peripheries' which are influenced by 'other parts of the world' (2009: 200).

The permanent exhibition comprises a variety of displays, including material objects, audiovisual installations projected on large or small screens, artworks and contemporary installations. Some objects are displayed in glass cabinets while others are presented uncovered—a display method that adds to the concept of boundaries, the separation of territories and where lines meet and end. For Balibar, there is a duality associated with borders in that they are both local and global—each line reflects a 'global order' and confers a 'universal' meaning upon local difference (2009: 200). In the context of the MuCEM's permanent

Figure 6.5. The interior space of the museum features organic shapes and reflections of natural light. Through the glass panels the Mediterranean sea and sky are visible. October 2015.
Photo A. Giovanangeli © A. Giovanangeli.

collection, the absence of precise lines or demarcations around some of the objects highlights questions about the Mediterranean and how to qualify a space that is not easily quantifiable.

The 'Figure of a Common History'

The museum's permanent collection is framed within the idea of the 'new' Mediterranean, as stated by the museum's director Bruno Suzarelli, quoted above. Indeed, a MuCEM press release in 2012 refers to 'une manière nouvelle de considérer la Méditerranée comme un espace d'ouverture et de partage, d'envisager une histoire commune, percevoir le dialogue des civilisations [...] façonner un nouvel espace public' (Dossier de presse, 2012: 4). Meanwhile, Suzzarelli also believes that the role of a museum of society, such as the MuCEM, is to present a dialogue between the local and the global: 'cette dialectique de l'identité et de l'altérité, du local et du global, qui caractérise nos sociétés à l'heure de la mondialisation et de l'ère numérique (2013: 9). These notions highlight the relation between the local and the transnational but also

Shaping Mediterranean Geographies

Figure 6.6. The MuCEM's permanent collection space.
Transparent curtains are a feature of the divisions between displays as well as the internal and external spaces of the museum, while glass cabinets reinforce the notion of boundaries and the separation of territories.
October 2015. Photo A. Giovanangeli © A. Giovanangeli.

mirror what French philosopher Jacques Rancière refers to as 'the future of the image', that is, the possibility of finding new paradigms to account for the relationship between objects and a common history.

The museum's quest for 'une histoire commune' is apparent throughout the exhibition. For instance, at the entrance a short film on a large screen presents four distinct aspects characterizing the Mediterranean and sets the context of the permanent collection: the honouring of plants and animals in the most ancient temple found in Turkey, the beginnings of monotheism in Egypt's Mount Sinai, the origins of citizenship in Athens and the exploration of new routes beyond Morocco. Different Mediterranean places are mentioned in the film. Countries of origin are also indicated in the texts adjacent to each object on display. Despite these references to geographic sites, specific places are not singled out, rather the collection is imbued with a general sense of the Mediterranean. Ancient and more contemporary earthenware pots on display in the section on agriculture are from France, Greece, Turkey and Serbia, yet they serve to illustrate their use with regard to shared eating practices in the Mediterranean: bread, olives and wine.

Adjacent to this Mediterranean narrative, however, exist the multiple junctions of the local and the transnational. In this same section on agriculture, alongside the earthenware pots stands a contemporary installation by Israeli artist Sigalit Landau titled *Water Meter Tree*, created in 2011.[6] Made out of water meters and metal water pipes in the shape of a tree, it refers to the problem of water management in the contemporary world that threatens food crops and the livelihood of farmers. Clearly the message of this installation is grounded in a Mediterranean narrative but also in a distinctly global setting. On the other hand, local references are found in the short film not far from this installation on fishing in the Mediterranean. The message of the video echoes the ecological issues in the installation by referring to the falling fish populations in the Mediterranean, yet makes a clear reference to Marseille when a local Marseillais fisherman in the film provides the viewer with advice on a distinct local seafood dish—the bouillabaisse—stating that 'au printemps il faut manger une bouillabaisse, c'est ça la valorisation des produits'.

Emilie Girard, one of the MuCEM's curators, states that the meaning of the objects on display in the MuCEM is generated 'par le regard et le discours donnés aux objets'.[7] For Girard, the discourse of the collection is designed around the principle that objects are 'like words in a sentence' and are therefore 'manipulated' to present an idea. This discursive approach has similarities with some of Rancière's ideas. In the *Future of the Image*, Rancière tells us that 'by drawing lines, arranging words or distributing surfaces, one also designs divisions of communal space' (2007: 91). It is thus by shaping the meaning of objects that a narrative is created around the Mediterranean.

These 'communal spaces' can be understood in terms of the connections they create with the local and the transnational. In the context of the MuCEM collection, these spaces have parallels with what social-cultural anthropologist Arjun Appadurai refers to in his *Modernity at Large* as a 'dialectical play between national and transnational allegiances' (1996: 167). From this perspective, locality creates contexts that extend ideas to broader areas and collective understandings. A further example of this relation between local and transnational

---

6 An image of this installation can be viewed at http://www.mucem.org/fr/water-meter-tree.

7 Thanks to Emilie Girard for her time and for her courtesy in answering the questions I had prepared for her during two one-hour interviews, the first conducted in Paris in 2012 and the second in Marseille in 2013.

concerns is evident in the museum's display on citizenship and human rights. The concept of citizenship is illustrated through various objects, installations and videos such as vases from ancient Athens, portraits from the merchant city of Venice, a contemporary video titled 'Istanbul, Istanbul' referring to the plight of exiles in Turkey. Here the evolution of democratic principles is situated in the Mediterranean space but evokes a dialogue between global questions on citizenship such as the passage of migrants and the notion of European belonging. Indeed, the effects of contemporary migratory practices playing out at the geopolitical margins of Europe and the Mediterranean put migrants at the very centre of Europeanization processes and 'migrants bring questions of citizenship and human rights' (Poehls, 2011: 340). Meanwhile, adjacent to these questions on citizenship, a significant proportion of this section is dedicated to the French Revolution. Iconic French objects such as the cockade, the Phrygian cap, the guillotine and a Marianne statue from Marseille are placed alongside each other. While universal in their outlook, strong national as well as Marseillais dimensions are present, with the local grounded in the city's connection to the nation as the 'birthplace' of France's national anthem and historical support of revolutionary ideology.

The MuCEM's narratives are clearly anchored in the local yet also present a transnational perspective that includes Turkey, North Africa, Europe, Israel and the intersection between Islam, Judaism and Christianity. This is further emphasized by one of the MuCEM's ethnologists, who explains that while the museum examines Euro-Mediterranean perspectives, its outlook will always be determined by its location in Marseille: 'c'est quand même vu de Marseille, vu de France, donc on reste quand même d'une certaine façon pris dans la problématique du lieu d'où l'on regarde les choses qui est le nôtre' (Mazé, 2014: 163). Clearly, this indicates that the transnational perspective of the MuCEM cannot be examined without consideration of the local context of the museum.

A 'New' Mediterranean

The symbolic positioning of the MuCEM on France's Mediterranean edge substantiates what Crang argues to be the political and contested nature of cultures—that is, cultures 'mean different things to different people in different places' (1998: 4). Clearly, power and meaning are written onto and through the landscape. The local objective of the

MuCEM is driven by Marseille's urban metamorphosis yet the museum also encapsulates the strategic role Marseille could play in connecting Mediterranean peoples and cultures, shifting European focus towards a geographic south.

Indeed, present-day urban strategies invest in building a local identity in Marseille around the symbolic centrality to the city's mythology of migrant flows and cultural interfaces in order to add legitimacy to the establishment of a modern economic city that is locally connected to its inhabitants. This locally constructed cosmopolitanism is illustrated by the idea of the Mediterranean as both a part of a local heritage and a narrative existing outside of France. Accordingly, the Mediterranean presented in the MuCEM embodies a 'parochial outlook' that 'values the local' (Tomaney, 2013: 659) as the site for reflection of a space inherently linked to transnational narratives around notions of mobility, citizenship, the environment and religion. The MuCEM identifies shared practices and rituals that go back to antiquity and predate the EU, while presenting a 'new' way of defining the Mediterranean as a borderless area possessing its own identity alongside and beyond Europe.

Bibliography

Appadurai, Arjun. 1996. *Modernity at large: Cultural dimensions of globalization*. Minneapolis: University of Minnesota Press.

Balibar, Etienne. 2009. Europe as borderland. *Environment and Planning D: Society and Space* 27(2): 190–215.

Blanchard, Pascal and Gilles Boëtsch. 2005. *Marseille porte sud. 1905–2005: Un siècle d'histoire coloniale et d'immigration*. Paris: éditions Jeanne Laffitte/Marseille: La Découverte.

Boura, Olivier. 2001. *Marseille ou la mauvaise réputation*. Paris: Arléa.

Bulley, Dan. 2009. *Ethics as foreign policy: Britain, the EU and the other*. New York: Routledge.

Chevallier, Denis. 2008. Collecter, exposer le contemporain au MuCEM. *Ethnologie française* 4(38): 631–37.

———. 2013. Introduction. Les musées de société: la grande mue du XXIe siècle. In Denis Chevallier, ed., in collaboration with Aude Fanlo, *Métamorphoses des musées de société*, 11–17. Paris: La Documentation française.

Colardelle, Michel. 1999. *Le musée et le centre interdisciplinaire d'étude des civilisations de l'Europe et de la Méditerranée. Etude préalable pour un projet de 'délocalisation' du MNAPT-CEF de Paris à Marseille*. https://www.vie-publique.fr/rapport/26213-le-musee-et-le-centre-interdisciplinaire-detudes-des-civilisations-de-l.

———, ed. 2002. *Réinventer un musée, le Musée des Civilisations de l'Europe et de la Méditerranée à Marseille.* Paris: Réunion des musées nationaux.

Conseil d'Etat. n.d. La Joliette au Titre d'Opération d'Intérêt National. *Rapport de Présentation au Conseil d'Etat Annexe 5,* 1–6. Archives Ville de Marseille, reference number 963W62.

Council of Europe. 2015. *The museum prize. Parliamentary Assembly Council of Europe.* Council of Europe. http://website-pace.net/en_GB/web/apce/the-museum-prize.

Cour des comptes. 2015. Le MuCEM: une gestation laborieuse, un avenir incertain. *Rapport public annuel 2015.* www.ccomptes.fr.

Crang, Mike. 1998. *Cultural geography.* London: Routledge.

Deleuze, Gilles and Félix Guattari. 1987. *A thousand plateaus: Capitalism and schizophrenia.* Minneapolis: University of Minnesota Press.

Discours de M. le Président de la République Vœux aux acteurs de la Culture, Nîmes, 13 January 2009. http://www.culture.gouv.fr/culture/actualites/conferen/albanel/prculture09.pdf.

Dossier de presse MuCEM. 2012. *MuCEM première, le MuCEM se dévoile,* June, 1–48.

Duncan, Carol. 1991. Art museums and the ritual of citizenship. In Ivan Karp and Steven D. Lavine, eds., *Exhibiting cultures: The poetics and politics of museum display,* 88–103. Washington DC: Smithsonian Institution Press.

Euroméditerranée. n.d. *Euroméditerranée.* Centre Décisionnel, Ville de Marseille. Archives Villes de Marseille dossier number 963W62.

Euroméditerranée à Marseille. 1996. *Euroméditerranée à Marseille, un grand projet d'aménagement et de développement.* Etablissement Public Euroméditerranée, April.

Euroméditerranée un projet stratégique. n.d. *Euroméditerranée. Un Projet stratégique pour l'aire métropolitaine marseillaise.* Archives Villes de Marseille dossier number 1040W14.

Freschel, Agnès. 2013. Voyage à l'intérieur du MuCEM. Entretien avec Bruno Suzzarelli, Directeur du MuCEM. *Zibeline.* http://www.journalzibeline.fr/voyage-a-linterieur-du-mucem/.

Grésillon, Boris. 2011. *Un Enjeu 'capitale' Marseille-Provence 2013.* La Tour d'Aigues: l'Aube.

Huntzinger, Jacques. 2010. *Il était une fois la Méditerranée.* Paris: CNRS.

Jaeglé, Yves. 2005. L'Adieu au musée des Arts et Traditions populaires. *Le Parisien,* 24 August. http://www.leparisien.fr/seine-saint-denis/l-adieu-au-musee-des-arts-et-traditions-populaires-24-08-2005-2006231768.php.

Krankenhagen, Stefan. 2011. Exhibiting Europe: The development of European narratives in museums, collections and exhibitions. *Culture Unbound* 3: 269–78.

Lazarus, Neil. 2011. Cosmopolitanism and the specificity of the local in world literature. *Journal of Commonwealth Literature* 46(1): 119–37.

Lebovic, Herman. 2014. The future of the nation foretold in its museums. *French Cultural Studies* 25(3–4): 290–98.
Maliszewski, Catherine. 2012. Le MuCem est un projet romantique. *M le magazine du Monde*, 29 June. http://www.lemonde.fr/m-styles/article/2012/06/29/le-mucem-est-un-projet-romantique_1726438_4497319.html.
Mazé, Camille. 2009. Les 'Musées de l'Europe', outils de production d'un ordre symbolique européen? *Regards Sociologiques*, 37–38: 69–80.
———. 2014. *La Fabrique de l'identité européenne. Dans les coulisses des musées de l'Europe*. Paris: Belin.
Morin, Edgar. 1998–99. Penser la Méditerranée et méditerranéiser la pensée. *Confluences Méditerranée* 28: 33–47.
Peraldi, Michel, Claire Dupont and Michel Samson. 2015. *Sociologie de Marseille*. Paris: La Découverte.
Peraldi, Michel and Michel Samson. 2006. *Gouverner Marseille. Enquête sur les mondes politiques marseillais*. Paris: La Découverte.
Poehls, Kerstin. 2011. Europe, blurred: Migration, margins and the museum. *Culture Unbound* 3: 337–53.
Poirrier, Philippe. 2000. *L'Etat et la culture en France au XXe siècle*. Paris: Le Livre du Poche.
Rancière, Jacques. 2007. *The future of the image*. Translated by Gregory Elliot. London and New York: Verso.
Rof, Gilles. 2014. 'Le MuCEM ne doit pas devenir un musée pour touristes', Jean-François Chougnet, son nouveau president. *Télérama*, 10 September. http://www.telerama.fr/scenes/le-mucem-ne-doit-pas-devenir-un-musee-pour-touristes,116708.php.
Suzzarelli, Bruno. 2013. Préface. Quels musées de civilisation(s) pour l'avenir? In Denis Chevallier, ed., in collaboration with Aude Fanlo, *Métamorphoses des musées de société*, 9–10. Paris: La Documentation Française.
Tomaney, John. 2013. Parochialism—a defence. *Progress in Human Geography* 37(5): 658–72.
Vigouroux, Robert. 1994a. Letter from Robert Vigouroux, Mayor of Marseille to French Prime Minister Edouard Balladur dated 8 February. Archives Ville de Marseille, dossier number 963W62.
———. 1994b. Supporting documentation attached to Letter from Robert Vigouroux, Mayor of Marseille to French Prime Minister Edouard Balladur dated 8 February. Archives Ville de Marseille, dossier number 963W62.
Watremez, Anne. 2013. Des approches renouvelées des sociétés et des cultures. Trente ans d'expérimentation pour les musées de société. In Denis Chevallier, ed., in collaboration with Aude Fanlo, *Métamorphoses des musées de société*, 21–34. Paris: La Documentation Française.

7

Marseille Provence 2013
A Social Facelift for an Old Lady?

Agnès Peysson-Zeiss

Marseille, the gateway to the Orient, a place of cultural exchange, has been a trading space between all major cities situated along the *Mare Nostrum* since its inception. As a port city, it is a lens opened onto the Mediterranean, a region which Fernand Braudel saw as 'Mille choses à la fois. Non pas un paysage mais d'innombrables. Non pas une mer, mais une succession de mers. Non pas une civilisation, mais plusieurs civilisations superposées' (1985: 351). Many from around the basin have crossed it, settled in it or travelled to and from it: Italians and Spanish in the 1900s, followed by a large Levantine population: Turks, Armenians and Greeks between 1915 and 1922. The end of the French-Algerian war in 1962 was marked by the arrival of a large population of *pieds-noirs*, fleeing newly independent Algeria. Around 150,000 settled in Marseille, a considerable number for a large city experiencing an economic crisis. It has been estimated that about two million people came from the Maghreb, particularly Algeria, during the 1960s (see Témime, 1995), adding to this already cosmopolitan city where a variety of languages and cultures coexisted. As a result of these successive migrations, Marseille had become a complex mosaic, filled with Maghrebi people but deprived of true connections to the rest of the Mediterranean.

When Melina Mercouri and Jack Lang, respectively Greek and French ministers of culture, launched the idea of the Capital of Culture in 1985, it was with the underlying aim of showcasing European cultures and bridging gaps between them. They argued for new cultural policies and strategies to attain cultural and economic renaissance in non-capital cities. Minister Mercouri presented the idea to the European Commission, and the European ministers of culture passed the resolution, creating the Capital of Culture programme with over 50 cities selected so far. Marseille's fate was about to change when it was unanimously elected as one of the two capitals with Košice in 2013—in the past, the honour had gone to Paris (1989), Avignon (1999) and Lille (2004). It may have come as a surprise to some but was a relief to many who identified this port city with poverty and crime-ridden *cités*. Due to its geography, Marseille has no *banlieues* but divisions exist between northern and southern quarters, creating a rift between its inhabitants. Keny Arkana, a rapper living in Marseille, highlighted the schism between the 'impoverished' (arrondissements 1–3 and northern areas) and 'wealthy' neighbourhoods (southern districts) in her song 'Marseille': '1-3, centre-ville, quartiers sud, quartiers nord. Marseille, Marseille'. Echoing her claim, Bernard Latarjet, the former president of Marseille-Provence, has spoken of the existing social divide; highlighting the fact that it is a microcosm of the issues facing Europe to explain why Marseille needed to attain the Capital of Culture status:

> Les vraies questions culturelles qui se posent à l'Europe, ce sont les migrations, le racisme, les rapports hommes-femmes, les religions, l'écologie. Marseille est sur la ligne de front des fractures de la planète. Il n'y a pas une ville plus cosmopolite. Des quatre villes candidates, c'est elle qui a le plus besoin du label capitale européenne de la culture, et elle peut servir l'Europe mieux que d'autres. (qtd. in Fabre, 2008: n. pag.)

As a result, both Marseille and its cultural twin city of Košice, in Slovakia, were selected and received a facelift to ready them as European Capitals of Culture for 2013. In a joint venture, the organizations Košice 2013 and Marseille-Provence 2013 (MP13) developed mutual cooperation underlining the fact that the two Capitals of Culture are shaped by their deep multicultural character and their geographic position at the crossroads of different cultures, whether as a port city for Marseille or landlocked as Slovakia is. Both cities are near multiple borders, within the European Union and in the Schengen zone. While Marseille displayed itself as a mediator of north-south cultural exchanges, Košice aimed at bridging the gap between eastern and western regions.

Each metropolis was hoping for a surge in civic pride that would endure, an associated economic and touristic development, city marketing and physical regeneration similar to what previous Capitals of Culture had experienced.[1] Following rap artist Keny Arkana's

---

[1] The amendments inserted to the European Union Treaty recognize that cultural associations are defined as members of civil society. As such, Article 2,

response to MP13 in her song 'Capitale de la rupture', we will examine whether the MP13 makeover brought about real change or was only undertaken for political expediency. Was MP13 only a way to allow the local government to 'kick out a portion of its citizens and gentrify the downtown', as Arkana feared?[2] I will offer a brief historical overview of the construction of MP13, by well-known literary figures, in order to understand the challenges of such an endeavour and determine whether the EU's Capital of Culture project is a pre-packaged, sterile identity maker created specifically for an international stage or if it will have genuinely long-lasting effects on the city.

If, historically, the various waves of immigration have shaped the cityscape and had a positive impact on its cultural, literary and artistic creations, has the 2013 cultural movement bridged gaps or mostly fostered segregation? Whether it be from the standpoint of travellers such as Flaubert, Cendrars and, more recently, Tahar Ben Jelloun, poets like Eluard and Cocteau, a citizen of the Mediterranean like Camus or a Marseillais like Izzo, all have seen Marseille through a different lens and tried to understand what it means to live in such a place. For Flaubert, Marseille was 'a Babel of all nations' where one will hear 'a hundred different foreign tongues' (all translations are my own).[3] Cendrars, despite the fact that he never lived in Marseille, understood that the city 'belongs to the one who comes from the sea [...] It is not a city where architecture, religion, literature, writing or fine arts are important [...] Nevertheless it is one of the most mysterious and most difficult world

paragraph 3 of the Lisbon Treaty provides for the respect of 'the richness of its [Europe's] cultural and linguistic diversity and sees to the safeguarding and development of the European cultural heritage'.

2 Keny Arkana, in 'Capitale de la rupture': 'Expulsés pour du business compte ceux qui restent / Esprit démolis comme ces murs qu'on a toujours tenus'.

3 Flaubert wrote: 'Marseille est maintenant ce que devait être la Perse dans l'Antiquité, Alexandrie au Moyen Age: un capharnaüm, une Babel de toutes les nations, où l'on voit des cheveux blonds, ras, de grandes barbes noires, la peau blanche rayée de veines bleues, le teint olivâtre de l'Asie, des yeux bleus, des regards noirs, tous les costumes, la veste, le manteau, le drap, la toile, la collerette rabattue, le turban et les larges pantalons des Turcs. Vous entendez parler cent langues inconnues, le slave, le sanscrit, le persan, le scythe, l'égyptien, tous les idiomes, ceux qu'on parle au pays des neiges, ceux qu'on soupire dans les terres du Sud. Combien sont venus là sur ce quai où il fait maintenant si beau, et qui sont retournés auprès de leur cheminée à charbon de terre, ou dans leurs huttes au bord des grands fleuves, sous les palmiers de cent coudées ou dans leurs maisons de jonc au bord du Gange?' (2007: 700).

cities to decipher'.[4] This sentiment is echoed by Ben Jelloun: 'Marseille is a mystery, a house with several doors and windows that are always open [...] Marseille is a migraine vivified by wind and an exodus of people. Exodus. Exile and hard work. But also the Formica of a narrow dream. Languages spoken but not heard'.[5] Is this Formica a durable dream with its laminated agglomeration of cultures, and all languages heard? The former Massilia is certainly multicultural and multi-ethnic and as such it has been featured in novels,[6] comic strips such as *Le Tour de Gaule d'Astérix* including all the Provençal clichés (pastis, pétanque and the accent), movies and songs—Kenza Farah, an R&B artist, in 'Sous le soleil de Marseille', embraced the city that 'welcomed her with open arms'. In the late 1980s and 1990s, music and the graphic arts paved

4 Blaise Cendrars: 'Je n'ai jamais habité Marseille et une seule fois dans ma vie j'y ai débarqué descendant d'un paquebot, le d'Artagnan, mais Marseille appartient à celui qui vient du large. Marseille sentait l'œillet poivré, de matin-là. Marseille est une ville selon mon cœur. C'est aujourd'hui la seule des capitales antiques qui ne nous écrase pas avec les monuments de son passé. Son destin prodigieux de vous saute pas aux yeux, pas plus que ne vous éblouissent sa fortune et sa richesse ou que ne nous stupéfie par son aspect ultra-ultra (comme tant d'autres ports up to date) le modernisme du premier port de France, le plus spécialisé de la Méditerranée et l'un des plus importants du globe. Ce n'est pas une ville d'architecture, de religion, de belles-lettres, d'académie ou de beaux-arts. Ce n'est point le produit de l'histoire, de l'anthropogéographie, de l'économie politique ou de la politique, royale ou républicaine. Aujourd'hui elle paraît embourgeoisée et populacière. Elle a l'air bon enfant et rigolarde. Elle est sale et mal foutue. Mais c'est néanmoins une des villes les plus mystérieuses du monde et des plus difficiles à déchiffrer' (1973: 58).

5 Tahar Ben Jelloun: 'Marseille est une énigme, une maison avec plusieurs portes et fenêtres toujours ouvertes. Quand un cheval entre dans la cour de cette maison il tourne en rond jusqu'à la folie et la chute. Dans sa crinière une araignée a tissé sa cage. Un jour une fenêtre s'est déplacée jusqu'à la mer. Un peintre qui passait par là s'arrêta et ferma les yeux le temps pour l'image de s'imprimer. Avec toutes ces ouvertures, ces écrans levés au-dessus de la Méditerranée et ces maisons de pierre les unes sur les autres, le vent s'ennuie, la lumière se perd et la ville sombre dans une grande fatigue. Être à ce point bousculé par des mains, des regards et des songes venus du Sud, fait de la ville un malentendu. Certes le cheval s'est trompé de cimetière et la Méditerranée a été complaisante avec l'Histoire. Calme et sereine, la mer assiste- en toute impunité – au déménagement des hommes. Car Marseille est une migraine que ravivent le vent et l'exode. L'exode. L'exil et le labeur. Mais aussi le formica du rêve étroit. Les langues parlées mais pas entendues' (1985: 219).

6 Alexandre Dumas père, *Le comte de Monte Cristo* (1844); Emile Zola, *Les mystères de Marseille* (1867); Jean Giono, *Mort d'un personnage* (1949); J.M.G. Le Clézio, *Désert* (1980); Jean-Claude Izzo, *Total Khéops* (1995).

the way for a new generation to find its space, using Marseille as a point of departure, a creative space. The city council was already committed to changing the view people had of Marseille and as such enacted a series of measures concerning art and the youth as part of 'an image policy [...] aiming at regaining and reversing the stigma associated with Marseille' (Lafargue de Grangeneuve, 2008: 184). The municipality and DRAC (Direction Générale des Affaires Culturelles) financed several organizations and sites such as the Cultural centre Mille Pattes (Noailles), the *café-concert* L'Affranchi, helping the promotion of new vocal artists. When the group IAM won at the Victoires de la musique in 1995, the city implemented a hip-hop policy to destigmatize rap music; bringing the northern quarters, a place that produced many young artists, into the spotlight, launching the golden age of Marseillais rap and positioning its *quartiers* on the national map. Marseillais hip-hop and rap music did grow for a number of years, focusing on questions of identity, artistic representation and advertisement of new artists, but with the decline in port activity and the economic crisis, city funding declined. If IAM, Psy4 de la rime and Keny Arkana have done well, signing with major music labels, other artists have not emerged on the national scene. The independent hip-hop and rap scene is still vibrant but without city funding there are fewer rehearsal spaces and less promotion of new voices in the city. The Logique hip-hop festival (1996–2002) is now long defunct, and MP13 did not feature much rap music besides the ephemeral WATT! project.[7]. However, 'the growth of cultural influence is a major theme of the Euroméditerranée project' (Culture et loisirs, n.d.: n. pag.), which has been promoting support for the existing network of centres contributing to the local livelihood of neighbourhoods. The venture intends to help the local artistic community, encouraging festivals such as La Fiesta des Suds, le Festival de Marseille, Le Festival de Jazz des cinq continents and le Festival des livres. According to geography professor Boris Grésillon,

> Marseille avait absolument besoin de tous ces équipements culturels. En 2011, dans mon livre, je dressais le constat d'une faiblesse cruelle dans certains domaines. Il n'y avait plus de paysage muséal, rien en danse classique [...] juste quelques forces dans le domaine du rap et des arts de la rue. (qtd. in Guien, 2014: n. pag.)

And Marseille did embark on the development of several major cultural centres located in different parts of the city: the Museum of

---

[7] A multicultural residency project organized by MP13 with Arab, American and French hip-hop, electronic and jazz musicians.

Civilizations in Europe and the Mediterranean (MuCEM), the Arenc Silo, the Regional Centre of the Mediterranean and the cultural hub of the Friche Belle de Mai. The Euroméditerranée project will continue its development programme until 2020 with a large-scale rehabilitation plan to turn Marseille into a major European metropolis. The 2013 Capital of Culture selection was timely, and, since MP13 was going to host European events, making Marseille centre stage of the European map, transforming it into an attractive and competitive metropolis.

Many doubted the viability of the Friche Belle de Mai[8] and of all the artistic initiatives undertaken in 2013 beyond the Capital of Culture moment. Others thought that it was just a publicity stunt, a legal way to evict the lower classes from the rehabilitated areas, gentrifying the downtown in its wake. Echoing Keny Arkana, Nicolas Burlaud argued in his documentary *La fête est finie* (2014) that culture and its 'Mediterraneanity' were just a pretext to attract investors to the area under the umbrella of Euroméditerranée, with the goal to homogenize the mosaic. For this documentarist, the MP13 project had a new type of conquest in mind: 'coloniser de nouvelles dimensions, de nouvelles épaisseurs de l'être'. Through a series of vignettes, interviews and images of the city and its inhabitants, *La fête est finie* contrasts the despair of the displaced populations with the city officials' desire to raise up Marseille to the stature of a European city regardless of its people's desires:

> [L]e cœur de cible n'est pas la population marseillaise mais des investisseurs, des partenaires privés, des promoteurs immobiliers dont la Ville de Marseille et Euromed ont besoin pour faire avancer leur projet. Et donc on dessine une ville qui ressemble à toutes les autres dans la concurrence acharnée que se livrent les villes moyennes pour devenir des mégapoles, des métropoles [...] Cette ville fait fi de la population marseillaise. (Burlaud, 2015: n. pag.)

From the metropolis to the individual, Burlaud's film attempted to recapture the city's mosaic, ever ephemeral, as it was erased in Marseille's facelift.

How did these makeovers affect the cityscape? Was there only a desire for erasure and palimpsest or was there more to the renovations? The Marseille Métropole projects had already been affecting Marseillais' life in a multiplicity of ways through the Euroméditerranée sustainable

---

8 A former tobacco factory transformed into a cultural complex displaying art in all disciplines.

urban planning project. The cultural mission of MP13 was part of a larger project initiated 20 years prior by national and local governments, charging the Euroméditerranée initiative 'with redeveloping and growing Marseille to such a degree that it becomes recognized as one of Europe's major cities. This social, economic and cultural development project of national significance [was] launched in 1995 [...] Euroméditerranée is the largest urban renewal project in Europe'.[9]

It is important to note that any political campaign comes with proponents and opponents. As such, there are two currents in the city: those who fully embraced 2013 and those engaged in a counter-campaign as soon as the announcement of the selection was made in 2008 because they felt their voices were not heard and neighbourhood associations were not taken into account. This raises the question as to which segment of the society wanted this honour and what it brought in terms of money, support and to whom? Who did it help in the long term? And what does 'culture' really mean in the Euroméditerranée vision?

As far as the official story is concerned, the idea was to convert underutilized industrial areas in the city centre into new economic, commercial and residential quarters. With these building projects, Euroméditerranée hoped to anchor the redevelopment schemes and signal Marseille's transformation to the rest of the world. As the project's own website claims, 'the recruitment of great architects is proof of the region's attractiveness and Euroméditerranée's success of the last decade'. It has equally promoted sustainable development in order to keep 'a social and generational mix in the Joliette area'.[10]

A crucial part of Marseille's urban transformation has been the commission of a series of impressive buildings designed by world-renowned architects. Not only does the association give the city an elite cultural cachet, these cutting-edge structures communicate a sleek modernity and access to capital that is not normally associated with Marseille. In the MP13 organization's own words, these projects serve to heighten Marseille's 'international allure'. The first of these architectural projects to be completed was the CMA-CGM Tower, located in the city's new central business district. Designed by Pritzker Architecture Prize winner the late Zaha Hadid, the building towers imposingly over the rest of Marseille's waterfront and proclaims Marseille's robust shipping industry (CMA-CGM is France's largest

9   https://www.euromediterranee.fr/actualites/aux-origines-deuromediterranee.
10 The harbour area at the heart of the Euroméditerranée rehabilitation project.

shipping company and the third largest in the world). Though the glass-and-steel structure is fairly typical of corporate headquarters, Hadid's sleek tower looks out of place in a relatively low-rise cityscape of sun-bleached townhouses and mid-century concrete housing blocks. This dramatic difference emphasizes a break with Marseille's past, effectively ushering in a new landscape of multi-billion euro construction and a sleek modern aesthetic, well received in the press. One of the more recent projects is the Tour La Marseillaise, the second tallest tower by renowned architect Jean Nouvel in the same neighbourhood completed in 2018. At the heart of the bustling Vieux-Port, Foster and Partners's mirrored Ombrière is intentionally less intrusive, as project director Spencer de Grey explains: 'the structure had to have a big, transformative impact when you approached it, but disappear into the background from a distance' (qtd. in Wainwright, 2013: n. pag.). Still, the fact that this elegant steel structure was designed by one of today's most internationally respected architectural firms, headed by Pritzer Prize winner Norman Foster, similarly communicates officials' attempt to rebrand downtown Marseille's visual identity.

Designed by Algerian-born French architect Rudy Ricciotti, the MuCEM opened in June 2013. Well known in the field, Ricciotti's awards include the Grand Prix National d'Architecture and the Légion d'Honneur. The MuCEM is the largest French national museum outside of Paris, and its mission is to celebrate the diversity of Mediterranean cultures and histories. This intention is carefully expressed in the building's design—balanced on 17-ton posts, it emerges from the sea and faces the Mediterranean, linking France to the rest of the basin. The exterior latticework resembles the *mashrabiya* screens used in the Maghreb to keep buildings cool, or even a fishnet, subtly referencing two iconic aspects of Marseillais culture.

With these building projects, Euroméditerranée sought to anchor the redevelopment schemes and signal Marseille's transformation to the rest of the world. Though some buildings attracted more criticism than others—notably, the *Guardian*'s Oliver Wainwright described Stefano Boeri's Villa Méditerranée as 'embarrassingly shouty' (2013: n. pag.)—officials are proud of each renowned architect they were able to attract and the city is resolutely pushing forward with its redevelopment plan. The construction of this starkly different cityscape is not only altering Marseille's urban fabric but, as redevelopment officials hope, will attract a new class of people and businesses, potentially changing the city's culture. Ideally, a capital of culture should benefit across the board from the appellation: urban regeneration and economic development, cultural renaissance, a steady increase in tourism, and a new image and identity.

In this regard, since the European Capital of Culture is 'designed to foster the contribution of cultures to the development of cities' (Creative Europe, 2020: n. pag.), Marseille seems to have achieved its objective with the renovations undertaken. To most, the city's renovations are positive. It is true that the Vieux-Port is bustling at night in the summer, the Ombrière protects from the fierce sun and the MuCEM has an undeniable attractivity; the Friche Belle de Mai and its rooftop comes to life with music, cinema and a dance floor bringing many people together. But one cannot help but wonder if this construction frenzy has changed the overarching goal of the city with the urban landscape as its main preoccupation, superseding the overarching economic goal of the industrial city that is Marseille.

Thus, the unofficial story emerges, the story of the people left behind. It is correct to assume that urban renewal attracts new businesses, which was the goal of the city administrators since the launch of the Euroméditerranée initiative, but has it truly helped the inhabitants? Euromed engaged in sustainable development, maintaining 'a social and generational mix in the Joliette area (30 per cent of the housing will be subsidized)',[11] but is that enough and what type of displacements are we to witness? What new identities are surfacing?

Already in a discussion with sociologist Bernard Organini, at the Institut Régional du Travail Social (the Regional Institute of Social Work, situated in Marseille's northern quarters) in 2013,[12] the latter argued that there were ways in which citizens and artists in Marseille

---

11   Euromed: 'Cette politique ambitieuse s'accompagne de la requalification des espaces publics et de la construction d'équipements nécessaires à la vie de quartiers (commerces, écoles, cinéma …). S'appuyant sur les principes du développement durable, la politique choisie s'attache à préserver une mixité sociale (30% de logements aidés) et une mixité générationnelle par les réalisations de résidences pour étudiants ou personnes âgées. Cette volonté d'équilibre et de mixité, ainsi qu'une offre de transport enrichie permettent de répondre aux exigences des habitants, des nouveaux arrivants et des actifs de la métropole marseillaise améliorant ainsi leur quotidien. La mixité au cœur de la politique de logement: Un objectif aussi simple qu'ambitieux: créer de nouveaux quartiers où chacun puisse, selon ses revenus travailler, se loger, se divertir, circuler […] Les logements s'adressent à tous, indépendamment de l'âge, situation familiale ou niveau de vie'.

12   The discussion happened during a visit I made to Marseille with a class I taught on migrations around the Mediterranean in 2013.

could work together to create an identity apart from that constructed by those concerned with the European Capital of Culture. This self-constructed identity, Organini argued, is fiercely anti-consumerist in nature, and is for that reason essential to the essence of the city and its active self-perception as a dynamic, productive society of intelligent, aware citizens. These projects act as societal exercises in understanding the dynamics of diversity and individuals' contribution to how a city defines itself. In issue 5 of *Esprit de Babel* (2013), Andrée Antolini, director of the Frais-Vallon neighbourhood's social centre, mentioned that 'working with artists allows for crossed glances with people who normally wouldn't contribute to these projects here [...] to find and confront these different worlds has become essential in this age'.[13] These collaborative efforts were a counter-campaign to the social and economic effects of the projects created in the name of the 2013 Capital of Culture at a neighbourhood level. In addition, the people interviewed in both Keny Arkana's documentary *Capitale de la rupture*[14] and Nicolas Burlaud's documentaries felt they had lost their voice and the city had turned away from its poorest inhabitants to create a new image for Marseille, 'cleansing' the city centre, displacing the poor to the northern quarters, thus increasing the divide.

While valuable as a creator of cultural dialogue on an international level, the European Capital of Culture project has created a pre-packaged, sterile identity specifically aimed at the international stage, lacking in diversity and a necessary grassroots-oriented social dialogue involving the city's inhabitants. In 2013, answering questions about her documentary, Keny Arkana stated that MP13 had promoted the dominant culture and was a marketing strategy devoid of humanity:

> [L]es grosses sommes reçues par la ville n'ont servi qu'au marketing et à la décoration de la ville pour en changer le standing. Mais les vrais problèmes et les vrais habitants ont été soit oubliés, soit carrément écartés [...] Au-delà des images de carte postale, Marseille est constitué essentiellement de cités et de quartiers populaires, qui sont actuellement confrontés à une misère réelle: si la jeunesse s'entretue aujourd'hui, c'est surtout parce qu'elle n'a jamais eu de perspective d'avenir, et n'a plus aucun espoir de s'en sortir [...] La rupture que j'évoque, elle est dans cette fracture qui se creuse entre l'image de Marseille que l'on vend et la réalité sociale qui vire au drame. (Granoux, 2013: n. pag.)

13 https://issuu.com/esprit2babel/docs/e2b_5_ok.
14 Arkana's mini-documentary *Capitale de la rupture* is available to view here: https://www.youtube.com/watch?v=CEg1jMeTIjQ.

In her eyes, it was only an excuse to give the city a makeover and gentrify the downtown, and took no account of the voices of the local populations. This is what Minna Sif, an author living in Marseille, has termed 'the other violence', speaking about projects undertaken without neighbourhood concertation. Today, there are many community-based projects in the neighbourhoods, but the *Esprit de Babel* publication reminds us that the inhabitants need a job.[15] The director of the Frais-Vallon social centre raised the question of the after-effects of MP13. She reiterated that local people were engaged in the various artistic processes and felt they had more of a say on what was going on. In this particular instance, in this particular neighbourhood, people were and still are involved.

In conclusion, will the cultures represented in Marseille be ultimately crushed or helped by the Capital of Culture label? Europe spent 400 million euros on the Capital of Culture project between 2007 and 2013 and Marseille-Provence invested 600 million euros on renovations and construction projects. If the city has undergone successful renovations, how are they affecting its citizens? Are efforts sustained and is Marseille becoming more attractive to businesses and tourists as have Lille, the Ruhr in Germany and Liverpool, which have seen an improvement in their image after their tenure as Capitals of Culture. During an interview with *Le Figaro*, Jean-François Chougnet, vice president of MP13, specified at the time that, for them: 'la grande question est de savoir comment faire pour que cela dure après [...] Pour l'instant, nous n'avons pas fait de scénario pour la suite', but the hotel infrastructure has improved (Bommelaer and Bavlier, 2013: n. pag.). 85% of the people polled felt that the image of Marseille has changed for the better, and the increase in tourism is felt with projects looming on the horizon; the city hosted some of the UEFA Euro 2016 finals and was the European Capital of Sport 2017 and will be a participant in the 2024 Olympic Games and a site for the Universal Exhibit 2025. Euroméditerranée is collaborating with Pôle Emploi to help with job creation and job seekers through their relationship with several schools in the city, such as the Kedge Business School. It also sponsors some students from impoverished neighbourhoods. Needless to say, these efforts seem far from sufficient but the hope is that Marseille's facelift lasts, bridges the rifts between its citizens in spite of their displacement, gives voice to more neighbourhood organizations and continues to bring work back to the city and its harbour.

15 https://issuu.com/esprit2babel/stacks/4b965bff76ac402ea7795476b1d6ef3f.

Bibliography

Ben Jelloun, Tahar. 1985. Marseille est une énigme. In *Le deuxième sud. Marseille ou le présent incertain*. Cahiers Pierre-Baptiste 4. Paris: Actes Sud.
Bommelaer, Claire and Ariane Bavelier. Marseille 2013: un pari sur l'avenir. *Le Figaro*, 4 January. https://www.lefigaro.fr/culture/2013/01/04/03004-20130104ARTFIG00607-marseille-2013-un-pari-sur-l-avenir.php.
Braudel, Fernand. 1985. *La Méditerranée: l'espace et l'histoire*. Paris: Champs Flammarion.
Burlaud, Claude. 2015. Interview du réalisateur sur Marsactu, 4 February. http://lafeteestfinie.primitivi.org/?p=565.
Cendrars, Blaise. 1973. *L'Homme foudroyé*. Paris: Gallimard.
Esprit de Babel. 2010–13. https://issuu.com/esprit2babel/stacks/4b965bff76ac4 02ea7795476b1d6ef3f
Euroméditerranée. n.d. https://www.euromediterranee.fr.
Fabre, Clarisse. 2008. Marseille, cité des migrations, sera capitale européenne de la culture. *Le Monde*, 17 September. http://www.lemonde.fr/culture/article/2008/09/17/pourquoi-marseille-sera-capitale-europeenne-de-la-culture-en-2013_1096062_3246.html#YRcAxZtRmVe3XZmO.99.
Flaubert, Gustave. *Voyages*. Paris: Arléa poche, 2007.
Granoux, Olivier. 2013. Marseille 2013 'Capitale de rupture' pour Keny Arkana. *Télérama*, 18 January. https://www.telerama.fr/scenes/t-l-charger-marseille-2013-capitale-de-la-rupture-pour-keny-arkana,92221.php.
Guien, Laura. Bilan: Marseille a-t-elle été une bonne capitale de la culture? *Slate*, 26 January. http://www.slate.fr/story/82671/marseille-capitale-europeenne-culture-bilan.
Lafargue de Grangeneuve, Loïc. 2008. *Politique du hip-hop: action publique et cultures urbaines*. Toulouse: Presses universitaires du Mirail.
Maisetti, Nicolas. 2014. *Opération culturelle et Pouvoirs urbains*. Paris: Harmattan.
Témime, Emile. 1995. Marseille XXe: de la dominante italienne à la diversité maghrébine. *Revue européenne de migrations internationales* 11(1): 9–19.
Wainwright, Oliver. 2013. Marseille's £6bn capital of culture rebirth. *Guardian*, 1 April. http://www.theguardian.com/artanddesign/2013/apr/01/marseille-capital-culture-architecture.

Music

Arkana, Keny. 2011. Marseille. *L'esquisse vol. 2*. Because Music.
———. 2012. Capitale de la rupture. *Tout tourne autour du soleil*. Because Music.

Filmography

La fête est finie. 2014. Dir. Nicolas Burlaud. France: Primtivi.

8

Bridges and Fault Lines in the Mediterranean City

Neighbourhood Memory in an Urban Walk in Marseille

Mark Ingram

> The Mediterranean speaks with many voices; it is a sum of individual histories.
>
> Fernand Braudel, Preface to the 1972 English edition of *The Mediterranean and the Mediterranean world in the age of Philip II* (I, 13).

Introduction

On a sunny July morning in 2014, a group of around 40 people assembled at the centre of the Frais-Vallon housing development in the thirteenth *arrondissement* of Marseille. Frais-Vallon is in one of Marseille's low-income 'northern neighbourhoods'. Part of the national expansion of public housing between 1954 and 1973, Frais-Vallon was built quickly in the early 1960s to house repatriates from the Algerian War and people living in substandard conditions in the centre of Marseille. Today it is home to a diverse population of roughly 6,000 people, many of immigrant descent, especially from North and West Africa and the Comoros Islands. The group was gathered there for a *balade urbaine* or 'urban walk' that was designed by the director of the Théâtre de la Mer theatre company, Frédérique Fuzibet, at the request of the Frais-Vallon social and cultural centres. As they waited, Fuzibet talked and laughed with the others, including *éducateurs de rue* and other social workers. Once the schoolchildren and their teachers arrived, the group moved slowly to their first stop at the base of an overgrown hilly forest known to Frais-Vallon residents as the Colline. Here, actors and residents recited poems about the neighbourhood, shouting to be heard above the noise of a nearby garbage truck. The *balade* was a series of performances linked by the procession that moved across the Colline, through another neighbourhood and back to its starting point five and a half hours later. The walk included a picnic lunch, dance and song in addition to presentations on neighbourhood history and on the flowers of the Colline (including tasting drinks made from them). Many of the texts performed and the conversations throughout the day centred on memories associated with the sites highlighted along the way.

This urban walk was a quintessentially local event—ephemeral performances marked by play and laughter most of the day. But it was also an attempt to express and valorize the memory of a particular neighbourhood at a time when the political stakes underlying the definition of the memory and heritage of 'popular neighbourhoods' have risen in France. Scholars have increasingly used terms such as 'segregation' and 'ghettoization' to describe peripheral urban areas with disproportionately high numbers of people of colour, primarily of North African descent (Mucchielli, 2010; Kokoreff and Lapeyronnie, 2013) and former prime minister Manuel Valls once described the profound isolation of such neighbourhoods as 'a territorial, social, and ethnic apartheid' (AFP, 2015: n. pag.). Efforts intended to empower residents include a 2014 law seeking to 'reconnaître et à valoriser l'histoire, le patrimoine et la mémoire des quartiers' (Loi n° 2014-173 du 21 février 2014). Artists, associations and local residents have celebrated the distinctive memorial qualities of low-income neighbourhoods as a way of promoting an image different from media portrayals emphasizing crime and alienation. In Marseille, neighbourhood arts projects were also important for the city's year as 'European Capital of Culture' in 2013. Noting the important immigrant heritage, the Marseille Selection File identified the 'Mediterranean' nature of its population as an asset, and stated that cultural life in Marseille is 'rooted in the community, spread across all parts of the city and close to its citizens' and is viewed by its leaders as 'an important means of social integration' (Association Marseille-Provence 2013, 2008: 18). In both the Capital of Culture programme and the memory work discussed in the 2014 law, the assumption has been that participation by residents in neighbourhood-centred arts projects serves an integrative social function.

Drawing on ethnographic fieldwork conducted intermittently between 2007 and 2015, this chapter examines one resident's participation and perspective on the urban walk described above. What kind of neighbourhood memory is put into play in urban walks such as these, and how is one to understand individual memory in relation to it? How did the walk serve as a bridging narrative by situating individual experiences within the broader social frame of the neighbourhood? Here, I consider these questions in the context of a heightened national discourse about how to confront the problems of French urban peripheries. Through focusing on this resident's interpretation of neighbourhood sites and history in the context of her personal life story, this chapter examines the performance of memory as a means of shaping social and political solidarity in ways that both align with, and depart from, the narrative frames provided by state authorities, local organizers and media reporting.

Memory and the National Context for *les banlieues*

As part of an extensive reform of urban policy in 2013, then minister of urban affairs François Lamy wrote a statement entitled 'In the popular neighbourhoods, the power of memory' that was published in the national newspaper *Libération*. While Lamy was replaced in 2014, his statement is valuable in that it acknowledges the political stakes underlying the memory and heritage of low-income neighbourhoods and articulates an ambitious agenda intended to provide a voice to marginalized communities. Describing his goals for future policies, Lamy stated that 'la mémoire des habitants des quartiers populaires' opposes 'l'invisibilité sociale', recounts the experience of contemporary France and thereby serves as 'un vrai levier contre les discriminations et pour l'égalité des territoires et des citoyens' (2013: n. pag.). Making reference to the landmark civil rights march in France in 1983, Lamy stated that:

> Trente ans après la Marche pour l'égalité et contre le racisme, une génération de militants pour la dignité des habitants va rappeler ses combats et faire le lien avec tous ceux qui depuis des années poursuivent sur le terrain, sous d'autres formes, la mobilisation pour l'égalité. Alors que le gouvernement s'est engagé dans une réforme de la politique de la ville et des politiques d'intégration, la mémoire a le pouvoir de remobiliser les consciences pour faire reculer les fractures urbaines et sociales. (2013: n. pag.)

Critics of the new initiatives on the memory of popular neighbourhoods argued that extensive historical research on these neighbourhoods already exists, and that ascribing a single *immigrant* identity to the *banlieues* neglects other sources of solidarity and mobilization (including labour unions and political parties of the left), and risks contributing to a stereotypical representation of these neighbourhoods at a time when understanding them better is especially important (Fourcaut and Tellier, 2014). Much critical scholarship on French urban policy concerning low-income neighbourhoods (the *politique de la ville*) has argued that policy and media representations of these neighbourhoods have contributed to their stigmatization: a change in perspective from 'neighborhoods in danger' to 'dangerous neighborhoods' (Dikeç, 2007: 93). Others describe the 'spatialization' of urban policy, arguing that a narrow focus on problems *within* these neighbourhoods neglects the broader sources of inequalities (including both economic and social sources such as 'residential' profiling) that extend beyond their borders (Tissot and Poupeau, 2005). Fabien Desage notes that terms such as 'apartheid' (as in the 2015 speech by Manuel Valls) reflect policies addressing 'déségrégation' and 'mixité sociale' within these neighbourhoods, 'alors même que leur "ségrégation" […] résulte de processus qui se déploient à une échelle plus vaste' (2015: 22). These studies argue that by overemphasizing factors localized within these neighbourhoods, and focusing on aspects of social cohesion (with the aid of concepts such as *exclusion* and *mixité*) rather than socio-economic inequality, policies have been ineffective and counterproductive in directing our attention away from the true engines of inequality in urban peripheries.[1]

Given the diversity within urban peripheries, the performances of 'neighbourhood memory' in urban walks are meaningful in part because they express a positive vision of the social environment of the neighbourhood, but also because they highlight individual and creative aspects of memory work that counter the presumed homogeneity (marked by segregation and isolation) of *banlieue* identity. In contrast to policies that attribute enormous agency to buildings (new housing) and institutions placed in these neighbourhoods (the 'decentralization'

---

[1] Similarly, after the 2015 terrorist attacks of January and November, some argued that a 'sous-culture des banlieues caractérisée par l'exclusion sociale et une image d'indignité de soi' are responsible for a specifically French variant of radicalization in Europe (Brucy et al., 2015). Studies of French jihadists show a broad diversity of origins among those attracted to radical forms of Islam in France (Messina, 2015; Thomson, 2014). Focusing too much on causes of radicalization *within banlieues* may lead analysts to underestimate this broader range of influence.

of theatres and museums, for example), these works focus on the active appropriation of urban space by residents. They are also 'bridges' in the sense that they highlight existing social relations and are opportunities for cultivating new connections with others.

Safia and the Colline

I first met the woman I refer to here as 'Safia' during research on the politics of community-based theatre in Marseille (Ingram, 2011; Ingram, 2015). Between 2007 and 2014, I travelled to Marseille six times for two- to three-week periods to conduct research. This chapter is informed by observation of Théâtre de la Mer performances in Frais-Vallon and other neighbourhoods, interviews with Théâtre de la Mer artists, the residents of areas where they have performed and the directors of the Frais-Vallon social and cultural centres. Others interviewed include Marseille-Provence 2013 (MP13) Capital of Culture administrators, and participants and social workers involved with other neighbourhood-centred arts projects. The urban walk considered here was not part of the MP13 agenda. The company proposed a project (involving exchanges between artists in disadvantaged urban areas in Marseille, Amsterdam and Tétouan, Morocco) that was included in the programme but the international residencies were cancelled because of a lack of funding. The Frais-Vallon urban walk is representative of the company's more than thirty years of work in low-income neighbourhoods of the city. It is one of many organizations in Marseille involved in creating community-based (and other) forms of art in these areas.

On 15 June 2015,[2] Safia and I spoke about her participation in the urban walk. Fifty years old and mother of two boys aged seven and 14, she works two jobs: as a doctor's secretary and as a bus driver. She has lived in Frais-Vallon for 14 years. It is mostly women and children who take part in the events organized by the Frais-Vallon social centre, which both hosted and helped to organize the urban walk. Safia described Frais-Vallon as 'a neighbourhood of poor people, basically' but Marseille is, as Peraldi, Duport, and Samson have noted,

> Une ville marquée par la forte présence de pauvres, certes, mais d'une pauvreté partout ou presque confrontée à des classes moyennes elles

---

[2] Statements by Safia are from interviews conducted on 30 June and 7 December 2015.

aussi plutôt précaires, formées d'employées du secteur public pour l'essentiel. Ce qui signifie que même si la grande pauvreté est relativement concentrée dans quelques lieux de la ville, on peut penser qu'une pauvreté diffuse touche, socialement et spatialement, une grande partie de la ville. (2015: 20–21)

Membership in neighbourhood and other associations in Marseille numbers in the thousands (Duport, 2007) and the authors note that some neighbourhoods have been sites of particularly dynamic associations and these areas have received more public funding. Their point is that funding has not necessarily gone to those most in need. They identify Frais-Vallon as one of the 'showcase' housing developments and it is true that there are poorer areas in the city, and that Frais-Vallon has attracted more media coverage than others. In 2012, when Manuel Valls (then minister of the interior) wanted to draw attention to a new police initiative designed to fight drug trafficking in 19 housing developments in Marseille, he was photographed arriving in Frais-Vallon, 'cité sensible des quartiers nord de Marseille'; he travelled there by *métro* and came out of the station 'en montrant son ticket sous le regard étonné des habitants' (AFP, 2012: n. pag.). But with regard to neighbourhood-centred cultural events, Frais-Vallon is particularly interesting precisely because of its especially active associational life. The activities of the social centre were crucial to Safia's early integration into the neighbourhood. She said she was greatly helped by a friend of hers who had worked at the social centre for 20 years:

> Moi la première fois quand j'ai atterri ici, je ne travaillais pas et je m'ennuyais … Alors, il fallait que je trouve quelque chose à faire. Donc, j'ai commencé à faire du bénévolat dans un Secours Populaire [a non-profit organization devoted to fighting poverty and discrimination]. Et c'est comme ça que j'ai appris qu'il y avait des sorties, des balades avec le centre social. Et une façon de pouvoir découvrir Marseille, que je ne connaissais pas.

Safia had grown up in Algeria, living from age two to seven in Algiers, and then until she was 20 in the town of Biskra on the edge of the Sahara. She said she had no desire to return: 'Ça a changé complètement … Je cherchais dans ma mémoire et je ne trouvais plus les lieux … Ma mémoire elle n'a plus de repères là-bas'. When I asked her later what the idea of 'the Mediterranean' meant to her, she told me that there are still things in her personality that she takes from her father and mother that have crossed the sea with her. When she thought of the Mediterranean, it was this personal family legacy she had in mind. Her father, for example, loved seeing people and having guests, something she underlined in her story about how she ended up in France:

> Il y avait une femme, une Française qui se promenait dans l'Afrique, dans le sud d'Algérie. Et un soir elle a atterri, mon père il avait un petit magasin. Il vendait des bijoux et tout ça ... Elle me demande 'Est-ce qu'il y a un hôtel?'. Il lui a dit 'vous pouvez rester tranquille, il y a un hôtel juste derrière'. Et l'hôtel en fait, c'était chez nous! Donc il l'a fait entrer ... Et ça lui a tellement plu qu'elle est restée 15 jours chez nous. Etcomme j'étais la seule qui parlait bien français avec elle, elle m'a invitée à venir en vacances. Voilà. Et je suis venue en vacances et je suis tombée amoureuse, et je suis restée! (laughs).

Safia settled first in Besançon (near the Swiss border) with her first husband, and later moved to Marseille to be closer to her younger sister. At first, she didn't like Marseille but now, she says, 'I wouldn't change it for anything'. Still, she contrasted the centre of the city, where 'there's no solidarity', with the social life of Frais-Vallon. She described one area 'behind Building B':

> C'est devenu le quartier général de tous les habitants de Frais-Vallon. Parce que c'est le seul endroit où ils amènent leurs enfants jouer. Et donc, du coup, il y a des barbecues, comme le ramadan maintenant, ils font une collecte ... et ils font à manger pour tous les pauvres ... Et tu vois, ce genre de choses on ne les trouve pas ailleurs.

Safia saw places such as this park as key 'points of reference' (*repères*) not only for the neighbourhood as a whole, but for her personally. She described the Colline, the wooded overgrown hill where the urban walk took place, as another of these sites:

> Quand on dit que les endroits ont une âme, c'est vrai ... Voilà, on n'a qu'à contempler les lieux et on sait qu'ils ont des choses à dire. Voilà. Comme la colline ... Au début, ... je me baladais dedans comme n'importe quel touriste on va dire ... et de la visiter avec des gens d'avant ... c'était quelque chose. Maintenant je ne la vois pas de la même façon, ça c'est clair, hein?

The original setting for the urban walk was the centre of Frais-Vallon. But residents wanted it at the Colline. Safia already had her own personal connection to the Colline. In talking about it as a place that had 'something to say', she described the ways certain places incite people to interpret them in terms of the past. But what she seemed to value most was the attitude—open, attentive to interpretation and deeper understanding—that such places provoke. During picnics and naps on the hillside with her children, she said,

> J'essaie de transmettre à mes enfants ... Quand je les vois par exemple qu'ils passent à côté de quelque chose. Tiens, le bassin qui est sur la colline ... Ils n'ont pas fait attention qu'il y a un bassin qui date d'il y a ... je ne sais plus combien de temps ... au fait, j'ai dit 'mais vous avez remarqué sur quoi vous êtes?'

Paying attention to how places 'speak', then, involved attending to the possibilities of interpretation, to aspects of a site's past heretofore unacknowledged. Safia was motivated in part by her own recent past, and in particular her escape from an abusive relationship. She had reached a point where she saw no way out and had withdrawn into a shell. Freeing herself was a major breakthrough and she said that she had regained her rich social life from before. Now, when she encourages her children to look differently at the Colline, it echoes her view on their surroundings in the neighbourhood as a whole. She wanted them to look beyond the buildings ('le côté bâtiment c'est le côté cynique, sinistre de ce quartier-là'). What she seemed to want to impart most urgently to her children was an ability to discover new perspectives even in difficult conditions that seem impossible to move beyond. For all of these reasons, Safia was one of the residents who most strongly pushed for having performances on the Colline. Situating the walk at this neighbourhood reference point was a means of drawing together many strands in her family and social life—her involvement with the social centre (which had helped her to find her place in the neighbourhood when she arrived), her experiences with her children and the social life she especially valued and viewed as a legacy of her parents.

The Théâtre de la Mer and the 'Fault Lines' of the Mediterranean

If one of the broader frames for understanding the memory of popular neighbourhoods is the national discourse on urban peripheries, another is the city-wide discourse on 'the Mediterranean' during the Capital of Culture year. As Michael Herzfeld has noted, the crucial question regarding this concept is, 'Who uses it and why? What are the political implications?' (qtd. in Ben-Yehoyada, 2013: 75). For Frédérique Fuzibet, the concept is useful in describing aspects of Marseille's immigrant heritage. In this respect, the Théâtre de la Mer, like Frais-Vallon, is itself profoundly 'Mediterranean'. It was founded in 1980 by three people, described by Fuzibet as: 'Akel Akian, un berbère du Rif marocain, Brigitte Bentolila, une Juive rapatriée d'Algérie, et moi-même. Une quatrième personne, Dalila Khatir, née de parents algériens dans une cité aixoise, a rapidement rejoint le groupe' (qtd. in Thomasson, 2014: 37).

Fuzibet was the only one not of recent immigrant origin. Her husband and collaborator, Akel Akian, passed away in 2012 and she is now the company's sole artistic director. Early on, the company performed works by North African authors as a way of highlighting a heritage often ignored or devalued. Over the years, their focus has turned to more collaborative exchanges and research into theatrical forms better able to express the singular aspects of orality and social life in disadvantaged neighbourhoods. Fuzibet described an early production on the Algerian War that was difficult because actors struggled to perform the roles publicly given the sensitive subject. A recent production of Medea grew out of Fuzibet's discovery that one of the women in her theatre workshops found out that her husband had another wife. Many of the women Fuzibet worked with were of immigrant descent and the production centred on Medea's identity as an exile, and as someone dealing with humiliation and anger. Here, through the myth of Medea, Fuzibet drew on a shared Mediterranean cultural heritage in Marseille but used it to address issues of inequality and injustice in the city today.

This is community-based theatre but without the assumption of a pre-existent community identity that is 'expressed' in performances. Rather, the theatre is a vector of exchange or encounter (*rencontre*). Fuzibet states that the principle of *rencontre* is to create relations among people who do not usually cross paths so that perspectives can be brought together and people can open up to multiple points of view. Speaking of Medea, Fuzibet said that the exaggeration in mythology of acts pushed to their extreme is a way of alerting us, of preventing us from being carried away by anger or depression:

> Il faut questionner ailleurs et autrement et prendre du recul, mettre en perspective. La difficulté principale que nos contemporains rencontrent est le manque de temps pour penser cette perspective. L'une des fonctions à nous, artistes, est de créer des fenêtres, des espaces de rencontres, d'interrogations, de paroles aussi; des endroits d'où on peut s'élever et apprendre à se déplacer, à se situer autrement, pour parvenir dans les lignes de failles. (qtd. in Thomasson, 2014: 45)

This effort to provide alternative perspectives, to suggest ways of rethinking one's habitual point of view has been a goal of the company with more serious works such as Medea, but it is also evident in their more ludic and site-specific works such as the urban walk. In a 2012 interview, Fuzibet described certain 'fault lines' as central to the 'Mediterranean' nature of Marseille:

> Il y a dans le bassin méditerranéen, un fonds commun, qui est en train de se fracturer … Une partie de l'avenir du monde se joue autour de ce bassin méditerranéen—pour moi, c'est une évidence. C'est complètement centré sur nous. Il y a des choses qui peuvent se dénouer si les choses se dénouent ici. (interview, 1 November 2012)

It is in part this conviction that motivates the artistic work of Fuzibet—she saw it as a crucial context for her and others' neighbourhood work, whether those tensions were acknowledged or not. 'Je pense qu'il y a des enjeux très importants—ces enjeux-là peuvent être l'objet d'un travail artistique—en tout cas nous, on y baigne tous les jours' (interview, 1 November 2012). It is this broader context that frames the two goals of the urban walk: for residents to reappropriate a public, common and ludic space, and to introduce new perspectives, to displace or shift existing ones, to 'déplacer les points de vue'. The emphasis on 'fracturing' provides a perspective different from the generally positive representation of the Mediterranean in the MP13 promotional materials. The walk was also an effort to address 'fault lines' by providing settings for expression, exchange and 'bridges', as in the case of Safia's social connections to others through this and other arts events organized by the social centre. These events are also bridges in another sense: providing connections to others through public discourse, and—as with the example of the earlier play on the Algerian War—finding ways to articulate perspectives otherwise neglected or silenced.

Memory in Performance: A *Neighbourhood* Memory?

Describing her work with the Frais-Vallon social and cultural centres, Frédérique Fuzibet explained that 'co-construction' with partners was a fundamental practice of the Théâtre de la Mer. She designed the urban walk collaboratively 'en partant des spécificités [...] de chacun de façon à vraiment faire place à la diversité des habitants et du tissu local' (personal communication, 24 June 2015). Working with residents, Fuzibet designed the circuit of the walk to extend into the more upscale Montolivet neighbourhood that borders Frais-Vallon. Part of Fuzibet's aim was to break down 'invisible barriers' and open up (*désenclaver*) Frais-Vallon (interview with Fuzibet, 13 June 2014).

Although frequented in the past, the Colline had been abandoned and because people were afraid to go there, there has been an effort to reclaim this as shared space. Fuzibet told me that because of the lack of shared space in the housing development due to various kinds of trafficking and insecurity, 'La Colline est devenue un espace de fantasmes, de rêves ... L'idée, c'est que ... les habitants, aidés par le Théâtre de la Mer, expliquent leur quartier, leur Colline' (interview, 17 June 2013). The company conducted writing workshops where residents wrote texts, and actors and residents performed them. She explained that part of this involved the 'reconstitution' of collective memory, something she viewed as particularly important in an area where, as in many of the housing developments in Marseille, there are no official street names. The result is that:

> Du coup les gens n'habitent pas au 9 rue Baudelaire, ils habitent à la cité des Flamants ... Pour un employeur, s'il y avait un nom de rue, ce serait complètement différent ... Ils seraient comme tout le monde qui habite dans un quartier différent. C'est important! Là, d'emblée tu es repéré.
> (interview with Fuzibet, 13 June 2014)

But people in the neighbourhood gave their own names to sites. She described a place called the 'stade rouge' because there used to be a stadium with red gravel; it was torn down, but local memory has kept the name. The lack of place names (and addition of community-created ones) is a particularly striking example of the affirmation of local perspectives and place meanings in a spatial environment deemed in much media and political discourse to be either devoid of culture (a 'badlands') or a negative influence. As Keith Basso has noted, place names are more than just referential labels:

> Because of their inseparable connection to specific localities, place-names may be used to summon forth an enormous range of mental and emotional associations—associations of time and space, of history and events, of persons and social activities, of oneself and stages in one's life. And in their capacity to evoke, in their compact power to muster and consolidate so much of what a landscape may be taken to represent in both personal and cultural terms, place-names acquire a functional value that easily matches their utility as instruments of reference. (1996: 76–77)

Part of the function exercised by terms such as 'le stade rouge', or even 'la colline' is the assertion of a distinctly local voice and frame of reference that unites residents as insiders—as 'native speakers' with their own perspective on the environment where they live.

Describing the urban walk, Safia talked about how people told stories about things they remembered from childhood: about a man who used to bring his horse to the Colline in the daytime and take him back home and upstairs in the elevator at night. Older people remembered childhood cabins they had built. For Safia, the walk truly expressed the memory of the neighbourhood:

> Pour chaque enfant de Frais-Vallon, l'enfant qui a 50–60 ans aujourd'hui ou l'enfant qui a cinq ans, ils ont le même—c'est comme un cordon ombilical avec la colline. Non, mais je vous assure. La colline, c'est le repère au fait, c'est le repère de Frais-Vallon.

During the walk, in a shaded grassy area, Safia read a text as part of a performance that Fuzibet introduced as 'Texts by women of Frais-Vallon, read by the women of Frais-Vallon!' Generally, readers presented work written by others even when their own poems were read. Safia read a poem by a woman from a rural area in North Africa, who was reminded by the greenery of the Colline of where she'd come from. Safia explained that she wrote when she was homesick and that 'son seul refuge—où elle pouvait pleurer dans son intimité—c'était à la colline ... Elle disait même quand elle ne pouvait pas sortir, elle ouvrait la fenêtre, elle pouvait regarder de loin les arbres de la colline'.

The Colline, then, was also sometimes a place of trans-Mediterranean 'dreams and fantasies'. While designed to provide a forum for individuals to speak publicly, the walk also situated those individual voices within the collective frame of the neighbourhood and—as readers presented the poems of others—the performance of someone else's perspective.

But while the neighbourhood was the organizing frame for the event, what seems most important here is *individual* memories rather than one shared collectively. By way of contrast, it is helpful to consider Maurice Halbwach's influential conception of social memory, in which 'the memory of the group realizes and manifests itself in individual memories' (1992 [1925]: 40), where a pre-existent social identity generates the memories that reflect and support it. As Alan Megill notes, 'for Halbwachs, the social identities in question already have a determinate existence before the collective memories that they construct' (2007: 47). It is this conception of social memory that seems to underpin certain descriptions of the memory of popular neighbourhoods in discourse about the 2014 Lamy law and it is precisely the lack of a clearly unified, single, pre-existent social identity within these neighbourhoods that provokes debate. Performances such as this urban walk highlight other aspects of memory—its dynamic and contingent qualities, the fact that memories 'are continually being adapted and rephrased to meet the needs of the present' (Jarman, 1997: 5). Megill, drawing on Fabian (1996), notes that 'it is the present that we remember: that is, we "remember" what remains living within our situations *now*' (2007: 54). There was a deliberate effort on the urban walk to see and sense places through memory, and to see and sense memories through place, but the form and content of the walk highlighted the creative nature of place-centred engagements with memory. What was central was not a pre-existent and collectively held view of the past, but rather an effort—through memories—to generate new perspectives on participants' existing social and physical environment.

One way of interpreting memory on this urban walk would be to highlight the social identity of the neighbourhood as a whole, in the way that Halbwachs viewed social memory as the expression of a pre-existent social identity. But in considering Safia's experience, what seems most important is not her representativeness with respect to a collective identity—even after 14 years, she still felt like an outsider in Frais-Vallon. While she shared with others the association of place and memory on the Colline, her own associations were quite personal and in her use of those memories she was less concerned with respect for a particular interpretation of the past than with her social relations in the present and the future. In other words, she 'remembered the present': her relationship with her children and what she sought to impart to them, and the people in the neighbourhood she knew and continued to see through activities such as the urban walk. The form and content of the walk highlighted the active appropriation of urban spaces by individuals and Safia's story directs our attention to the dynamic, creative and collaborative nature of this place-centred memory work.

Conclusion

In this chapter, I have focused primarily on one person's perspective as a way of highlighting the individual appropriation of memory in community-based arts projects devoted to neighbourhood heritage and memory. 'Senses of place', as Basso has noted, 'while always informed by local knowledge, are finally the possessions of particular individuals. People, not cultures, sense places' (1996: xv–xvi). In the context of national debates about the *banlieues* and the memory of popular neighbourhoods, Safia's perspective directs our attention to the 'bridging' qualities of memory work in the present, and the social value of such work beyond the expression of a single, putatively pre-existent and collectively shared memory and identity. Given that media representations of urban peripheries often emphasize a lack of community and the negative social influence of such neighbourhoods, and that policy approaches have emphasized the problems situated *within* such neighbourhoods rather than the broader extra-local factors that extend beyond their borders, it is especially important to acknowledge internal dynamics that foster collaboration and work against the kind of isolation and alienation that urban policies have targeted.

This urban walk was very much a collaborative work lasting three years and building on an extensive aesthetic infrastructure of dynamic and creative partnerships, including the Frais-Vallon social and cultural centres, institutions that provide solidarity and support for newcomers and others in the neighbourhood, as they did for Safia when she first arrived 14 years previous. Ricky Burdett, who has examined grassroots projects in over twenty cities around the world in the last ten years, speaks of how 'the potential for social integration and democratic engagement of socially excluded urban residents is often realized through small-scale 'acupuncture' projects [...] that [bring] people and communities together in ways that formal planning processes have uniquely failed to do' (2013: 350). Such projects encourage 'flexible and resilient open networks that optimize the democratic potential of their urban residents' (Burdett, 2013: 365). Safia described the importance of the urban walk this way:

> C'est un quartier quand-même qui reste un quartier difficile. C'est comme ils appellent, ... c'est les quartiers nord. Il y a beaucoup de délinquance, il y a beaucoup de trafic de drogue ... Par contre, ça reste cette colline-là par rapport à cette fameuse balade où il y a eu beaucoup de choses beaux envoyées ce jour-là même d'autres jours—de la danse, des trucs artistiques, qui ont pu être jouées sur la colline, et ça donnait une autre dimension.

If, as with the concept of 'the Mediterranean', we look at how memory is *used* on the urban walk, what seems most important is the cultivation of new perspectives. Of course, memory is always a generative process. As de Certeau said, memory is 'like those birds that lay their eggs in other species' nests': it 'produces in a place that does not belong to it. It receives its form and implantation from external circumstances [...] its mobilization is inseparable from an alteration' (1984: 86).

Rather than specific content tied to place—the national character of the more spatially focused subjects (such as Reims, Lascaux or the Eiffel Tower) in Pierre Nora's study of memory and identity in France (1984–92), for example—it is this quality of alteration, of displacing points of view, that was highlighted on the urban walk. It encouraged new perspectives on existing social and spatial boundaries, suggested bridges across divisive fault lines and fostered a kind of initiative, creativity and inventiveness so often absent in policy and media representations in the past, but so important to future social and economic progress in these neighbourhoods.

Bibliography

AFP. 2012. À Marseille, Manuel Valls prend le métro. *Le Point*, 12 October. http://www.lepoint.fr/societe/a-marseille-manuel-valls-prend-le-metro-12-10-2012-1516289_23.php.
——. 2015. Manuel Valls: il existe 'un apartheid territorial, social, ethnique' en France. *Le Point*, 20 January. http://www.lepoint.fr/politique/valls-il-existe-un-apartheid-territorial-social-ethnique-en-france-20-01-2015-1898010_20.php.
Association Marseille-Provence 2013. 2008. *Marseille-Provence 2013 selection file*. Marseille: Horizon Group.
Basso, Keith. 1996. *Wisdom sits in places: Landscape and language among the Western Apache*. Albuquerque: University of New Mexico Press.
Ben-Yehoyada, Naor. 2013. The sea of scales and segments. Interview with Hashim Sarkis and Michael Herzfeld. In Antonio Petrov, ed., *New Geographies 5: The Mediterranean*, 59–80. Cambridge, MA: Harvard University Press.
Braudel, Fernand. 1972 [1949]. *The Mediterranean and the Mediterranean world in the age of Philip II*. Berkeley: University of California Press.
Brucy, Anne et al. 2015. Face à la radicalisation, l'Europe doit s'unir et se renforcer. Interview with Farhad Khosrokhavar. *CNRS, Le Journal*. https://lejournal.cnrs.fr/articles/face-a-la-radicalisation-leurope-doit-sunir-et-se-renforce.
Burdett, Ricky. 2013. Designing urban democracy: Mapping scales of urban identity. *Public Culture* 25(2): 349–67.
de Certeau, Michel. 1984. *The practice of everyday life*. Translated by Steven Rendall. Berkeley: University of California Press.

Desage, Fabien. 2015. Pas de quartier(s) pour les 'grands ensembles'? Banlieues populaires, ségrégation résidentielle et reformulation de la question sociale dans la France contemporaine. *Cahiers français* 388: 22–28.

Dikeç, Mustafa. 2007. *Badlands of the republic: Space, politics and urban policy*. Oxford: Blackwell.

Duport, Claire. 2007. Notables, militants, entrepreneurs: une histoire sociale du militantisme dans les cités. PhD thesis, LAMES/CNRS. http://www.transverscite.org/Notables-militants-entrepreneurs.html.

Fabian, Johannes. 1996. *Remembering the present: Painting and popular history in Zaire*. Berkeley: University of California Press.

Fourcaut, Annie and Thibault Tellier. 2014. Les quartiers populaires vont-ils perdre la mémoire? *Métropolitiques*, 10 January. http://www.metropolitiques.eu/Les-quartierspopulaires-vont-ils.html.

Halbwachs, Maurice. 1992 [1952]. *On collective memory* (excerpts from *Les Cadres sociaux de la mémoire*). Edited and translated by Lewis Coser. Chicago: University of Chicago Press.

Ingram, Mark. 2011. *Rites of the Republic: Citizens' theatre and the politics of culture in southern France*. Toronto: University of Toronto Press.

———. 2015. Emplacement and the politics of heritage in low-income neighborhoods of Marseille. *International Journal of Heritage Studies* 22(2): 117–30.

Jarman, Neil. 1997. *Material conflicts: Parades and visual displays in Northern Ireland*. New York: Berg Publishers.

Kokoreff, Michel and Didier Lapeyronnie. 2013. *Refaire la cité. L'avenir des banlieues*. Paris: Seuil.

Lamy, François. 2013. Dans les quartiers populaires, le pouvoir de mémoire. *Libération*, 27 June. http://www.liberation.fr/politiques/2013/06/27/dansles-quartiers-populaires-le-pouvoir-de-memoire_914244.

Loi n° 2014-173 du 21 février 2014 de programmation pour la ville et la cohésion urbaine. http://www.legifrance.gouv.fr/affichTexte.do?cidTexte=JORFTEXT000028636804&categorieLien=id.

Megill, Alan. 2007. *Historical knowledge, historical error: A contemporary guide to practice*. Chicago: University of Chicago Press.

Messina, Marine. 2015. Qui sont les Français sur la piste du djihad? *Le Monde*, 26 March. https://www.lemonde.fr/les-decodeurs/article/2014/11/19/qui-sont-les-francais-sur-la-piste-du-jihad_4524774_4355770.html.

Mucchielli, Laurent. 2010. Les émeutes urbaines dans la France contemporaine. In Laurent Mucchielli and Xavier Crettiez, eds., *Les violences politiques en Europe. Un état des lieux*, 141–76. Paris: La Découverte.

Nora, Pierre, ed. 1984–92. *Les lieux de mémoire*. Paris: Gallimard.

Peraldi, Michel, Claire Duport and Michel Samson. 2015. *Sociologie de Marseille*. Paris: La Découverte.

Thomasson, Anne-Lise. 2014. Art et société plurielle. L'aller-retour. Entretien Frédérique Fuzibet, Yan Gilg. In *Nouveaux regards. Identités, parcours & mémoire*, 33–52. Marseille: Le Bec en l'Air.
Thomson, David. 2014. *Les Français jihadistes*. Paris: Les Arènes.
Tissot, Sylvie and Franck Poupeau. 2005. La spatialisation des problèmes sociaux. *Actes de la recherche en sciences sociales* 159(4): 4–9.

PART III

Mediterranean Beyonds

PART III

Mediterranean Beyonds

9

Between the Comoros Islands and Marseille

Trans-Mediterranean Bridging Narratives in the Works of Salim Hatubou

Silvia Baage

The coast and ports of southern France have a long history of attracting foreigners. In the twentieth century, the port city of Marseille established itself as a destination for immigrants of various backgrounds, as David Abulafia[1] and Janine Renucci[2] indicate. Hailing from Mediterranean and non-Mediterranean locations, their experiences differ vastly from Cézanne or Pagnol's romanticized descriptions of Marseille's exuberance, light and sea. How are immigrant experiences in Mediterranean urban centres contextualized by contemporary francophone Mediterranean migrant writers whose works can be 'autobiographiques, proches de l'auto-fiction ou fictifs' (Moura and Lalagianni, 2014: 6)? What narratives do they produce?

This chapter will consider the exemplary case of a non-Mediterranean immigrant, Salim Hatubou (1972–2015), a writer of Comorian origin who settled in Marseille at the age of ten and lived there until his sudden death in March 2015. His works primarily deal with current issues in his native land and Marseille, and present a particular case of bridging narratives in contemporary French literature. These bridging narratives can be read through David Abulafia's distinction between

---

1 'But population movements that originated far beyond its shores have also had a significant political and social impact. New, non-Mediterranean populations become temporarily or permanently installed in its cities or employed as cheap labor in the countryside' (Abulafia, 2011: 629).

2 'Un Corse sur deux vivrait hors de Corse [...] La Provence—Côte d'Azur rassemble plus de la moitié des expatriés, les Bouches du Rhône en particulier [...] Marseille a le privilège d'être la plus grande ville corse' (Renucci, 2001: 34).

the Mediterranean as a body of water on the one hand, and the paths of human interactions across similar bodies of water on the other:

> 'Mediterranean' means that which is between the surrounding land. Yet historians and geographies of 'the Mediterranean' may concern themselves mainly with the lands that surround the Mediterranean Sea and the peoples who have inhabited them, to the extent of paying rather little attention to the bonds that have linked the opposing shores of the Mediterranean World. (2005: 64)

Abulafia's comparative approach connects the Mediterranean region and various broader conceptions of a 'Mediterranean' including the Indian Ocean, based on the notion of connecting seas, transformation and exchange between opposing shores. This shift from Horden and Purcell's micro-level analysis towards a macro-scale comparative study has interesting implications for literary works produced by contemporary diasporic authors such as Salim Hatubou.

I posit that Hatubou's works represent an important contribution to the study of trans-Mediterranean *francophonies*. Drawing on *L'Odeur du béton* (1999) and *Hassanati: de Mayotte à Marseille* (2005), this study will start by examining Hatubou's use of Abulafia's conceptually similar 'Mediterraneans' to analyse the flow of migration from and to Marseille. The following sections will consider Hatubou's use of bridging narratives through several lenses, including the concept of exile in postcolonial migrant literature, and spatial practices, as outlined by Michel de Certeau. Hatubou's act of bridging between the Comoros Islands and Marseille contributes to a new understanding of the themes of travel and migration in French and francophone literature. As such, bridging narratives cross geopolitical and sociocultural boundaries that facilitate an understanding of the contrasting yet intertwined realities of a Mediterranean *ville-monde*.

Hatubou's Mediterraneans: The Mediterranean Sea and the Indian Ocean

In *Hassanati* and *L'Odeur*, Hatubou depicts a contradictory image of the Mediterranean by focusing on the port city of Marseille. In his young adult novel *Hassanati*, the 13-year-old narrator, Sambafum, who lives in Mayotte, becomes infatuated with Marseille because of his beautiful teacher, Madame Delaroche, who will soon leave to return to Marseille: 'J'ai lu dans un livre que Marseille est une ville qui a 2600 ans [...] on l'appelle aussi *Massalia* et c'est la première ville comorienne' (Hatubou, 2011: 14). While the nine chapters unfold on the Indian Ocean island of Mayotte, Marseille becomes of primary interest for Sambafum, who critically reflects upon various socio-economic problems of his native island, including the lack of access to public transportation to schools, life-saving medication for AIDS for the storyteller Sédali and the teenage pregnancy of Hassanati. The destiny of these characters diverges as Sédali's disease is left untreated, but Madame Delaroche is able to help the teenage mother Hassanati. Sambafum takes a particular interest in the future of his long-time friend Hassanati, from the moment she stops attending school due to the responsibilities of motherhood, until the moment of her departure for Marseille with Madame Delaroche. He agrees with his teacher's decision: 'Elle et son bébé vont venir avec moi à Marseille [...] Je pense qu'elle aura sa chance là-bas' (Hatubou, 2011: 47). Hassanati's story is representative of the trajectory of the Comorian diaspora settled in Marseille.

Based on Abulafia's notion of 'Mediterraneans' as human relationships across a body of water, the plot of Hatubou's young adult novel juxtaposes two conceptually similar 'Mediterraneans' that foreground different forms of connection and movement. In Mayotte, connection and movement remain a challenging endeavour. The story unfolds within the aftermath of Mayotte's splitting from the Comoros Islands, which gained their independence in 1975 while Mayotte remained under French control. Mayotte's separation from the Comoro archipelago thus drove a divide between four formerly united islands whose inhabitants are currently kept apart by virtue of French citizenship: 'tous les enfants des 4 îles, étaient frères de sang et d'Histoire' (Hatubou, 2011: 23). The geopolitical situation that Abulafia refers to as the 'Indian Ocean Mediterranean' causes dispersion and therefore contrasts with the idea of free movement. Hassanati's joining of the Comorian diaspora in Marseille is therefore necessary to secure her future. The novel ends with a significant time lapse in which the narrator reveals that he, too, has settled in Marseille and that Hassanati has become his wife:

> Les années ont passé. Chaque matin, à Marseille, je regarde les bateaux quitter le Vieux Port et je pense aux barges de mon enfance [...] Je m'appelle Sambafum et j'ai trente-deux ans aujourd'hui. Je viens de traverser le champ de mon enfance mahoraise et la belle Hassanati, devenue ma femme, a été la lumière de cette traversée comorienne.
> (Hatubou, 2011: 67)

If Marseille becomes the refuge for these two young Comorian immigrants, this positive end contrasts with the negative images of Marseille conjured up by a returnee talking about his bad experiences in southern France right before Hassanati is about the leave:

> Tu vois, mon frère, [...] tu crois que là-bas, de l'autre côté de la mer, c'est l'Eldorado, ta terre promise. Détrompe-toi, mon frère. Tu sais combien il y a des gens qui vivent dans la misère? [...] Ce n'est pas que je veuille t'empêcher d'aller trouver le bonheur à Paris ou à Marseille [...] j'étais là-bas, moi, j'avais vendu toutes les terres de ma famille pour partir et je suis resté au chômage pendant des années. Sais-tu où je vivais? Dans un ghetto. Oui, mon frère, un quartier écrasé sous le béton, la crasse, les odeurs puantes et ... (Hatubou, 2011: 64)

While the narrator does not provide any details of the socio-economic condition of his life with Hassanati, the plot of *L'Odeur* (1999) focuses specifically on the issues Comorian immigrant families face in the Mediterranean urban centre of Marseille, and more specifically, the ghetto.

The plot unfolds over the course of ten chapters, and an epilogue, to tell the story of Karim, a recent graduate of the Institut Universitaire de Technologie and unsuccessful jobseeker. He was born and raised in Belle-Ville (*quartier nord*), a housing project located on the outskirts of Marseille. As the plot unfolds, he succumbs to despair and violence that clearly do not reflect the image of the Eldorado often upheld in the Indian Ocean Mediterranean. Karim describes the city of Marseille in a way that does not fit into Jean-Claude Izzo's image of 'Marseille, la lumière et la mer' when the latter speaks of the ease with which one can appropriate the city: 'L'accueil. Car Marseille est faite d'ailleurs, d'exils, et elle se donne sans résistance à ceux qui savent la prendre, l'aimer' (1998: 14). Despite the meaningful connections Karim develops across the ethnic community of the *quartiers nord*, his search for a job consistently stalls as he keeps receiving rejection letters, despite his stellar academic performance. In an act of self-defence, he punches a potential boss because the latter verbally and physically threatens him in an attempt to make Karim leave his office. After Karim is released from prison, his mother insists that he return with her to the family's native Comoros Islands: 'Ne dis pas de bêtises, mon fils, des racines ne poussent jamais sur du béton' (Hatubou, 1999: 143).

As the title evokes, Hatubou uses the imagery of concrete walls, along with the asphalt of the streets, to build the plot around a synaesthetic structure, combining a visual and olfactory cue. This strategy creates a perspective that highlights the experience of the Comorian diaspora in Marseille. During his plane ride into exile, Karim sulks, 'Pendant que l'oiseau de fer survole les nuages, je défile tout le film de ma vie dans ma tête. "*Belle Île*" est loin, mais l'odeur de son béton reste tatouée dans le tréfonds de mon cœur' (Hatubou, 1999: 154). He is well aware that staying in Marseille is no longer an option, yet he finds himself unable to envision himself away from the concrete walls of his childhood:

> J'essaie d'imaginer les collines, les chemins boueux, les femmes qui pilent les feuilles de manioc [...] les enfants qui courent derrière des poules capricieuses [...] tout ce petit monde de Milépvani, le village campagnard dont mes parents sont originaires [...] Mon imagination me trahit parce que le béton de Marseille me retient. Irrévocablement. Marseille et Milépvani, deux femmes, différemment belles, majestueuses dans leurs neufs lettres de noblesse. Comment divorcer de la première pour la seconde? Comment rester fidèle à l'une sans trahir l'autre? (Hatubou, 1999: 155-56)

As the plot concludes, Karim is unable to connect these different worlds. Similarly, the narrator of the young adult novel *Hassanati* does not provide any information on the quality of life in Eldorado. Therefore, cross-reading both novels, as well as other texts, is revealing for a comparison of their visions of the different 'Mediterraneans'. Hatubou's focus on the process of migration to and from the Comoros Islands and the port city of Marseille creates an important link between two bodies of water that are normally not connected, despite the obvious conceptual similarities that exist for Abulafia. In that sense, Hatubou's works display the problematic cultural blends of the Mediterranean region, as Jean-Marc Moura and Vassiliki Lalagianni posit for contemporary francophone trans-Mediterranean writing: 'À la croisée des cultures et des langues de la Méditerranée, l'œuvre des écrivains et des écrivaines francophones se donne à lire aujourd'hui comme une contribution importante à l'appréhension actuelle de la migration, de l'errance, voire du nomadisme qui caractérisent l'extrême contemporain' (2014: 18). How do Hatubou's narratives absorb the themes of migration and exile that are prevalent in contemporary writing of the francophone Mediterranean, as Moura indicates?

Hatubou's Mediterranean Bridging Narratives: Exile in Postcolonial Migrant Literature

Moura and Lalagianni consider the appearance of new forms of intercultural dialogue a logical consequence of texts that are produced in the Mediterranean, 'qui a connu sous des formes diverses le colonialisme, l'Empire, la décolonisation et les guerres d'indépendances [...] la Méditerranée, croisement complexe de culture, a connu des affrontements, des heurts et des bouleversements identitaires' (2014: 8). Within this context, Hatubou creates a particular form of narrative that illuminates the position of Marseille at the crossroads of geographically close civilizations by exploring unmapped territories and trajectories of those shuttling back and forth between two seemingly unconnected locations, Marseille and the Comoros Islands. Cédric Fabre highlights this uncommon link by including Hatubou in his collection *Marseille Noir*, where he describes Hatubou's contribution through the uniqueness of a plot 'qui s'étire entre une cité des quartiers nord et les lointaines Comores [ce qui] est assez éloignée des habituelles histoires' (Fabre, 2014: 15). However, I suggest a closer reading of this supposedly random spread of actions that unfold between Marseille and the Comoros Islands through a focus on Mediterranean bridging narratives that take on various forms in Hatubou's works. Analysing this complexity of cultural crossings and clashes also facilitates an understanding of Hatubou as a migrant writer.

While the themes of exile and migration are clearly associated with postcolonial migrant literature, Hatubou's trajectory as a migrant writer needs to be distinguished from the ways his characters experience them in *L'Odeur*. For Michel Gironde, the experience of exile is associated with the impossibility of returning to the native land. While both Hatubou and his main character Karim fit the profile of the second-generation Comorian diaspora with parents who settled in southern France, Karim, unlike Hatubou, was born and raised in the housing projects of Marseille. However, in real life, at the age of ten, Hatubou perceived concrete as a sad reality of urban life when he first arrived in Marseille, as he stated in an interview: 'J'étais une fleur fanée, dans ce quartier où tu ne retrouves plus tes repères' (Hatubou and Jourdana, 2014: 181). For Karim, this feeling of alienation is rather common, though the author claims his right to use the notion of exile in the context of extreme poverty: 'ce mot exil [...] on l'utilise à propos de personnes victimes de guerres et/ou de persécution, et comme aux Comores, il n'y a ni guerre ni persécution, il ne peut s'appliquer à ma situation [...] on peut être persécuté par la misère sans l'être par les armes' (Hatubou and Jourdana, 2014: 180). Hatubou's approach to extreme poverty as a form of exile becomes particularly meaningful in the context of intercultural dialogues in the Mediterranean setting and, more specifically, in a city Fabre describes as 'une ville tissée comme un filet qui emprisonne ses proies, une cité d'errance et d'attente' (2014: 14). As a matter of fact, shifting from the context of geopolitical persecution to sociocultural injustice and alienation sheds light on the fact that poverty is a recurring theme in both visions of Hatubou's 'Mediterraneans' in which the paradoxical position of Marseille as simultaneously Eldorado and hell take on a central role.

Quoting Pierre Nepveu, Moura and Lalagianni's definition of migrant literature ('écriture migrante') specifies that 'le narrateur/ personnage entretient avec l'écriture un rapport particulier puisque, par son intermédiaire, il entreprend d'acquérir une certaine compréhension de la situation d'exclusion ou de marginalité dans laquelle il se trouve' (2014: 6). The aspects of exclusion and marginalization are particularly important in a process Iain Chambers describes as 'uneven politics of memory': 'These all reside in the postcolonial archive, in the stunted translations of alterity and the uneven politics of memory' (2008: 23). Hatubou's works must therefore be interpreted as an integral element of this postcolonial archive. Gironde considers Hatubou as an exemplary case of a creative performance of exile: 'ayant quitté très jeune son île pour Marseille, [il] construit son propre pont mémoriel en élaborant inlassablement les récits entendus pendant son enfance' (Gironde, 2014: 12). This form of Mediterranean bridging narrative through traditional storytelling can be observed in *Hassanati*, where it enters into direct competition with the television and alcohol. It is therefore important to note that these types of valued leisure activities do not exist within the context of *L'Odeur*.

The dialogic structure of *L'Odeur* points to a different form of storytelling or creative performance of exile at work in Karim's description of Marseille. Snippets of conversations permeate the plot. The blend of verbal utterances, miscommunication and monologues illustrate what Abulafia calls the fragmentation of the Mediterranean, with the subsequent wave of xenophobia and racism that preceded the arrival of the Comorian diaspora in Marseille:

> Perhaps 900,000 French Algerians left in the months before or after independence, including both the descendants of settlers and Algerian Jews, with vast numbers settling in Southern France. They were followed by a wave of native Algerian immigrants, and immigration

from Morocco and Tunisia [...] Rather than creating a new *convivencia*, the presence of a teeming North African population unlocked ugly, xenophobic sentiments in Southern France, accentuated by memories of the terrorism of the FLN. (2011: 622)

It is precisely within this context that we find the second form of bridging narratives in Hatubou's work.

Hatubou explained his commitment to memory as a need to talk about the difficult trajectories of the Comorian diaspora: 'notre parcours migratoire est semé [...] de tragédies' (Hatubou and Jourdana, 2014: 191). Besides the written preservation of his grandmother's tales in *Contes de ma grand-mère*, Hatubou's diligent commitment to the task of memory manifests itself in the contextualization of tragic events such as the brutal murder of Ibrahim Ali, who was attacked in Marseille by a 17-year-old billposter for the Front National on 21 February 1995. *L'Odeur* is dedicated to 'Ibrahim Ali, pour que nul n'oublie' (Hatubou, 1999: 161) and the plot features the rather unpleasant figure of the attacker as a secondary character. The text can therefore be read as an auto-fictional account of the context within which the 21 February incident occurred. The narrative draws on Karim's daily observations as he moves around different neighbourhoods of Marseille and thus represents what Michel de Certeau calls a spatial story: 'Every story is a travel story—a spatial practice [...] These narrated adventures, simultaneously producing geographies of actions and drifting into the commonplaces of an order, [...] organize walks' (2002: 115–16). Karim's spatial practices of everyday life take on an epistemological function.

Bridging Narratives as Spatial Stories: Marseille's Urban Tableaux and Frontiers

Karim's descriptions of Marseille are reminiscent of Michel de Certeau's distinction between place as 'instantaneous configuration of positions' and space as 'practiced place' (2002: 117). This opposition between 'either *seeing* (the knowledge of an order of place) or *going* (spatializing actions)' (de Certeau 2002: 119) creates a series of *tableaux* and *movements*. However, Karim is far from partaking in Jean-Claude Izzo's vibrant *tableau* of Marseille's 'rues, bruyantes, excubérantes comme toutes les villes du Sud', where one can 'se laisser porter par [cette ville], par ses rues, par ses collines, oui, tellement urbanisés il est vrai, que l'on oublie que Marseille est faite de collines qui descendent vers la mer' (1998: 15).

Hatubou's Karim describes the noise and exuberance of Marseille's streets with quite different connotations. He comes across typical places such as Izzo's *tableaux* of the seashore and its Vieux-Port as gateways to the Orient.[3] However, Karim's *tableau* ridicules this imaginary cartography:

> Des touristes asiatiques marchent sur un passage piéton, les uns derrière les autres comme des enfants en colonie de vacances. Ils s'arrêtent et commencent à filmer et photographier les bateaux accostés au Vieux-Port. La brise emporte les odeurs de la mer et les abandonne dans les entrailles de mes narines. (Hatubou, 1999: 125)

While perceiving the odour of the sea, Karim's observations focus less on picturesque scenery than on capturing sounds, including conversations and music, witnessing patterns of behaviour and identifying other sensory cues such as smells and tastes only to reiterate numerous aspects of the image of 'Marseille, la belle cosmopolite' (Hatubou, 1999: 76). These descriptions function as what Michel de Certeau calls the 'theater of actions' (2002: 123) in that they point to tensions within practised places of the urban landscape that seem to prevail on both sides of the Mediterranean Sea.

In her comparison of urban spaces in Paris and Marrakech, Yamina Sehli foregrounds the theatricality of social life. She associates the openness of large streets and intersections in modern Western urban spaces with 'indifférence et […] matérialité' (Sehli, 2014: 84) while the tight, entangled streets of North African Mediterranean cities allow to 'préserver l'intimité de la famille' (Sehli, 2014: 83). Her analysis particularly focuses on the social function of the café:

> Le café devient le lieu commun par excellence à toutes les cultures et à toutes les géographies. Ainsi le café parisien et le café marocain sont similaires […] puisqu'ils constituent indéniablement un lieu d'échanges dans les deux cultures. Le café est surtout un lieu de passage, de transition […] un espace polyphonique dans le sens où il réunit des personnes de différentes conditions et de différentes cultures. (Sehli, 2014: 85–86)

Within Hatubou's series of practised places, the streets and cafés of Marseille play an important role. Mistrust governs interactions between peoples of different origins in shared spaces such as the street, contrary

---

[3] 'À ce moment, vous découvrirez la mer. Et la baie. Immense, belle […] le vrai voyage ne peut commencer qu'ici. Marseille reste porte de l'Orient' (Izzo, 1998: 17).

to the notion of privacy common in the Marrakech. In streets such as La Canebière, the police immediately dissipates a crowd gathering around an Asian woman who talks loudly about her problems before addressing the indifferent crowd: 'C'est ça, circulez, circulez, vous ne devez rien voir, sinon le keuf vous conduira au poste' (Hatubou, 1999: 75). While children are being taught to ignore human eyesores in the urban landscapes, suspicion is even more evident on the bus:

> Dans le bus, une jeune fille blonde regarde deux vieux magrébins qui discutent en arabe; un grand Noir observe la jeune fille blonde; un vieil homme coiffé d'une casquette basque, le nez rouge, dévisage le grand Noir; et moi j'observe ce petit monde qui se regarde en chien de faïence, les yeux remplis de méfiance. (Hatubou, 1999: 133)

Similar scenes unfold during Karim's visits to the Agence Nationale de l'Emploi or local cafés such as Le Samaritaine, providing him with food for thought as he listens to the stories of poorly integrated *harkis* who claim their right to French citizenship.

Karim's practice of everyday cosmopolitan life in Marseille cannot be situated in Arjun Appadurai's deterritorialized world of the postnational era. He comments that 'le centre-ville continuera à être le centre de nos extrêmes. Ton Sud et mon Nord' (Hatubou, 1999: 104). These extremes trigger an imaginary lovemaking scene as Karim observes a blond woman in a café with African braids, which leads him to reflect upon 'métissage culturel [...] malgré les vingt pour cent d'électeurs marseillais qui balancent leurs voix à l'extrême droite [...] L'ignorance culturelle aussi est en marche. Mais tout cela me dépasse [...] Je [...] regarde admirablement la jeune blonde. Sans qu'elle le sache [...] je lui fais l'amour' (Hatubou, 1999: 114). The segregation of *une ville-monde* becomes even more evident during Karim's interactions with friends from various Mediterranean origins as tensions are particularly prevalent in the shared public space of housing projects, located north of central Marseille. These housing projects represent boundaries.[4] The concrete walls of Belle Ile function as a barrier between the 'Haves' and the 'Have Nots': 'Ma famille reste accroupie à "*Belle Ile*", un quartier Nord de Marseille—trait d'union entre une cité classée défavorisée par les institutions et un bidonville' (Hatubou, 1999: 11).

---

4 'Stories are actuated by a contradiction that is represented in them by the relationship between the frontier and the bridge, that is, between a (legitimate) space and its (alien) exteriority' (de Certeau, 2002: 126).

While the plot points to local attempts to alleviate tensions, institutionalized services fail at both the human and administrative level. According to the social worker, Karim is too young to receive certain forms of assistance. Temporary relief can only be obtained in the rue Thubaneau, where Christine, who holds a Bachelor's degree in Communications, fights unemployment by selling her attractive body: 'je tends mes cuisses, mon ventre, mes seins et mon sexe aux passants. Je gagne de l'argent. Je paie mon loyer, mes factures, mes fringues, ma bouffe et je fais des petites économies' (Hatubou, 1999: 99). Unlike Christine's fairy tale of restoring her honour by leaving the rue Thubaneau for good, Comorian men have dreams of obtaining honour and status far away from Marseille: 'Moi, ce que je veux, c'est de faire mon mariage traditionnel. Juste pour avoir ma place dans la société. C'est tout. Après, je retournerai à La Savoine pour vivre avec la mère de mes enfants' (Hatubou, 1999: 152). This ambitious dream leads countless Comorian men to resort to criminal activity in Marseille to be able to finance big wedding ceremonies (*le grand mariage*) in their native land.

Given the accumulation of *tableaux* and *movement* across spatial divides, Hatubou's bridging narratives can be read as a particular form of travel literature. His works fit the paradigms of a new genre, auto-fiction, in twentieth- and twenty-first-century literary French studies of the French-speaking world. This genre revolves around what Charles Forsdick calls the francophone postcolonial traveller in France whose itineraries draw on deceleration and domestic journeys (2005: 156–96). The meanderings of Hatubou's protagonists through the streets of Marseille or the rural towns of Mayotte therefore require a closer reading of these types of movement through a supposedly homogenous Mediterranean urban centre, Marseille, and its conceptually similar counterpart, the Comoros Islands. We will turn to Michel de Certeau's foundational essay on spatial practices, 'Walking the City', to describe operations and stylistic figures associated with movement that can be situated within Timo Obergöker's topography of the contemporary extreme.[5]

---

5 Obergöker writes: 'Être contemporain [...] revient à faire face à la part d'ombre de notre époque [...] c'est se trouver de l'autre côté d'une fissure qui permet de regarder le spectacle du monde' (2011: 7).

Pedestrian Rhetoric in the Mediterraneans of the Contemporary Extreme

For Obergöker, the city, its margins and rural France are representative spaces of the topography of the contemporary extreme in that they translate the struggles of 'le réinvestissement du lieu et de la recherche d'une stabilité et d'une cohérence là où tout semble flou et se dématérialise de plus en plus' (2011: 21). These sites are equally relevant to trans-Mediterranean studies about the Comorian diaspora. Both *L'Odeur* and *Hassanati* focus on modernity and change that originate from the outside. Hatubou's Karim follows the 'thicks and thins of urban texts' (de Certeau, 2002: 93) through physical movement in the streets and as a victim of the bureaucratic system. He experiences the operations that control urban practices to make them 'a place of transformations and appropriations, the object of various kinds of interference but also a subject that is constantly enriched by new attributes, it is simultaneously the machinery and the hero of modernity' (de Certeau, 2002: 95). For the Mediterranean urban centre of Marseille as well as the divided archipelago of the Comoro islands, the language of power and redistribution repeatedly points to the incommensurability of romanticized French ideals of *liberté, égalité, fraternité*, in both Metropolitan France, as well as its 101st department, or fifth DOM, Mayotte.

The descriptions of operational functions in both 'Mediterraneans' reflect Obergöker's development of representative examples that include 'une sensibilité très à droite' (2011: 12). This anti-immigration sensibility manifests itself through words and images, or, more precisely, stylistic figures that illustrate Michel de Certeau's comparison of the act of walking to a speech act: 'The walking of passers-by offers a series of turns (*tours*) and detours that can be compared to "turns of phrase" or "stylistic figures"' (de Certeau, 2002: 100). Karim consistently walks under the gaze of a personified city: 'Je lève les yeux et là-haut, sur une colline, Notre Dame de la Garde veille sur Marseille. Mais qui veille sur notre peau basané?' (Hatubou, 1999: 95). Every chapter features similar personifications of the city or its sights that watch Karim without interfering:

> Marseille, elle, regarde la nuit tomber dans le cœur des hommes et s'inquiète. Alors, elle raconte son Histoire, celle des différentes tribus qui l'ont enfantée ou qu'elle a enfantées, elle ne sait pas trop, la belle Phocéenne. Elle ne pleure pas, Marseille, mais regarde simplement les vaseux souiller les murs. (Hatubou, 1999: 67)

These personifications draw attention to the contrast between Mediterranean history and its current issues. Within the realm of pedestrian rhetoric, walls do indeed take on an important role because they function as one of two primary stylistic figures in 'Walking the city', the synecdoche[6] and asyndeton.[7] Marseille's concrete walls bear racial slurs and thus function as a synecdoche in that they stand for the attitude of the whole city. Contrary to the graffiti, the abbreviations on administrative forms become an asyndeton that draws attention to the bureaucratic world that has turned into a succession of dysfunctional places.

In the Indian Ocean Mediterranean, operational functions and stylistic figures are grounded in domestic and international politics that foreground anti-immigration. In *Hassanati*, as well as other texts that cannot be analysed here, the image of the rock is constantly present to refer to the fragmentation of the Comoros Islands, whose population now needs a French passport to enter Mayotte legally. In addition to the asyndeton of the rock that is intensified through the teacher's name, Madame Delaroche, Sambafum identifies the malfunctioning of Mayotte through the image of scavengers: 'Parce que tout est question de business et le Sud n'a pas d'argent ou plutôt le Sud a de l'argent mais dans les comptes de ses dirigeants corrompus' (Hatubou, 2011: 23). Local authorities are equally corrupt as they watch over the land of the poor like 'charognards dans les savanes africaines' (Hatubou, 2011: 52). They immediately jump on any opportunity to purchase it, as selling land is the only means to finance the process of migration. As Obergöker indicates, 'L'espace rural est ainsi tout sauf reclus, il est le point de convergence où diverses lignes de fuite confluent' (2011: 14).

It is therefore even more surprising to encounter symbols of hope in marginalized spaces such as rural areas of Mayotte or the *quartiers nord* of Marseille, outside of ephemeral pleasures at rue Thubaneau for Karim or long nights of storytelling for Sambafum. In *L'Odeur*, foods such as bread and couscous stand for the non-Western Mediterranean community, specifically Oummi's and Rabah's Algerian origins, thus representing an important synecdoche. This figure of style is complemented by Karim's reference to his father's old car, which stands for his dream of social ascension, or what Obergöker describes as the 'emblème de la modernité et de la mobilité' (2011: 14).

6 De Certeau writes: 'In essence, it names a part instead of the whole which includes it' (2002: 101).
7 De Certeau: '*Asyndeton* is the suppression of linking words […] In walking it selects and fragments the space traversed' (2002: 101).

Modernity and mobility are further illustrated through the role of education and literature. While in the young adult novel *Hassanati*, Sambafum values education, along with the act of reading, writing and oral traditions, Karim, on the other hand, consistently questions the functionality of his academic degree by analysing the useless words on his diploma. As basic units, words can both cause disruptions (asyndeton) and build bridges (synecdoche). Throughout the plot, education and eloquence are sources of miscommunication and misunderstanding. As such, they create brief moments of comic relief for those who have mastered the difficulties of the French language, as opposed to people from different sociocultural origins who confuse words. Words also appear as synecdoche in the form of intertextual references to texts that denounce the abuses of postcolonialism, as Moura and Lalagianni indicate for Mediterranean migrant authors. Writers such as Samir, Hatubou's fictional double, are called upon to raise awareness about ethical issues in both 'Mediterraneans'. This becomes particularly evident at the end of both novels, where they embrace an even broader vision of the 'Mediterranean' and its shared ethical issues.

The Global Mediterranean and the Notion of the Symbolic Return

Karim's sad account of the Comorian diaspora in Marseille attests to the problematic existence of divides that are considered common for the Mediterranean region. Abulafia goes as far as to identify the Mediterranean as 'probably the most vigorous place of interaction between different societies on the face of the planet' (2011: 648). But Karim knows that similar phenomena are at work in other conceptually similar Mediterranean regions, as Abulafia would put it. The third Mediterranean vision outlined in both of Hatubou's texts is Abulafia's 'Global Mediterranean'. At the end of both novels, each narrator conjures up images of racial discrimination and terrorism in the conceptually similar 'Mediterranean' space of North America. In *Hassanati*, Samba's world turns upside down when watching the footage of 9/11 the day of Hassanati's departure:

> Je ne voulais pas la laisser partir [...] c'est vrai qu'elle allait en France, pas en Amérique, mais finalement, quel coin était à l'abri de la folie des hommes? Jusqu'ici, je pensais que notre petit archipel de quatre îles était éloigné du monde, mais c'était faux, nous étions tous reliés les uns aux autres. (Hatubou, 2011: 66)

The notion of connecting Mediterraneans is furthermore reiterated in Samba's goodbye poem to Hassanati: 'J'ai [...] recopié *I have a dream* (J'ai fait un rêve) de Martin Luther King. Moi aussi, j'ai rêvé qu'un jour tous les frères de mes quatre îles se donneraient la main pour former une belle nation' (Hatubou, 2011: 67). In that sense, *Hassanati* puts forward a bridging narrative that connects the conceptually similar spaces of the Indian Ocean and the Americas, while maintaining that the Mediterranean of southern France is an Eldorado. However, in *L'Odeur*, Hatubou links the south of France and the South of the United States:

> Dans le sud des Etats-Unis, le Ku Klux Klan sème la terreur; du haut de leurs chevaux nerveux [...] Dans le sud de la France, des colleurs d'affiches sèment la terreur, à l'intérieur de leurs voitures puissantes [...] En Amérique, au pays du Klan, des hommes en cagoules brûlent des croix [...] En France, au pays des droits de l'Homme, des hommes excités par les discours haineux de leurs chefs veulent brûler d'autres hommes [...] Nous sommes en février mil neuf cent quatre vingt quinze. Les masques de la nuit vont d'un Sud à l'autre. (Hatubou, 1999: 159)

Between experiences of terrorism, corruption and racial segregation, all 'Mediterranean' spaces similarly struggle with issues that become particularly complex in the Mediterranean region, as outlined by Edgar Morin. For Morin, the Mediterranean region faces 'à la fois la crise du Passé, la crise du Futur, la crise du Devenir. Ces crises sont en même temps la crise du développement et la crise de notre ère planétaire' (1998: 37). He therefore suggests situating the Mediterranean region within a global context of interconnecting issues and solutions: 'Elle porte en elle la crise du monde tout en vivant sa crise singulière. De même que le monde nécessite une mondialisation de compréhension et de solidarité, la Méditerranée nécessite une méditerranéisation de compréhension et de solidarité' (Morin, 1998: 41). Hatubou's texts thus point to a prevailing lack of mutual understanding and solidarity, with some minor exceptions, thus reiterating Amin Maalouf's vision of the Mediterranean region as 'une entité à construire' (1998: 89).

The open end of each novel invites the reader to imagine a successful migration process to and from Marseille, while a cross-reading of both texts, as well as several other works, reveals the harsh realities on either side of the migration process. However, the reader is led to question the functionality of Hatubou's visions of 'Mediterraneans'. When comparing these two novels, it is striking to note that Marseille is portrayed in a positive light from the outside, that is, when the plot evolves around characters who migrate to the supposedly homogenous Mediterranean urban centre of Marseille. Yet, when the plot focuses on the Comorian diaspora in a divided *ville-monde*, specifically the *quartiers nord* of Marseille, the narrator remains surprisingly ambivalent about the actual outcome of the process of returning to the Comoros Islands.

In *L'Odeur*, Hatubou differentiates between two types of return. The first is a temporary return that has numerous implications for the status and identity of the returnee. The second is what is referred to as 'le retour définitif', meaning that the returnee leaves Marseille for good. While the narrator denounces those whose only motivation is to return to improve their status in Metropolitan France through *le grand mariage* in the Comoros Islands, Karim's return raises questions about the process itself as well as his future: will he find salvation, peace and comfort upon his return to a non-native land? The newspaper article about Mourad's success in local Comorian politics is promising, yet for Karim, uncertainty is more reassuring than envisioning a future in the current climate of what Morin calls 'la zone sismique méditerranéenne' (1998: 38), especially after the killing of Ali, which triggered the novel in the first place.

The theme of the return refers to both a physical and a mental process that is reminiscent of Forsdick's reference to the 'striking diversity of a plurality of *banlieues* while nevertheless seeking continuities between its fragments' (2005: 187). With this shift towards what Aimé Césaire coined as the return to one's native land, Hatubou's Mediterranean bridging narratives open up a new space in French and francophone literature of the contemporary extreme to consider anew the harsh realities of the *quartiers nord* of Marseille and the rural landscape the Comoros Islands. As such, Hatubou's representation of the Mediterranean and non-Mediterranean immigrants in Marseille absorbs what Obergöker calls the 'nouveaux épisodes comme l'histoire coloniale et la Guerre d'Algérie, [qui] seront abordés de manière originale [...] Se pose également la question de la séparation entre la littérature française et francophone' (2011: 10). The question of belonging is present throughout the novel, for Algerians and Comorians of three different generations. In addition, Hatubou's Comorian origins take the question of belonging to the level of literary production and distribution. A still young and emerging[8] literary

---

8 For more information about contemporary Comorian literature, see Ali Abdou Mdahoma (2012), Abdoulatuf Bacar (2009), Isabelle Mohamed (2011), and Jean-Luc Raharimanana (2011).

production of a divided archipelago in the Indian Ocean, Hatubou's texts seemingly fit into this category, as well as that of that of migrant writing of the Mediterranean region that currently lacks the visibility and status of its counterpart on the other side of the Atlantic, that is, Quebecois migrant literature. Can the Comorian diaspora claim African heritage, following the lead of Léopold Sédar Senghor's *Anthologie de la nouvelle poésie nègre et malgache de langue française* (1948), considering that its literary production is still absent from African anthologies, as Ali Abdou Mdahoma shows? Hatubou's shift towards the notion of return can be contextualized within the category of what Odile Cazenave refers to as the post-Afrique sur Seine generation.[9] Situating Hatubou within this post-Afrique sur Seine generation helps reiterate the author's commitment to the Comorian community of Marseille and the writers of the Comorian diaspora that goes beyond the depiction of migration towards Metropolitan France. *L'Odeur* decries the silencing of harsh realities that exist on either side of the migration process, a phenomenon that first developed with Ousmane Sembène's *La Noire de ...*, similarly denouncing the myth of Metropolitan France, as Cazenave underlines.

A prolific writer, Salim Hatubou was considered a leading figure of an emerging literary production. His representations of trans-Mediterranean experiences, along with his involvement as an activist in Comorian literature and the Comorian diaspora in Marseille, was consistently praised not only in the 2015 obituaries and announcements of his death, but also prior to his unexpected passing. Hatubou adopted a transnational approach by juxtaposing untold stories of Mediterranean and non-Mediterranean communities that unfold in three conceptually similar 'Mediterraneans'. However, as the failure of Karim's ambitious friend Samir indicates, the act of writing these stories is a challenging endeavour. Yet Hatubou, like his fictional doubles, reiterates the importance of creating bridges that foster what Morin calls a feeling of shared identity: 'Il n'y a de vraie communication que s'il y a non

---

9   Cazenave writes: 'j'ai voulu revenir sur [...] les configurations nouvelles qui me paraissaient se dégager sur le plan des formes esthétiques chez nombre d'auteurs diasporiques [...], que ce soit en termes de direction de regard d'écriture des axes spatiaux-temporels—'hier'/'aujourd'hui'; 'ici'/'là-bas'—et autres fondamentaux de l'inscription de la jeunesse et de la migrance dans le contexte postcolonial [...] cette notion, absente ou reléguée à l'arrière-plan dans la génération Afrique sur Seine, dans un désir de porter le regard sur le *hic et nunc* implicite de l'expérience de migration, voire un regard dirigé sur demain, reparaît aujourd'hui dans la fabrique textuelle des romans francophones des dernières années mais dans une configuration nouvelle' (2014: 173–74).

seulement compréhension mutuelle des différences, mais aussi, en-deçà des différences, un sentiment d'identité commune' (1998: 44).

Bibliography

Abdou Mdahoma, Ali. 2012. *Le roman comorien de langue française*. Paris: L'Harmattan.
Abulafia, David. 2005. Mediterraneans. In W.V. Harris, ed., *Rethinking the Mediterranean*, 64–93. Oxford: Oxford University Press.
———. 2011. *The great sea: A human history of the Mediterranean*. New York: Oxford University Press.
Bacar, Abdoulatuf. 2009. *Comment se lit le roman postcolonial? Cas des Îles Comores: la République des imberbes et le bal des mercenaires*. Levallois-Perret: Editions de la Lune.
Cazenave, Odile. 2014. Dire le retour sans le dire tout en le disant: nouvelle configuration des motifs exiliques et d'expatriation. In Jean-Marc Moura and Vasiliki Lalagianni, eds., *Espace méditerranéen: écritures de l'exil, migrances et discours postcolonial*, 173–83. New York: Rodopi.
de Certeau, Michel. 2002. *The practice of everyday life*. Translated by Steven Rendall. Berkeley: University of California Press.
Chambers, Iain. 2008. *Mediterranean crossings: The politics of an interrupted modernity*. Durham, NC: Duke University Press.
Fabre, Cédric. 2014. Marseille calling. In *Marseille Noir*, 9–15. Paris: Akashic Books.
Forsdick, Charles. 2005. *Travel in twentieth-century French and francophone cultures*. Oxford: Oxford University Press.
Gironde, Michel. 2014. Penser et écrire l'exil. In *Méditerranée & exil aujourd'hui*, 9–13. Paris: L'Harmattan.
Hatubou, Salim. 1999. *L'Odeur du béton*. Paris: L'Harmattan.
———. 2011. *Hassanati de Mayotte à Marseille*. Paris: L'Harmattan.
Hatubou, Salim and Pascal Jourdana. 2014. Ouverture: entre les Comores & Marseille. Dialogue avec Salim Hatubou. In Michel Gironde, ed., *Méditerranée & exil aujourd'hui*, 179–92. Paris: L'Harmattan.
Izzo, Jean-Claude. 1998. Marseille, la lumière et la mer. In Michel Le Bris and Jean-Claude Izzo, eds., *Méditerranées: une anthologie*, 13–18. Paris: Flammarion.
Maalouf, Amin. 1998. Construire la Méditerranée. In Michel Le Bris and Jean-Claude Izzo, eds., *Méditerranées: une anthologie*, 89–93. Paris: Flammarion.
Mohamed, Isabelle. 2011. Salim Hatubou, écrire pour vivre et faire vivre un espace. In Jean-Luc Raharimanana and Magali Marson, eds., *Les Comores: une littérature en archipel*, 269–84. Lecce: Alliance Française.

Morin, Edgar. 1998. Penser la Méditerranée et méditerranéiser la pensée. *CONFLUENCES Méditerranée* 28: 33–47.
Moura, Jean-Marc and Vasiliki Lalagianni. 2014. Écrire l'exil et la migrance à l'ère postcoloniale. In *Espace méditerranéen: écritures de l'exil, migrances et discours postcolonial*, 5–19. New York: Rodopi.
Obergöker, Timo. 2011. Pour une topographie du romanesque contemporain. In *Les lieux de l'extrême contemporain. Orte des französischen Gegenwartsroman*, 7–21. Munich: Martin Meidenbauer.
Raharimanana, Jean-Luc. 2011. Les Comores: une littérature en archipel. In Jean-Luc Raharimanana and Magali Marson, eds., *Les Comores: une littérature en archipel*, 9–13. Lecce: Alliance Française.
Renucci, Janine. 2001. *La Corse*. Paris: Presses universitaires de France.
Sehli, Yamina. 2014. Exils à Paris & Marrakech—Mohammed Dib et Tahar Ben Jelloun. In Michel Gironde, ed., *Méditerranée & exil aujourd'hui*, 81–89. Paris: L'Harmattan.

10

Trans-Mediterranean *Beyroutes*

Claire Launchbury

In the annals of Lebanese legend, Beirut has been destroyed and rebuilt seven times in the course of its 5,000 years of continuous habitation.[1] It developed as a settlement on the eastern coast of the Mediterranean to facilitate trade to and from the inland metropolis of Damascus. Rivalled as the primary port on the eastern Mediterranean by Haifa and Jaffa in the south and Tripoli in the north, Beirut has long held a contingent relationship with its shore and sea. Although Beirut was destroyed by a tsunami in 551 CE, the Mediterranean Sea has provided trade, escape and diversion for its many and varied inhabitants. A passage in Etel Adnan's most famous work of the civil war, *Sitt Marie-Rose* (1977), compellingly observes that Beirut will have soon become nothing more than 'une épave soudée à ses rochers' and notes how the merchant ships waiting to dock in the port and leaving their lights on all night creates the sense that 'Beyrouth a l'air de s'être déplacé, d'avoir glissé sur la mer' (2010 [1977]: 23). The arrival of the war is also described in watery metaphors of deluge or flooding and foundering by Amin Maalouf: 'Notre pays au mécanisme fragile prenait l'eau, il commençait à se détraquer; nous allions découvrir, au fil des inondations, qu'il était difficilement réparable' (2012: 35).

This sense of the city and country as being somehow unmoored or ruined, wrecked on the rocks and difficult to repair is revisited in Samir Khalaf's 2012 study of the post-war *état présent*, *Lebanon Adrift*. For Khalaf the excesses in Beirut which he sees illustrated

---

1   This chapter was written and went to press before the devastating explosion of 4 October 2020.

175

in the unregulated building of beach resorts, among other urban manifestations, demonstrate a predilection for 'the tawdry and the absence of aesthetic restraint', and are ultimately symptomatic of the 'aberrant attributes of the perennial state of being *adrift*' (2012: 241). While Khalaf's sense of 'adrift' points to something rather different, as I discuss below, the trope of Beirut as untamed when reflected by the external gaze of Western commentators takes us back to more orientalist instincts: these are people who saw the turn to violence during the civil war as some sort of organic, unstoppable process or read it—tacitly if not openly—as a failure of a civilizing European colonial influence unable sufficiently to contain or repress the othered, orientalized barbarian of their exotic and erotic imaginations. We are left with little more than a projection of a return to a European atavistic primality repressed, and which is perpetually articulated in such gazes upon the territories of the eastern Mediterranean.

This chapter demonstrates how Beirut is a series of urban paradoxes. Operating simultaneously as something adrift, free-floating in the Mediterranean which borders its shores, yet also as the hub of a transnational capital and its exchanges. In thinking through both how to navigate the city and to reclaim it, we see attempts to tame urban space semantically through an agenda of familiarization, or how its pervasive official and unofficial securitization and surveillance makes for alert citizens with adept urban ruses. This allows for an examination of different ways of seeing and understanding the city, and how these have been articulated. I also discuss how capital flows have influenced urban dynamics across the pre-war, civil war and post-war city. Reflecting on grassroots social movements that have challenged both political and economic orthodoxy, the chapter closes by thinking about how, if Beirut is a playground, can the excesses be contained, or should they even be so?

Is it possible to define Beirut in its own terms without the gaze of the *voyageur en orient*? Is it possible to counter the habitual practice of taking theories from the global North and using them to read for 'facts' in the global South? I hope to suggest in the analysis of these trans-Mediterranean confluences that it is possible to work *in theory*, alongside transnational streams of discourse, emulating Fadi Bardawil's compelling intention to 'hold the tension' between narrative and theory: 'to avoid both highlighting an interconnectedness, which does not take power into account, and an erasure of interconnectedness, which is itself a symptom of power' (2020: 7). Some look to the mid-century innovations in architecture that were built in the city as a lost modernist heritage subsequently overshadowed by the neo-Oriental pastiche and façadism of the rebuilt downtown (Kassab, 2015). In trying to trace the routes of the 'trans-Mediterranean' dynamics of this city, I am drawn to the notion of hybridity and dialectics in how the very active partitive article in the clichés mentioned below both gives and takes, with varying degrees of irony, representations of the aphanisic relationship between colonizing West and colonized East. The fragility of the comparison is marked by a perpetual fading reinforcing Edward Said's forceful and later tacit observation that there are 'cultures and nations whose location in the East, and their lives, histories, and customs have a brute reality obviously greater than anything that could be said about them in the West' (2003 [1978]: 5). Attending to the trans-Mediterranean in Beirut involves teasing out multiple layers of mediation between knowledge and power, residual influence on language from the former metropole; and how the routes of global capital can help to explain some of the roots of civil conflict.

Urbicide

In her examination of how urban materiality responds to geopolitics, Sara Fregonese (2009) explores Beirut's 'urbicide', and the inevitable and extreme changes rendered to the urban fabric during the civil war. She notes how discourses exterior to Lebanon have simplified the complexities of the situation, employing machine metaphors as well as fatalistic ones, so that the war was framed as the result of a fatal mechanism, an unstoppable chain of events, the sectarian 'barbarism' of a failure of sovereignty to keep the sects in check or to keep the terrorists out, paraphrasing Israeli Foreign Minister Shimon Peres, who identified a Palestinian and Syrian threat in January 1975 (Israel Ministry of Foreign Affairs, 1975). If fighting is described as uncontrolled, it is also understood as instinctive—as though it exposed the natural inclination of an Arab society once the colonial European civilizing framework crumbled. French political views on the situation early on during the civil war demonstrate this particularly well. In the French Assemblée Nationale on 6 May 1976, Minister of Foreign Affairs Jean Sauvagnargues made a speech stating that France had a particular duty to 'prévenir l'éclatement d'un pays qu'elle a contribué à créer, auquel elle est attachée par tant de liens et dont l'indépendance et l'intégrité sont si évidemment les éléments indispensables de l'équilibre et de la stabilité de la région, dans son ensemble' (*Journal officiel*,

1976: 2698). Taking the credit for its independence and integrity, former premier Michel Debré in the same debate states how Lebanon 'était également le symbole exceptionnel d'une tolérance et d'une paix qui éclairaient de leur lumière cette partie du monde' and how France, in addition to helping create the state as Sauvagnargues claims above, must 'rappeler notre ancienne vocation protectrice de la communauté chrétienne, mais aussi et surtout nos liens spirituels profonds avec les deux communautés' (*Journal officiel*, 1976: 2714). Maurice Couve de Murville again cites the particular responsibility France has in regard to Lebanon 'tant le Liban est proche de la France, tant sont multiples et étroits les liens qui unissent les deux peuples. Cette amitié profonde, la part que nous avons prise jadis à la création du Liban sur la base d'un accord entre chrétiens et musulmans nous imposent des responsabilités plus évidentes qu'à quiconque' (*Journal officiel*, 1976: 2702). As the 'accord' between the 'two communities'—which simplifies considerably the confessional diversity of Lebanon—brokered by France is fractured, Lebanon becomes an untamed figure in need of patriarchal structure.

These Franco-Lebanese links still persist in France's dominance in leading the case for financial aid such, as the to-date embargoed CEDRE (Conférence économique pour le développement, par les réformes et avec les entreprises) Capital Investment Plan funding donated following the Paris conference of 2018, the high-level networking between the families of Chirac and Hariri, and within the generally politically right-leaning francophone Maronite communities who hosted Marine Le Pen prior to the presidential elections. The Front National and this community are far from strangers to each other as militant *frontistes* joined the right-wing militias in fighting during the civil war. Indeed, in the first round, the electoral *circonscription* in Lebanon in April 2017 showed Le Pen achieving marginally fewer votes than Macron, by far the bulk of the vote going to centre-right Fillon but nevertheless a sizeable vote from a community that joyfully termed itself *francophile et francophone* in a chorus to the far-right candidate during her visit in February 2017 and who would have lost their right to dual citizenship had she won. In the second round Le Pen still managed almost a third of the vote against Macron (Élection présidentielle, 2017).

Another mechanism by which Western observers try to tame Beirut is semantically, and while this has been exploited for its potential to attract tourism from within Lebanon, there is a rich history of placing the city in association with many different elsewheres. These range from the hackneyed clichés which portray the city as the 'somewhere-else' of the Middle East. Clichés such as the 'Paris of the Middle East' speak to nostalgic reminiscence of pre-war conspicuous consumption and the leisure of the international jet set. Or as a shorthand for the particular ways in which finance and transnational capital operate in Beirut formulations such as 'the Monte Carlo of the Middle East', 'the Singapore of the Middle East' or the 'Switzerland of the Middle East', all of which point, with lesser or greater degrees of irony and accuracy, to gambling, free ports, banking secrecy and *laissez-tout-faire* economics with their concomitant tax avoidance and corruption. As I show below, capital has always had a physical impact on the cityscape of Beirut. Indeed, as Najib Hourani (2015) has shown explicitly, the dynamics of two principal rival financial networks, petrodollar financialization, globalization and financial crash provided the civil war with roots just as deep as those already existing sectarian, religious or political tensions.

Global capital has had an almost equal impact on the urban fabric of Beirut as the destruction caused by the urbicide of the civil war. Transnational capital flows from the Gulf and from wealthy expats in the diaspora who help maintain the 'sovereign wealth fund', and while serious economic crisis is imminent, this has combined in the past to make a resilient banking sector despite a series of systemic shocks. Ma'an Barazy's study *Lebanon Finance 2.0* is as much a tribute to Banque du Liban governor Riad Salameh, who has held the post since 1994, as it is an analysis of Lebanon's financial management. Barazy describes how 'many press reports have portrayed Salameh as the governor of an island of stability among rough seas' (2012: 19) and having made the Banque du Liban a 'safe haven' notably, the economy had immunity in the 2008 global financial crash, having evaded sub-prime markets.

Global Capital and Trans-Mediterranean Flow

Political and financial circulation are most visible in the 'skyline of empty apartments' (Sakr-Tierney, 2017) as familiar in Beirut as along contemporary London's South Bank, as Gulf investors deposit monies in real estate with a value far beyond the reach of Beiruti residents, representing an urban manifestation of the neoliberal principle of prioritizing commodities over people. As Sakr-Tierney notes, 'development discourse conceives the post-war economy's dependence on foreign financial inflows and as a destination for real estate investment as inevitable, as unquestioned as the law of scarcity and the banking system's resilience when the effect has been to consolidate political and financial power among warlords-turned-politicians' (2017: 76). It is precisely this nexus of liberal wealth and political power held by the same small cohort of men that has held Lebanon in a sort of post-war stasis behind the uprisings since 17 October 2019.

David Harvey notes how the neoliberal turn which restored class power to the very richest in society manifests in cities in the visibility of the sharp polarization between those with money and status and those without; this distribution of power is 'indelibly etched into the spatial forms of our cities, which increasingly become cities of fortified fragments, of gated communities and privatised public spaces kept under constant surveillance' (2012: 15). Their impact is visible as Sakr-Tierney states that 'transnational capital circulations constructed and reconstructed Beirut many times over' (2017: 77). Protection of these property rights becomes the hegemonic form of politics and Harvey, following Park and Lefebvre, argues that the right to the city is not simply the right to access the resources that it offers, but 'it is a right to change and reinvent the city after out heart's desires', all of which is foreclosed by the neoliberal configuration of Beirut's city space (2013: 4). Indeed, capitalism is particularly insidious in the ways it inveigles itself into communities, encouraging the poor to sell assets that the rich would not; or promoting progressive sounding micro-financing schemes which rely on women's social relations to spread and enforce repayment.

Barazy, an international expert for UNIFEM, developed a microfinance fund for women in Lebanon. It was designed to be a means of encouraging women active in the informal sector to work in mainstream economic development. The microfinance initiative provided financial services to low-income women entrepreneurs, focusing on 'female' activities such as handicrafts (Husseini, 1997). While there was certainly a benefit in the programme's assessment of issues surrounding gender inequality in relation to access to banking, it arguably does not address the structural issues or inequalities that capitalism itself fosters by investing in gender-assigned projects, nor issues of inequality specific to Lebanon, such as the status of Palestinian refugees or the frequently precarious and dangerous situation faced by migrant domestic workers. As Harvey points out, these are myths of progressive projects which merely push the problems somewhere else (2012: 21). An additional pernicious consequence of approaching development through access to credit is the archetypal suturing of debt and discipline in late capitalism which leads both to precarity and the suppression of dissidence. This generally fulfils Western geopolitical objectives rather than actively helping to improve social mobility or

Trans-Mediterranean *Beyroutes*

encouraging the innovative restructuring that civil action can achieve from the grassroots.

Transnational financial dynamics transcended political and sectarian divisions during the civil war, as anthropologist Najib Hourani (2015) has clearly outlined. This nexus of capital, colonial legacy and power concentrated in the hands of oligarchical families has typically been overlooked in studies which assess the civil war solely in terms of religion or politics. It demonstrates a persistent geopolitics of capital in which the circulation of commodities, the trade in real estate, and the banking sector have operated. While certainly in the years following independence and before the civil war, the economic sector proudly presented itself as a merchant republic with Beirut as a trading capital, a haven for shoppers and pleasure seekers (Gates, 1998), other factors were at work with a shift in power 'unmistakably passing to financial tycoons' (Yusuf Sayegh qtd. in Hourani, 2015: 139). Famous family names, such as Sursock, Chiha, Pharoun and Obegi, operated expansive networks across the Mediterranean, due to the legacies of the Ottoman empire and mandated era and their centralized administrations. Michel Chiha was one of the primary authors of Lebanon's post-independence Constitution, his brother-in-law and Lebanon's first President, Henri Pharoun, designed the Lebanese flag, and the Obegi family began in textile dyes before founding one of the largest banks, Crédit libanais, while the Sursock family eventually gave their name to an entire district in Beirut. What Hourani demonstrates is that, first, there was significant rotation between these financially powerful families and politics and, second, that collaborative transactions and alliances would take place between people who were otherwise opposed in daily political life (2015: 140). Post-independence, the Lebanese economy retained its transnational and, indeed, trans-Mediterranean power basis with major banks now operating as joint ventures with either American or European partners, of which the latter were predominantly hexagonal institutions originating as branches of French colonial banking, such as Crédit Foncier d'Algérie et Tunisie (Fransabank) or Compagnie Algérienne (Banque Libano-Française), offering mediated access by Western financial institutions to burgeoning Gulf markets.

During the civil war, the constellation of militia-run civil organizations, banking, families and religious organizations were also operating through transnational axes. While both the Jumblatt-led Druze militia and its organizations were efficient, and Amal, a Shi'a resistance militia, drew upon connections in Iraq and Jordan, the financial networks and capitalist profiteering of the Gemayel dynasty's

Kata'eb Party led by Roger Tamraz were arguably the most extensive. Harvard-educated Tamraz operated across networks in the United States, Saudi Arabia and France. In 1982, he was appointed by Amin Gemayel to head the semi-nationalized Intra-Investment, which had huge infrastructure holdings including MEA-Air Liban, the national carrier, the Beirut Port Company and indeed the second largest shipyard in France, La Ciotat, exemplifying the trans-Mediterranean connections at work between global capital and urban global capitals. Once in power, Gemayel established his sectarian economic planning arm as a government department, COFER (Council for Foreign Economic Relations), not only to deal with foreign economic affairs but also to circumnavigate regulatory state structures and conventional banking practices controlled by the central Banque du Liban. Hourani notes that the civil war, far from making global financial interest shy away from the troubled state, was in fact a magnet for capital, with the conflict being secondary to the liberalization of the Lebanese sector (2015: 145). In this way, Rafic Hariri, despite many competing analyses, was also a canny transnational operator. Holding dual citizenship in Lebanon and Saudi Arabia, and with close ties to the Saudi royal family, Hariri's involvement was not so much in infrastructure, at least in the beginning, but in the transnational networks associated with petrodollars.

Operating as a Saudi mediator between the different sectarian factions of the civil war, Hariri became both an incredibly rich construction contractor and a politically indispensable Sunni whose close friendship with Jacques Chirac helped sustain his inroads into political and economic power in France, the 'historical guarantor of a Christian-dominated Lebanon' (Hourani, 2015: 151). Hannes Baumann's study *Citizen Hariri* explores how this trans-Mediterranean affinity between Hariri and Chirac worked geopolitically both in the liberation of French hostages during his premiership between 1986 and 1988, and in Hariri's substantial donation to the Institut du Monde Arabe in Paris. In return, French diplomatic efforts expedited a rapid end to the 1996 'Grapes of Wrath' conflict with Israel (Baumann, 2016: 139–40). Chirac resided in a Hariri-owned residence on the Île Saint-Louis in Paris and a street in the central downtown district, where Hariri's contracting expertise flourished and his company, Solidere (a portmanteau of Société libanaise de développement et reconstruction), made its largest urban impact, is named after the former French prime minister and president.

What Hourani elucidates most clearly is that the transcendent power of capital overrode political and sectarian affiliations. While Hariri kept his distance from the Kata'eb leadership and evaded the decisive far-right shifts of Geagea's Lebanese Forces in the mid 1980s, mutual economic interests maintained hidden collaborations even as fighting continued on Beirut's streets. The rise and fall of Kata'eb's political and economic power nexus alongside the rise and rise of Hariri articulates some of the major dynamics of the Lebanese civil war:

> It was more about deeply networked and illiberal elites seeking to protect a colonial order atop which they have lived in relative luxury. It was about their willingness, and that of second-tier elites, to be sure, to kill to preserve or penetrate that order, especially as the petrodollars poured in. It was about Gulf oil states seeking the same, in the face of Western powers eager to retain control of the region, its resources and indeed, the global economy. The war was a struggle for politico-economic power among the powerful themselves. It was the average Lebanese who paid the price. (Hourani, 2015: 157)

These power moves by the illiberal elite did not go unnoticed by the Lebanese fighters on the ground, though the early years of the civil war in particular saw several aspects of the conflict articulated in overtly anti-capitalist terms with an explicitly urban manifestation. In an interview, a former National Movement (the coalition of various leftist and pan-Arab parties) militia fighter describes how the Holiday Inn and its possession during the Battle of the Hotels also aligned with their movement's anti-capitalist agenda (Fregonese, 2009: 315). The vast and dominating Holiday Inn building represented international capital and the bourgeois system, in addition to its strategic importance in establishing the front, or green line. This point is illustrated by a 1976 propaganda poster of the Al Mourabitoun, the Nasserite, secular though predominantly Sunni militia opposed to the Christian Maronite majority, which depicts one of their soldiers smashing the Holiday Inn with the butt of a rifle, smashing the symbol of fascist treachery (Fregonese, 2009: 316).

Urban Bridges

While internationalism undergirded the influential spheres of Beirut-based left-wing intellectuals, there were especially strong trans-Mediterranean routes established, in particular, through texts in translation. Bardawil's genealogy of Socialist Lebanon, a relatively short-lived Marxist groupuscule (1965–70) which involved figures such as Waddah Charari, Ahmad Beydoun and Fawwaz Traboulsi, demonstrates how these figures, in a fairly typical postcolonial *parcours*, followed the second language of their schooling, private education in Lebanon typically being delivered in French or English, with postgraduate metropolitan study in France or the United States. While direct political engagement might have been relatively short lived and their attention shifted to formalized academic careers in history and sociology, most notably in the public Université Libanaise, they participated in production, dissemination and translation of a network of publications and publishing houses including Editions Maspero, *Le Monde diplomatique* and *Les Temps modernes*. Bardawil is keen to stress that it was not solely through these relatively official routes of metropolitan exchanges with Paris that engagement with and circulation of texts took place, but also in the way this 'globally interconnected world, which was fashioned by the practice and travels of militants as well as the intense circulation and translation of texts, did not always transit through metropolitan universities, periodicals, and publishers. It was also fostered by the art festivals, publications, and intellectual, political, and military institutions of the nonaligned and socialist worlds' (2020: 13). Indeed, the theorizing transcends the active partitive object I mentioned above, it is not a global North to South translation but, as Bardawil forcefully argues, 'a part and parcel of the arsenal of revolutionary politics which was rendered possible by a deeply held belief in a shared horizon of an emancipation to come' (2020: 14).

In the next part of the chapter, I examine the urban bridges that facilitate or inhibit rights to the city. Returning to Khalaf's study on the unmoored and adrift dimensions to both Lebanon and Beirut, let us turn to his desire to see the transformation of consumers into citizens. As he noted in 2012—and the current financial crisis and uprising are testament to the endgame of his analysis—Lebanon has been embroiled in all the unsettling forces of globalism and the intensification of consumerism and commodification. Class and identity are being cast adrift to be replaced by individualized manifestations, the allure of kitsch and spectacle, a distance between the lifestyle promises of the building site hoardings and the impossible bridge between such representations and a reality beset by malfunctioning infrastructure, entrenched structural inequality and the very quotidian difficulties of simply getting around the urban space. There is a strong resentment felt by an urban population tied up in endless traffic jams as corteges of security vehicles with blackened windows carry politicians smoothly through the disrupted city (the experience of which they do little to enhance), adding their own road closures and additional congestion. Such a scene opens Philippe Aranctingi's 2005 film *Bosta*, a Lebanese 'Strictly Dabké' where touring *dabké* dancers use a 1943 bus that has broken down. The camera pans along the traffic jam to show a cross-section of Lebanese united in their frustration at the question 'Where is the state? (*wayn al-dawla?*), which in itself is a broad question since it asks who has the authority to make things work, to make the city unstuck? At this moment a motorcade of police cars and limousines sails past on the opposite carriageway. Hannes Baumann uses this scene in part as a vignette to contrast to the explosive motorcade that assassinated Rafic Hariri in 2005, but also to note that 'despite its absence—or because of it—the Lebanese state establishes a hierarchy, distinguishing those who travel freely from those stuck in an eternal traffic jam' (2016: 1). This oxymoronic absent-presence or present-absence of the state in Lebanon is as pervasive as it is perplexing. There is a state in Lebanon, there are ministries for public transport, there is a minister of rail even though the trains have not run since the outbreak of the civil war in 1975.

While there is plenty of discourse about the absent state in Lebanon and how it manifests in a discursive sense of the unstated and unsaid, particularly in terms of recognizing the events of the civil war officially, it overlooks the heavily securitized power that it holds and how quickly it becomes visible at moments of civic tension and rebellion (Hassan, 2008). It also overlooks the transversal connections between the neoliberal elite who employ private security and surveillance. Indeed, the rebuilt central business district built and maintained by the private company Solidere employs its own security service, the 'hawks' that sit at street corners. The link between this employment and precarious casual labour is brilliantly and humorously depicted by Ahmad Ghossein in his short film *White Noise*, where a hapless security guard undertakes his first night duty under the 'ring', the bridge formed by the overpass at the site of the old green line which marked the demarcation line, and is driven to both exhaustion and insanity by the myriad strange events that take place. It is striking that this film is one of the very few to actually take in footage of the central district, the management is extraordinarily cautious in letting cameras in. The axis of precarious worker and neoliberal wealth is rendered clear.

There is no understating the exhilaration that Beirut is capable of engendering. Judith Naeff is grateful for the 'existential unsettlement and liberating frenzy' of Beirut in her investigation into its perpetually 'suspended now' (2018: viii). Rayess Bek's track 'Schizophrénia' from his album *L'Homme de gauche* (2010) depicts the split life of someone divided between Beirut and the Parisian *banlieue* and it is the psychological affect of return that I want to consider in an attempt to understand the dynamics at work in the city. Ghassan Hage, one of the most perspicacious of Beirut's chroniclers, examines the 'urban jouissance' he ascribes to multiple urban discourses that speak of the buzz or quiet pleasure that 'is woven into the texture of everyday life' (2018: 88). This is indissociable with both chaos and uncertainty provoked in subjecthood and extant as an objective reality, the party life and pursuit of pleasure in spite of the daily difficulties that life in Beirut poses. Hage's urban jouissance celebrates the sort of astonishment one feels that things happen at all in spite of situations which would otherwise foreclose them, in comparison to places, in his case Australia, where efficient systems falter when anything slightly anomalous happens. Hage illustrates his point with the way drivers, especially recently returned expats, diligently, indeed performatively, respect the traffic signals that Beirutis habitually ignore. But this joy and exhilaration found in those for whom Beirut is a 'parenthèse' has a counterpart in those who, far from being unmoored, feel contained, trapped by virtue of passport or lack thereof and unable to leave at will when life proves too difficult. Paternal descendants of former *fonctionnaires* of the colonial administration inherited French citizenship, leading to a large number of dual citizens in the Christian communities of Lebanon, creating a hierarchy of those who can leave, from dual nationals through Lebanese-only citizens to Palestinian refugees whose statutory limbo has been in place since 1948. While the exceptional status of Palestinian refugees is not to be confused with placing them in a separate moral or indeed policy domain, they remain involuntarily displaced people, durable modes of resolving their condition, such as return, integration or resettlement elsewhere, are uniquely unavailable. The refugee camps and, as we see below, other areas of Beirut such as Dahiyeh in the south are examples of Fregonese's concept of hybrid sovereignty (2012) where the standard national government's jurisdiction either does not apply—Ramadan describes the refugee camps as sites of sovereign abandonment (2013: 72)—or is superseded by particular political actors such as Hezbollah. These different subjectivities make for very different experiences of Beirut. Nevertheless, the city is composed of an urban fabric which includes integrated yet divergent zones, enclaves but also different forms of dislocation, both spatial and temporal, which together provoke an affective invigoration of the chaos in which everyone seems complicit.

Monumental Surveillance

Surveillance plays an important role in the temporal-spatial dimensions of the city too. There are unwritten rules which delineate forbidden spaces as well as the overt and outright prohibition of entering others, even if access sometimes seems arbitrarily conceded depending on the informal assessment of the soldier guarding. The area near the Capuchin cathedral is strictly guarded due to its proximity to the Grand Serail and similarly the synagogue in Wadi Abu Jamil has restricted access due to the residence of former prime minister Saad Hariri being located there. Not simply is access monitored, sound recording and photography are strictly enforced but not necessarily by state actors such as the police or Lebanese army: the private security hawks employed by Solidere or by owners of private capital real estate development routinely forbid photography.

There is a correlation between civil war ruins that work as accidental monuments, navigation points, and their role in surveillance both in the psychic imaginary of city inhabitants and in their continued role as military sites, notably the Holiday Inn and the Bourj el Murr. The significance of the memory of these buildings was highlighted in the response to interventions by Jad el Khoury, who uses the soubriquet Potato Nose. His decoration of bullet holes and explosion impacts on the Holiday Inn was roundly condemned in 2015, not least since the intervention was presented as a subversive act of street art, but it was later discovered that the artist had received permission from the Lebanese Ministry of Defence (Stoughton, 2015). In response to public protest the paintings were whitewashed. In 2018 el Khoury installed brightly coloured balcony shades made of laminated cotton that are found on domestic buildings in Beirut in the open window spaces of the Bourj el Murr. In contrast to the Holiday Inn, this intervention was felt to be a positive contribution to the accidental memorial, the pretty blinds fluttered as the wind flowed through the tower, giving it life and colour, as though the building was breathing. This time it was the building's owner, Solidere, who insisted on the early removal of the installation in 2019. This is a vignette which epitomizes the conflicting desires of urban memory, intervention and the private, neoliberal demands of a corporation. Rana Eid's beautiful cinematic essay on sound, *Panoptic*, explores surveillance and memory with particular focus on the Bourj el Murr, the unfinished tower block which seems to survey the city, policing and warning as an encoded memorial to the civil war. A photo essay by Nasri Sayegh plays on the translingual frames of the word *murr*

(مُرّ)—it means 'bitter' in Arabic and its translation into French gives *amère* in the feminine, from which we find both *mère* and *mer* in *Mes nuits sont plus amères que vos jours* (2018). Sayegh juxtaposes images of the building with the sea (*mer*), and plays on the homophony of *mère* as mother, in his photo-book.

Travelling across a city is a quotidian affair. Regular routes are created between home and work. So, while Murr looks out over the city as a symbolic panopticon, digital surveillance is much more informative. Harvesting geolocation data transmitted by mobile phones proves just how simple it is to trace the everyday itineraries of someone by following these regular trajectories, and how easy it is to notice when the regular pattern varied, to suspect nefarious activity was afoot, an extra-marital affair, membership of clubs; the betrayal of secrets, of double lives. While this is in effect a sped-up version of the 'filoche' of the routine detective work of old, citizens are giving up this information freely and largely unaware that such identifying data is available for analysis by private or government organizations. Security in Beirut, according to a 2012 article by Mona Fawaz et al., is built upon 'constructed threats' which restrict mobility and free circulation in urban space, blocking the right to the city. No-parking zones, detours, blocked streets, no-photo zones, all with varying degrees of authority behind them, inhibit urban citizens in their daily interactions with the city. In a trajectory which follows the neoliberal façadism of Beirut's central district in its reconstruction, urban scholars document an extreme and increasing presence of securitizing material. A militarized presence is common in the city, in the form of armed soldiers, tanks, barbed wire and high walls. However, city subjects use their own informal measures to calculate heightened security on particular days according to the news cycle, or in particular zones according to the number of security personnel and vehicles, surmising that a politician or other VIP is present. Seasoned Beirut residents have an enhanced security literacy. While incidences of habitual city crime such as muggings and thefts are low, the abduction, assault and murder of British Embassy worker Rebecca Dykes in 2017 alerted citizens to the dangers faced by women in the city. It is clear that the 'architecture of security is an integral element of the city that works to entrench socio-spatial divisions and shapes the daily experiences of dwellers along gender, class, race, and religious/sectarian social hierarchies' (Fawaz et al., 2012: 187). One of the most striking early images of the 17 October 2019 uprising was a protestor who had climbed up the high pole staring down the security camera placed upon Riad el Sohl Square. The circulation of this image demonstrates how central places, and in particular the frequently empty ones, of Beirut become strategic sites of protest: Gezi Park in Istanbul, Tahrir Square in Cairo, République in Paris, not to mention Sahat Al Nour in Lebanon's Tripoli, tied together in a global, transnational imaginary of protest.

Joana Hadjithomas and Khalil Joreige's 2009 feature, *Je veux voir*, which centres on a road trip taken by Rabih Mrouré and Catherine Deneuve, opens with the iconic French star leaving the Phoenicia Hotel in a place where photography is policed by the hotel security not simply because of potential infringements of privacy but because the establishment does not wish to be associated with images of the ruined Holiday Inn which stands behind it. In a later scene demonstrating the thwarting of the gaze, the camera filming Catherine Deneuve is repeatedly knocked out of the hand of the operator. Yet how cinema permits that which it is normally forbidden is a persistent theme of the film, as they take Deneuve south to the border with Israel encountering roads and zones that are typically off-limits. As an essay in what cinema makes possible, Hadjithomas and Joreige are engaging with a rich theme in Lebanese cinematic practice, and the legitimized filming of an otherwise prohibited scene recalls Schlöndorff's filming of *Die Falschung* on the front line during the civil war, where the fighting stopped to let the cameras in.

Ziad Douieri's film *West Beyrouth* deliberately titled in a combination of English and French, begins with the outbreak of the civil war, depicting the assassination of bus passengers on 13 April 1975. The coming of age film depicts cross-sectarian friendship between two teenage boys, Tarek and Omar, and an orphaned Christian girl called May. Tarek obsessively films in Super 8 with occasional *mise-en-abîme* moments such as the filming of the bus attack featuring throughout. As the city is divided and schools are closed, the young adults find great adventure in crossing the front line, including encountering a notorious brothel run by the formidable Umm Walid in the central Beirut red-light district subsequently destroyed in the post-war reconstruction. Etel Adnan, reviewing the film, notes how it made her see 'the good things we lost, things that survived the war, but not the "after war"' (1998: n. pag.). Rafic Hariri commands respect from Adnan but she describes a lost innocence as the ravages of neoliberalism seem so caustic and so unforgiving in their ramifications, to a degree that was worse than the civil war. The nebulous end of the conflict, famously encoded as 'no victor no vanquished', led to 'disenchantment with the war and, mainly, with the fact of having lost the war, the feeling of a great defeat felt by every group who participated in that war (nobody felt victorious in that mess), made people apathetic to anything daring and creative. The only activity therefore which kept any interest is the endeavour of making money' (1998: n. pag.). Such madness of unrestrained and unregulated real estate projects out of the financial grasp of the middle classes—as property investment for the global elite whose urban footprint, in spite of their conspicuous absence, is significant. While Adnan credits Hariri for reinvigorating the state, especially in areas such as telecommunications and electricity, she identifies problems where the government meets local culture, and predicts the revolution to come:

> Being still weary about war, [the Beiruti] will not revolt in a foreseeable future, but nobody knows what could happen if the frustration keeps growing and if the city itself, materially speaking, becomes a stifling forest of cement, with no places for public recreation and no alleviation of the tremendous traffic jams that by themselves are changing social intercourse by making a simple visit to a friend an insoluble nightmare. (1998: n. pag.)

Commentators frequently acknowledge that the post-war destruction of central Beirut was worse than the damage done in 15 years of civil conflict. Joana Hadjithomas and Khalil Joreige's early film *Autour de la Maison rose* (1999) depicts the way capital bought up real estate without care for the refugees and inhabitants of a *palais* the contractors intend to redevelop into a shopping mall. Displacement is not simply the relocation of residents elsewhere for the reconstruction to take place, it has also shifted city industries and whole communities of residents and their networks. In the next section, we consider how to recover the city.

Reclaiming the City

In response to both widespread political corruption and unregulated building and demolition in Beirut, grassroots activists have united behind environmental causes to improve the day-to-day life of urban citizens. This includes campaigns to access green spaces in Beirut, notably Horsch Beirut, or making additions to the urban furniture of the street. Mona El Hallak has focused on Ras Beirut and the area around the American University of Beirut campus, as well as on her significant role in the project at Beit Beirut in Sodeco Square. Creating alternative maps of the city that focus on networks of literature or bookshops, the maps highlight alternative places, creating virtual malls where people visit rather than consume, spending time and not spending money. The role of these socially conscious action groups, within which I include Beirut Madinati, who have growing political traction in the city, mark a shift in emphasis from clientelism to citizenship. While Khalaf (2012: 50) felt this was playing around the edges when major structural reform of power and sovereignty is required, he observed that protests for secular rights—Laïque Pride or the founding of the Green Party of Lebanon back in 2004 with the slogan 'the earth knows no religion'—gave some a sense of hope. His pessimism was that the escapist refuge into realms of 'gaudy dreams and sleazy consumerism' would act as further symptoms of denial of any consequences seen in the ecological and environmental impact of this *je-m'en-foutisme*, and in another nod to navigation, the 'hazardous motorways—let alone the conventional etiquettes and proprieties of public driving!' (2012: 241). Khalaf here engages with a development trope that Kristen Monroe associates with driving, specifically the 'chaos' of driving (2016: 100). She studied a driving school in Beirut where lessons, *théorie* and *pratique* are undertaken in French using educational videos from the former metropole. Informing the students of the *décalage* they would experience between what they learned *en théorie* and their learning *en pratique*, Monroe observed that 'France was positioned as a kind of role model and served a teleological function' (2016: 100), where driving habits were 'modern' and 'civilised'.

The ramifications of traversing the city and how it is done and thinking about how modes of transport interact with the everyday are indissociable from the construction of the civic sense of the city, and how such failures have inspired grassroots (with greater and lesser degrees of success) to try and set up their own solutions to gaining cheap and easy transit across the cityspace of Beirut. While thinking about bus or rail transport might seem mundane or edging into the murky world of the enthusiast, their axiomatic potential to provide coherence to a city, to give its citizens the right to access it, are extremely important, not least on the most simplistic level because it identifies function and provision, the presence of a state or municipality dispensing with taxpayers' money and investing in services for them.

It is a long-established cliché for a lazy journalist to report conversations with taxi drivers as keen insight, but as anthropological informants concerning the everyday, their input is invaluable and in Beirut the shared carpool *service* provides an additional opportunity to talk to other passengers, too. As Monroe notes, these vehicles are places of intergroup interaction and a 'kind of everyday civic forum' (2016: 105). All of which attests to the fact that 'getting around Beirut [is] about more than merely getting somewhere; it was about how people encountered the very formation of their civic culture in a city wounded by war and, once again, on the razor's edge' (2016: 7). Anyone who has walked the streets of Beirut will be familiar with the sharp double klaxon of the *service* taxi driver who crawls the curb to pick up passengers heading in the same direction. There is a very real intersection of capital and flow through the capital in the planning of routes around fuel consumption exacerbated by issues of the Lebanese currency being pegged to the US dollar. Petrol is sold by cartels in US dollars, but prices are fixed for individual consumers in Lebanese lira, leading to lively black-market currency exchanges. Drivers make perpetual calculations involving fuel consumption, distance and potential congestion in a situation where their income is low and their living costs high. There is also a criminal black market in fake red plates, the identifying number plates issued by the transport ministry for taxis. The *service* operate largely along main routes and there is often a lot of confusion about certain districts when looking for specific locations. This can be due to sectarian affiliation where East Beirut-based drivers are unfamiliar with the West, but also down to an absence of the street furniture which allows one to navigate independently: street names, building numbers, and road signs are far from consistently present in the city. On his return to an unnamed Beirut, Amin Maalouf's adrift protagonist, Adam, in the judiciously entitled novel *Les Désorientés* (2012), reflects on the difficulty of finding his way 'dans cette ville aux rues sans plaques, sans numéros, sans trottoirs, où les quartiers portaient des noms d'immeubles, et les immeubles les noms de leurs propriétaires' (2012: 28). Beirut has therefore very subjective and diverse cartographies, be they political, affective or economic; indeed, semantic route maps bring poetic and transport links together, axiomatic links between places, lives and everydays.

The principal mapping company of Beirut is Zawarib, which translates as 'ginnel' or 'alleyway'. It produces as street atlas like a London A–Z, largely developed for expats and visitors. As a cartographic project it is extremely precise, but it also features titbits of information in the margins. Zawarib also has an underlying mission to improve public transport including a transit map of Beirut's putative bus network, minibuses and vans which charge 1,000 LL a journey. It maps predominantly a Beirut of pleasures and leisures for a Western gaze. This is most clear on the Zawarib website (www.zawarib.org) and mobile app, where searches can be made by keywords—including rubrics such as

Trans-Mediterranean *Beyroutes*

'vibrant', 'western', 'sexy' or 'louche' covering the main city sites of socializing: Hamra, Ras Beirut, Gemayzé, Mar Mikhael and Badaro.

Amsterdam-based collective Archis, a 75-year-old organization, coordinated a fascinating guide to the city entitled *Beyroutes* in association with Studio Beirut, published in January 2010. It resulted from various initiatives including an Archis RSVP 'tactical intervention', a project which is an extension of their *Volume* magazine, edition #22, which centred on 'The Guide' as its topic:

> Beyroutes presents an exploded view of a city which lives so many double lives and figures in so many truths, myths and historical falsifications. Visiting the city with this intimate book as your guide makes you feel disoriented, appreciative, judgmental and perhaps eventually reconciliatory. Beyroutes is the field manual for 21st century urban explorer. (Beyroutes, 2010: n. pag.)

Beyroutes features essays by urban scholars and artists. There is a humorous cut-out pocket guide to visiting Dahiyeh, by Zinab Chahine, describing the southern suburbs controlled by Hezbollah and typically off the Western tourist's agenda (2010: insert between 82–83, n. pag.). This is counterposed by a chapter by Mona Harb, 'Story of a Name', on the political history and development of the same area (2010: 57–61). Photo-texts exhort the visitor to examine the details of buildings, the overlooked modernist architecture, to admire the beautiful ironwork (Gardner and Hulshof, 2010: 84–89). Other essays look at street names, notably those which end in '-ian' signifying a name from Armenia in Bourj Hamoud (Harès, 2010: 82). In several ways, *Beyroutes* chimes with Khalaf's observation that the city has transitioned from battleground to playground. It exposes the duality of Beirut and its Janus-like population. A place of privileged creation, resourceful and resilient pluralism *and* a fractious and precarious polity bent on self-destruction but, as he points out, rarely are these two opposites understood as operating as lived dialectical realities for Beiruti citizens (Khalaf, 2012: 257). During the civil war, Beirut and Lebanon had became metonymic shorthand for destruction, random assassination, danger and, post-war, for the 'catchy and sensational clichés' of licentious playground, permissive, uncensored pleasures for tourists and visitors. By drawing down on these two extremes, Khalaf proposes instead the metaphor of Beirut as playground 'more relevant for the liminal, protean and liquid state of being adrift'. A playground inspires adjectives such as 'open, gregarious, accommodation' place of experimentation and invention but also at the mercy of the vicissitudes of excess. This 'neutral' metaphor neither adulates not abnegates—permitting analysis of both the shadows and the everyday, beyond a heuristic tool, the playground metaphor offers cathartic and redemptive features—rules of the game, the civility and commitment of homo ludens (Khalaf, 2012: 257). The playground also invokes, in a very Kleinian sense, the ability to contain, a place where excessive impulses are retained. Khalaf states 'some of the enabling features of a playground—that is, those of fair plays, teamwork, equal recognition and the sheer exuberance of doing one's thing without encroaching on the rights and spaces of others—can all become vectors for the restoration of civility' (2012: 258).

Trans-Mediterranean gazes, inward and outward, interact with determinations on the ground; in a perpetual exchange between outside observations, the juxtapositions of the diaspora, those who come back and those who leave. Beirut's dualities link to the hybrid identities and the tilt towards one side of it or the other. Ghassan Hage terms this the 'primal injury of migration', which in Lebanese society seems deeply repressed, resurfacing only in the scenes of 'tears at the airport' (Hage 2019), suggesting a whole new set of ties, relations and moorings, connections between staying and leaving, dislocation and relocation. The Beirut band Ziad and the Wings sing about wanting to escape the city to the 'ocean' in their track of the same name, but being thwarted by the traffic and a circular railway. It reminded me of the loss of the Mar Mikhael railway bridge which crossed the rue d'Arménie until a lorry carrying a shipping container drove into and destroyed it. This metaphoric clash of transit types, one long since abandoned and the articulated lorry carrying goods that travelled into the city by sea in some failure of infrastructural coexistence left adrift, unmoored, all at sea.

In his preface to Khalaf's essay, Ghassan Hage notes the semi-subversive yet pervasive incidence of smoking in Lebanon—he notices not simply cigarettes, which are extremely cheap, but, to his surprise, the widespread use of *narguilé* or shisha across classes and generations in a way he had not observed before the civil war. Riffing on Khalaf's theme of being adrift, Hage suggests that smoking like this is a form of 'escapism and a kind of narcissistic folding oneself onto oneself to seek a sense of immunity from the traumatising environment' (2012: 8). His psychoanalytical interpretation identifies this as regressive and infantile, marking a desire to step away and withdraw from the social with the waterpipe presenting both womb-like sound in the watery gurgles, the suckling-at-the-teat action of smoking, the umbilical cord of the pipe and the 'soft buzz' of the aromatic tobacco all overtly symbolic. For me, it demonstrates the soporific effects of mooring, where a *narguilé* functions as a sort of umbilical cord tethering the orally fixated to their primary object relation. And it does no harm to stretch the analogy and consider the psychoanalytic frame of the postcolonial relation in Lebanon particularly in its extant links to former mandatory power, the ramifications of which I discussed above in relation to the circulation of global capital. It also raises an important question about the mooring ties that stop Beirut, and Lebanon, from floating into the mid-Mediterranean, the bridges to other urban centres, the *passerelles* that permit passage from vessel to shore.

Bibliography

Adnan, Etel. 1998. Letter from Beirut: Lebanon loses what war did not destroy. *Al-Jadid* 4(24). https://aljadid.com/content/letter-beirut-lebanon-loses-what-war-did-not-destroy.

———. 2010 [1977]. *Sitt Marie-Rose*. Beirut: Tamyras.

Barazy, Ma'an. 2012. *Lebanon finance 2.0: A tribute to Governor Riad Salameh*. Beirut: Data and Investment Consult Lebanon.

Bardawil, Fadi. 2020. *Revolution and disenchantment: Arab Marxism and the binds of emancipation*. Durham, NC: Duke University Press.

Baumann, Hannes. 2016. *Citizen Hariri: Lebanon's neoliberal reconstruction*. London: Hurst and Company.

Chahine, Zinab. 2010. How to survive in Dahiya. In *Beyroutes*, n.p. [insert between 82–83]. Amsterdam: Archis.

Fawaz, Mona, Mona Harb and Ahmad Gharbieh. 2012. Living Beirut's security zones: An investigation of the modalities and practice of urban security. *City and Society* 24(2): 173–95.

Élection présidentielle—Retrouvez les résultats du premier tour pour les Français de l'étranger. *France-Diplomatie*, 2017. https://www.diplomatie.gouv.fr/fr/services-aux-francais/voter-a-l-etranger/resultats-des-elections/article/election-presidentielle-resultats-du-premier-tour-pour-les-francais-de-l.

Fregonese, Sara. 2009. The urbicide of Beirut? Geopolitics and the built environment in the Lebanese civil war (1975–1976). *Political Geography* 28: 209–318.

———. 2012. Beyond the 'weak state': hybrid sovereignties in Beirut. *Environment and Planning D: Society and Space* 30: 655–74.

Gardner, Edwin and Janneke Hulshof. 2010. Creative modernism: come closer, love is in the details. In *Beyroutes*, 84–89. Amsterdam: Archis.

Gates, Carolyn. 1998. *The merchant republic of Lebanon: Rise of an open economy*. Oxford: Centre for Lebanese Studies.

Hage, Ghassan. 2012. Preface. In Samir Khalaf, *Lebanon adrift: From battleground to playground*, 7–11. London: Saqi.

———. 2018. Inside and outside the law: Negotiated being and urban *jouissance* in the streets of Beirut. *Social Analysis* 62(3): 88–108.

———. 2020. On belonging to a country that cannot keep its children. *Public Source*, 18 February. https://thepublicsource.org/belonging-to-a-country-that-cannot-keep-its-children.

Harb, Mona. 2010. Story of a name. In *Beyroutes*, 57–61. Amsterdam: Archis.

Harès, Pascale. 2010. …ian. In *Beyroutes*, 82. Amsterdam: Archis.

Harvey, David. 2012. *Rebel cities: From the right to the city to the urban revolution*. London: Verso.

Hassan, Salah. 2008. UnStated: Narrating war in Lebanon. *PMLA* 123(5): 1621–29.

Hourani, Najib. 2015. Capitalists in conflict: The Lebanese civil war reconsidered. *Middle East Critique* 24(2): 137–60.

Husseini, Randa. 1997. Promoting women entrepreneurs in Lebanon: The experience of UNIFEM. *Gender and Development* 5(1): 49–53.

Israel Ministry of Foreign Affairs. 1975. 58 Reply in the Knesset by Defence Minister Peres on Syria's role in Lebanon, 6 January. https://mfa.gov.il/mfa/foreignpolicy/mfadocuments/yearbook2/pages/58%20reply%20in%20the%20knesset%20by%20defence%20minister%20peres.aspx.

Journal officiel de la République francaise. 1976. Assemblée nationale—1er séance du 6 May.

Kassab, Maroun Ghassan. 2015. Beirut modernism: Theoretical framework and case study. PhD thesis, University of Sydney.

Khalaf, Samir. 2012. *Lebanon adrift: From battleground to playground*. London: Saqi.

Maalouf, Amin. 2012. *Les Désorientés*. Paris: Grasset.

Monroe, Kristen. 2016. *The insecure city: Space, power and mobility in Beirut*. New Brunswick: Rutgers University Press.

Naeff, Judith. 2018. *Precarious imaginaries of Beirut: A city's suspended now*. Basingstoke: Palgrave Macmillan.

Ramadan, Adam. 2013. Spatialising the refugee camp. *Transactions* 38: 65–77.

Sakr-Tierney, Julia. 2017. Real estate, banking and war: The construction and reconstructions of Beirut. *Cities* 69: 73–78.

Stoughton, India. 2015. The scars of war on Lebanon's Holiday Inn. *Al Jazeera*, 30 December. https://www.aljazeera.com/news/2015/12/scars-war-lebanon-holiday-inn-151219082356997.html.

Studio Beirut. 2010. *Beyroutes: A guide to Beirut*. Amsterdam: Archis.

Music

Koudaih, Wael and Rayess Bek Orchestra. 2010. Schizophrénia. *L'Homme de gauche/Khartech Aa Zamann*. CHICHprod.

Zeid and the Wings. 2011. Ocean. *Asfeh*. 22D Music.

Filmography

Autour de la Maison rose. 1999. Dirs. Joana Hadjithomas and Khalil Joreige. Canada/France/Lebanon: CCT, Canal (II), Canal Horizons et al.

Bosta, l'autobus. 2005. Dir. Philippe Aractingi. Lebanon: Fantascope Production.

Je veux voir. 2008. Dirs. Joana Hadjithomas and Khalil Joreige. France/Lebanon: Abbout Productions.

West Beyrouth. Dir. Ziad Doueiri. France/Norway/Lebanon/Belgium: 3B Productions, ACCI, Centre National du Cinéma et de l'Image Animée et al.

White Noise. 2017. Dirs. Ahmad Ghossein and Lucie La Chimia Said. Lebanon/France: Lebanon Factory.

11

Multilingual Pilgrimages
Language and Trans-Mediterranean Cultural Identity in Ismaël Ferroukhi's *Le Grand Voyage*

Gemma King

Introduction

In a cultural climate attuned to the complexities of migration, integration and intercultural conflict, a number of contemporary French films foreground multilingualism as a central feature and theme. In a range of twenty-first-century films, such as Philippe Lioret's *Welcome* (2009), Jacques Audiard's *De battre mon cœur s'est arrêté* (2005) and Ladj Ly's *Les Misérables* (2019), complex and empowering representations of North African and other migrant languages have begun to appear on the French screen. It is true that dialogue in languages other than French has been included in a select number of films across the history of French cinema, from Julien Duvivier's *Allô Berlin? Ici Paris* in 1932 to Jean-Luc Godard's *Le Mépris* in 1963 and beyond. However, not only is multilingualism vastly more present in contemporary French titles, but there has also been a marked increase in the number of films which represent the use of multiple languages as a means to (re)negotiate intercultural power relationships. Exploiting their knowledge of a wide range of languages, from rival *lingua francas* such as English to traditionally marginalized languages in the European context such as Arabic, multilingual characters offer a counter-perspective to dominating ideologies of the role and status of the French language.

A key example of this phenomenon can be found in Ismaël Ferroukhi's Arabic, Bulgarian, English, French, Italian, Serbo-Croatian and Turkish-language film, *Le Grand Voyage* (2004). The film follows a young Franco-Maghrebi man, Reda, as he drives his father across Europe and into the Middle East, to fulfil the latter's lifelong dream of making the *hajj*; the Islamic pilgrimage to Mecca. In contrast to cinematic movements of the 1980s and 1990s that explored Franco-Maghrebi identities within the framing of the metropolitan French *banlieue*, *Le Grand Voyage* displaces its second-generation *beur* protagonist from the urban French periphery to the international road. Through the narrative framing of a dysfunctional road trip, the film places at its centre trans-Mediterranean flows of culture and power, and the negotiation of Franco-Arab identities and languages. Despite taking place mostly beyond the confines of the Hexagon, Ferroukhi's film reconsiders what it means to be Moroccan in modern France, to inhabit such a diverse space as the Mediterranean and to have power—and speak a power language—in the contemporary world.

In the context of a political system struggling to come to terms with the reality of the contemporary refugee crisis, the European continent is frequently conceived of as a sealed, hostile space. In such a space, the mobility of non-Europeans is systematically policed and curtailed. Despite the somewhat paradoxical mission of the European Union, which facilitates border crossing between nation states within its territory, the contemporary European continent is presented as politically and physically closed. As many European nations move to close their borders to migrants and refugees from beyond the continent, political and cultural discourse is coming to be dominated by the concept of 'Fortress Europe', a notion which Dominic Thomas sees as striking 'at the very heart of contemporary discussions pertaining to migration and belonging' (2014: 447). Mobility is open to those moving between European nation states, but closed to those seeking to enter them from beyond its borders.

Yet, as Carrie Tarr (2007) has argued, borders can be porous, and despite the powerful metaphors of dominant political discourse, the walls of Fortress Europe can indeed be transgressed. In *Le Grand Voyage*, the politics of movement play out in ways that reject the configuration of the fortress. Instead, the film represents flows of cultural capital that operate not only in Eurocentric terms, but in polycentric (that is, dispersed and multipolar) ones. Ferroukhi's characters may traverse their Mediterranean world via linear road travel, yet this world is one which calls to mind Deleuze and Guattari's philosophy of the rhizome, which offers a frame for understanding 'connections between semiotic chains, organizations of power, and circumstances relative to the arts, sciences, and social struggles' in a non-binary, non-hierarchical way (1981: 7). In this world, characters do not simply seek to move from the periphery to the centre, nor do they only travel from the global South to Western Europe. Thus, the concept of Fortress Europe does not hold up to scrutiny in Ferroukhi's film. Instead, the film's titular voyage, comprising both the father's migration from Morocco to France (which occurs long before the film's events but is referenced in the narrative) and the father and son's pilgrimage from France to Mecca, can be better understood not through metaphors of Europe but in terms of a broader Mediterranean sphere. *Le Grand Voyage* does not simply portray a linear margin–centre passage, but a multi-decade, pan-continental journey comprising North Africa, Western and Eastern Europe and the Middle East. This journey decentres Europe from the privileged position of sole vantage point or intended destination. Instead, the characters travel in a trans-Mediterranean semicircle that undermines the validity of dominant discourses surrounding the unilateral concept of Fortress Europe. This opens up the way for discussion of a more polycentric understanding of a diverse and multilingual space.

Le Grand Voyage

Described by Mireille Rosello as a 'babelized road movie' (2011: 258), *Le Grand Voyage* depicts a transcultural, translingual and transcontinental pilgrimage. The film begins in a working-class suburb of Lyon, where a young French-born man, Reda, lives with his Moroccan-born parents. When Reda's ageing father decides to make the *hajj* pilgrimage while his health still permits it, he pulls his son out of school and demands he drive him thousands of kilometres to Mecca in their small, dilapidated car. As father and son travel through France, Germany, the Baltic States and Turkey towards the Muslim spiritual capital, their generational, linguistic and cultural differences are laid bare. The narrative is punctuated by clashes in the pair's world views and moral codes. Their journey, which physically comprises a circuit from Lyon to Mecca yet also symbolically incorporates the father's earlier migration from Morocco, traces a curve around the Mediterranean rim, and explores the complexity of the multiple identities, languages and power centres that characterize the region. Upon arriving in Mecca, and before undergoing a tragic event, Reda and his father are eventually able to attain a level of mutual understanding and to bridge the seemingly insurmountable gap that divides them. This negotiation takes place on Saudi Arabian soil, yet reveals much about transcultural experiences in France, and undermines traditional understandings of Franco-African relationships.

Upon its release in 2004, *Le Grand Voyage* received only a modest commercial response in France, but enjoyed a positive critical reception. The film received an '83% fresh' rating on Rotten Tomatoes, was nominated for a BAFTA prize and won the 'Luigi de Laurentiis' Best First Film Award at the 2004 International Venice Film Festival. However, despite these successes, *Le Grand Voyage* was an extremely challenging project for Ferroukhi and his team to realize. The production was fraught with challenges: six years of preparation were required to gain sufficient funding, and filming was thwarted by curfews in Serbia and visa difficulties in Saudi Arabia. Shooting was particularly complex for the scenes set in Mecca. Indeed, after much negotiation, Ferroukhi became the first film-maker in history to gain permission to film within the city during the *hajj* (Jaggi, 2005). The result is a pared-back yet emotive film, with an understated style and a semi-autobiographical narrative (Ferroukhi's father also made the *hajj* from France by car). At the heart of the film is the role of language. Indeed, linguistic difference and cultural contact not only dominate the film's plot, but define its central relationship, which Ferroukhi has described as being about 'break[ing] down barriers' (qtd. in Jaggi, 2005: n. pag.). In *Le Grand Voyage*, characters speak different languages, yet language difference is represented not as a barrier or a hindrance, but an opportunity for creative and meaningful exchange.

Throughout its septilingual dialogue, *Le Grand Voyage* uses linguistic diversity as a barometer for depicting shifting cultural capital. Unlike many earlier films, which often gloss over the reality of linguistic, religious and social differences between first-generation immigrants to France and their more integrated children, *Le Grand Voyage* delves into these differences, in an attempt to understand the trans-Mediterranean francophone migrant experience. Furthermore, language is consistently used by the film's characters to shape and navigate intergenerational and intercultural relationships. As Jaggi writes, 'it becomes a film about language and communication across gulfs of faith, culture and generation, between migrant and second-generation *beurs*, orthodox and non-believer' (2005: n. pag.). In these ways, language becomes both a point of contention and a means of bridging the space between disparate figures.

Language is primarily representative of generational difference in *Le Grand Voyage*; the father cannot speak French well, while his son cannot speak Arabic, understanding only some Moroccan dialect. However, from the beginning of the film, while Reda shows no active interest in learning his parents' tongue, he is content to converse with them (he in French, they in Arabic) and does not criticize, mock or discourage them from their native language use, as the vast majority of second-generation children in twentieth-century French films tend to do. In this portrait of convivial intergenerational communication across languages, the preference for one language by one generation and another by the other does not necessarily prohibit functional communication. As Rosello explains, 'Reda and his dad have a relationship to language that tolerates, if not welcomes, different levels of competence and different uses of different languages. His dad speaks one language and understands his son in another' (2011: 267). Thus, while the film's narrative tension frequently hinges on linguistic difference, communication is enriched, rather than limited, by multiple language use.

The film's multilingual dialogue also tells us much about cultural capital and social power in the many environments through which the protagonists pass. As they travel through Europe, Reda's multilingual repertoire carries great value, as he negotiates for his father in French and English. (The father can in fact speak some French, but is generally unwilling to do so, and unable to convey complex information.) In Western and Central Europe, these two dominant Western *lingua francas* suffice for Reda to handle accommodation and automotive issues, various purchases and complex passport problems. On several occasions, the father's unwillingness or inability to communicate in French is represented as a hindrance. This dynamic reflects Claire Kramsch's claim that 'monolingualism is a handicap' (2007: 102). In almost all cases of multilingual French film, ignorance of French is directly disadvantaging, and fluency in French provides access to resources and the potential for gaining and wielding social power. In the same way, *Le Grand Voyage* posits knowledge of the French language as relevant and valuable on contemporary European soil. In addition, it follows in the footsteps of a long line of French films, from Mehdi Charef's *Le Thé au harem d'Archimède* (1985) to Rabah Ameur-Zaïmeche's *Wesh-wesh, qu'est-ce qui se passe?* (2001), which depict the children of first-generation migrants as more linguistically adept, more open to learning and using the French language and subsequently better positioned to integrate into the reality of public life in France than their parents.

However, this normative picture of language politics is not the only framework within which multilingualism is explored in *Le Grand Voyage*. For as they near their ultimate destination, the value of Reda's and his father's respective linguistic abilities begins to shift. In these spaces, it is the father who communicates with officials, negotiates money, food and shelter arrangements, donates aid to the needy and befriends locals and fellow pilgrims. Significantly, he must also interpret for his son, from the standard Arabic spoken among pilgrims to the Moroccan dialect Reda partly understands (but does not speak). By the time they arrive in Mecca, Reda is at a loss to communicate with others, while his father interacts freely with those around him. In this new context, Reda's competency in French and English has no currency: Arabic is the reigning language. Consequently, mainstream spoken Arabic comes to occupy the place of a *lingua franca*, directly replacing the role Reda's native French and learned English had formerly played. Indeed, in this environment Reda becomes linguistically dependent on his father for the first time ever, in an inversion of the status quo of their metropolitan French life. The relationship between Moroccan father and French son is subsequently transformed, and Reda comes to view his father's history and identity in more complex and empathetic ways (Gott and Schilt, 2013: 7).

In numerous scenes, knowledge of more than one language is not only useful, but essential. Yet the film does not merely valorize knowledge of Western languages, but knowledge of a range of *lingua francas* including Arabic, in concert with more localized languages, such as Moroccan dialect. As I have explored in previous publications, the Arabic language has historically occupied a marginalized and devalued position in French cinema (King, 2015). However, in *Le Grand Voyage* Arabic is portrayed as equally worthy of the status of 'world language' typically enjoyed by languages such as English and French. Unsurprisingly, French and English are important languages in the film. Yet their importance is far from universal; they are not the *only* valuable linguistic resources available to the characters, nor are they *unconditionally* valuable throughout the journey. Rather, value is attributed to a diverse network of both official and improvised linguistic codes, a value system dependent on location and cultural context. Indeed, even the imprecise and unofficial practice of mime operates as a useful bridging code in one key scene, in which Reda's father negotiates with an unofficial Serbian money changer. Using the word 'change' as a linguistic tag, combined with the gestures of pointing, shaking heads, counting on fingers, smiling and shaking hands, the father manages to obtain a better exchange rate than Reda, who initially attempts to speak to the man in English:

> Money changer: *The man greets Reda's father in unsubtitled Serbo-Croatian, before realizing his client does not speak his language.* [English] Change?

Father: [English] Change? [French] Euros.
The two men hold up their hands and count rates on their fingers in silence. Reda steps in.
Reda: [French] Wait, wait, wait. [English] Excuse me, do you speak English?
The currency exchanger ignores him; his father pushes him aside. The two men continue to barter through mime, until they nod to agree on a rate.
Money changer: [English] Change.
They exchange the money, shake hands and depart.
(dialogue 00:29:40–00:30:56)

For Rosello, this improvised form of transcultural contact is symptomatic of this Mediterranean region's 'fragmented and often chaotic mosaic of linguistic encounters [composed] of micro-encounters between individuals for whom languages are both a challenge and an opportunity to invent new modes of communication' (2012: 215). Such scenes demonstrate the possibility of communication despite linguistic misunderstanding: in such cases, mime and body language are more effective than official *lingua francas*, and become functional replacements for verbal contact.

In this scene, just as dealing with an unofficial currency exchanger leads the father to obtain a superior exchange rate to that offered by the nearby *bureau de change*, so too do unofficial communication tactics yield better results than Reda's attempt at interacting in English. The result is a progressive view of language relations, in which not only dominant languages, but peripheral and even improvised communicative forms, possess the potential to advance the situation of their users. *Le Grand Voyage* thus explores the complex linguistic economy that shifts around the Mediterranean rim, as its characters forge new trans-Mediterranean relationships and connections that resist Eurocentric discourse. The film imagines the Mediterranean as a polycentric space where the European, African and Asian continents converge, portraying a West–East movement that avoids mapping a binary South–North voyage. Of course, it is important not to ignore that the father's knowledge of Arabic grows in value in proportion to the distance he gains from metropolitan France. Yet the film foregrounds the potential of even the most historically disenfranchised languages to empower their speakers, and explores the complexity of the Franco-Maghrebi experience of immigration, integration and cultural identity in non-hierarchical ways.

Movement and Trans-Mediterranean Identities

Despite its amateur tone and semi-improvised dialogue, *Le Grand Voyage*'s plot is tightly structured in its depiction of an ambitious border-crossing journey. Yet, despite the plot's physical focus on the move from Western Europe to the Middle East, the film is more concerned on a thematic level not with the connection between Lyon and Mecca, but with that between Morocco and France. As Reda reluctantly escorts his father on his journey, he gradually gains a more profound perspective on his father's experience of migrating from North Africa to France, and the sacrifices, cultural clashes, linguistic challenges and identity shifts which form the backdrop to his own life in France. The characters' pilgrimage charts a direct course to Mecca. Yet, in doing so, the film prompts Reda and the viewer to ponder a deeper understanding of the cultural, linguistic and identitary flows along a very different Mediterranean course: that between Western Europe and the Maghreb.

In the vast majority of French films which deal with international migration, the relationship between metropolitan France and the migrant's country of origin is mapped as that between centre and periphery. In films as diverse as Yamina Benguigui's *Inch'Allah dimanche* (2001), Michael Haneke's *Code inconnu: récits incomplets de divers voyages* (2001) and Costa-Gavras's *Eden à l'ouest* (2008), among countless others, non French-born characters aim for upward economic mobility by travelling to France. These films are also characterized by movement, yet this movement is almost always linear and binary: from the country of origin (generally in North Africa) towards the Hexagon. Most frequently, characters head to the country's metropolitan centres; usually Paris (*Eden à l'ouest*, *Code inconnu*) and occasionally Marseille or Lyon (*Inch'Allah dimanche*). Such perpetual periphery-centre mapping has a powerful impact on the representation of culture, power and movement in these films.

Upon arriving in France, characters in such films usually experience a combination of social isolation, cultural or religious discrimination, economic disadvantage and geographical marginalization. Film-makers frequently return to the motif of the *banlieue* as both the geographic and symbolic margin of French society, and migrant characters' othering is frequently explored through their cinematographic framing in this exilic environment. Those more naive characters who arrive in France with romantic ideals, such as in Abdellatif Kechiche's *La Faute à Voltaire* (2001), tend to undergo a profound disillusionment with

Language and Trans-Mediterranean Cultural Identity

Figure 11.1. Journey map and film still.

their host country. Yet, while the reality of migrant life in metropolitan France is rarely represented in a favourable light, and while characters may dream of returning to their homeland (the most privileged even doing so, if only temporarily, in films such as Tony Gatlif's *Exils* (2004)), the Hexagon is mapped as an inherently privileged space. Such films are critical of the postcolonial contemporary universe, and interrogate the myriad challenges that first-generation migrants, and their French-born children, experience in attempting to integrate into French society. Yet, while these films depict the migrant experience in a range of complex ways, they nonetheless map a traditional configuration which posits France (and usually Paris) as geographic and existential centre. Other Mediterranean spaces, from North Africa (*Inch'Allah dimanche*, *La Faute à Voltaire*) to Eastern Europe (*Code inconnu*) and the Middle East (*Eden à l'ouest*), are represented as less desirable locations, spaces from which characters depart, rather than where they arrive.

By contrast, *Le Grand Voyage* focuses on the act of moving *away* from France. The young Reda will inevitably return to France, but it is his journey away from his country of birth with which the film is concerned. He is also highly unlikely to return via the same route or mode of transportation, rendering the road trip a one-way voyage. Paris also has no role to play in the story, and the cinematography employed to represent Lyon is neither stark nor oppressive. The film does not problematize, or even depict, the French *banlieue* (while Reda's family are far from wealthy, they live in a comfortable suburban house). France is not shown to be the object of the characters' efforts. This opens the film up to a rhizomatic mapping of the Mediterranean region and allows for a more complex understanding of transnational relations and movements. As Will Higbee explains, such 'postcolonial discourses in film are concerned with challenging fixed, Eurocentric assumptions around cultural identity and the nation' (2007b: 51).

For Reda and his family, France has become (or has always been) home, a place to which they aim to return. But the film itself casts its gaze to the Middle East. In her analysis of *Le Grand Voyage*, Carrie Tarr sees this as an important 'move further towards the deconstruction and dismantling of a Eurocentric vision of the world [...] which not only acknowledges the voices and gazes of those previously confined to the periphery, but also enables cultures (or ethnicities) to be seen "in relation"' (2009: 291). Reda's father risks (and ultimately loses) his life in a quest to reach a particular place. But, unlike *Eden à l'ouest*'s Elias or *La Faute à Voltaire*'s Jallel, that place is not France. This reconfiguration updates French cinema's representation of the standard migrant character's trajectory, and evokes Patricia Caillé's work on transnational, polycentric cinemas, which 'enable us to interrogate relationships of power and domination in a digital and post-industrial age, at a time when the accrued circulation of cultural commodities and people (either forced or voluntary) affects the terms of the polarity between nation and migration' (2013: 242).

This updated trajectory cannot be properly understood without examining the place of religion in the film. Where many contemporary French films neglect the religious dimension of Franco-Maghrebi migrant life in France, choosing to focus more closely on issues of sociocultural isolation or institutional discrimination, Ferroukhi uses Islam to link such disparate locations perched around the Mediterranean Sea as Morocco, France, Turkey and Saudi Arabia. It is true that films such as *Inch'Allah dimanche* and Karin Albou's *La Petite Jérusalem* (2005) include characters with a strong connection to religion (Islam and Judaism, respectively), and who engage in prayer and other religious practices. Yet these practices are mostly undertaken within the home. *Le Grand Voyage* is not only one of the first films to depict inhabitants of France embarking on the *hajj*, but also one of the first to depict characters undertaking Islamic practices in the public sphere, without incurring discrimination from mainstream French or other Western characters. The result is an unusually optimistic picture of religion in France, Europe and the broader Mediterranean space. It should be noted that the father is automatically disapproving of Reda's relationship with his French girlfriend. Yet, despite this clash of social views, *Le Grand Voyage* not only films a sympathetic Muslim character's experience, but presents Islam—much like language—as possessing the potential to unify characters of disparate histories and origins. This is set in contrast to films such as *La Petite Jérusalem*, where religious difference serves primarily to carve rifts between non-religious, Christian, Jewish and Muslim populations of the same Parisian *banlieue*.

Reda is the chief protagonist in *Le Grand Voyage*, and the film's only character to be named. For the most part, we experience the film's events through his eyes, and are posited to empathize most with the young man. Reda is certainly portrayed as a more sympathetic, complex and well-rounded character than his strict father. Yet in the evocation of a series of pan-Mediterranean movements, both in the current Lyon–Mecca pilgrimage and the past Morocco–France migration, the father's story emerges as an equally important element of the film, speaking to the complexity of the contemporary Mediterranean condition. His life of migration and movement touches on a range of important questions relevant to contemporary Europe and its neighbours. These range from trans-European border crossing (crucial to debates in the context of the current refugee crisis), to economic migration from the former French colonies in North Africa to metropolitan France, to the relationship between Europe and the Middle East, to debates surrounding religion versus secularism in France. *Le Grand Voyage* may present Reda as its protagonist, and the character best-adapted to life in contemporary France, but his father embodies a wider range of contemporary trans-Mediterranean experiences.

Conclusion: Polycentrism and the Mediterranean

Clustered around a common body of water, but home to a disparate range of national, cultural, religious and economic power centres, the Mediterranean is the ideal motif for understanding the polycentric flows of people, capital and ideas in the contemporary world. The region is home to complex configurations hinging on concepts of emigration/immigration, East/West, North/South, Islam/*laïcité*, first-generation migrants/second-generation children, migration/pilgrimage and centre/periphery. In this setting, *Le Grand Voyage* presents a dispersed picture of contemporary cultural relations, portrayed not only through multiple language use but through the experiences of characters with plural, trans-Mediterranean identities. The film sees transnational movement and cross-cultural identity as interconnected, and irons out the tensions in its central relationship through a series of multilingual exchanges. Primarily funded by and produced in France, Ismaël Ferroukhi's debut feature certainly understands the history of (post)colonial linguistic hierarchies, and represents the French language as essential knowledge on French soil. French and English are also shown to be useful bridging languages in the broader Western world. However, multilingualism permeates the film on many levels, and the film's portrayal of language is not necessarily detrimental to its main Moroccan-born character. Instead, the father's language use challenges Eurocentric notions of linguistic power, and portrays alternative *lingua francas* such as Arabic as equally useful and empowering, albeit in very different geographical and cultural contexts. For Ferroukhi, all languages are potentially important, as are all spaces.

Against the backdrop of escalated political tensions in the region, *Le Grand Voyage* conceives of the Mediterranean, from Morocco to France to Central Europe and the Middle East, as a non-linear space transcendent of simplistic postcolonial configurations. As an expanse of land clustered around an eponymous sea, the region is simultaneously centre and void, both unified and unanchored by the body of water at its heart. The Mediterranean and its disparate inhabitants, to borrow Will Higbee's words, thus offer 'a way of thinking about knowledge, culture and power relations that rejects the idea of an epistemology structured around notions of hierarchy or fixed centre or binary structure' (2007a: 86–87). The film's characters lead lives deeply informed by the (post)colonial relationship between the French North and the Maghrebi South. Yet they are also engaged in complex flows of culture and capital that lead them on a pan-continental journey around the Mediterranean and encompass a range of economic and cultural power centres. From Lyon to Mecca to Marrakech, *Le Grand Voyage* sees the Mediterranean as characterized by a plurality of voices and spaces in which traditional metaphors of centre versus periphery are no longer sufficient to understand the globalized, shifting, contemporary world.

Bibliography

Caillé, Patricia. 2013. 'Cinemas of the Maghreb': Reflections on the transnational and polycentric dimensions of regional cinema. *Studies in French Cinema* 13(3): 241–56.

Deleuze, Gilles and Félix Guattari. 1981. *A thousand plateaux: Capitalism and schizophrenia*. Minneapolis: University of Minnesota Press.

Gott, Michael and Thibaut Schilt. 2013. Introduction. In M. Gott and T. Schilt, eds., *Open roads, closed borders: The contemporary French-language road movie*, 1–18. Bristol: Intellect.

Higbee, Will. 2007a. Beyond the (trans)national: Towards a cinema of transvergence in postcolonial and diasporic francophone cinema(s). *Studies in French Cinema* 7(2): 79–91.

———. 2007b. Locating the postcolonial in transnational cinema: The place of Algerian émigré directors in contemporary French film. *Modern and Contemporary France* 15(1): 51–64.

Jaggi, Maya. 2005. The long and winding road. *Guardian*, 7 October. http://www.theguardian.com/film/2005/oct/07/1.

King, Gemma. 2015. Code-switching as power strategy: Multilingualism and the role of Arabic in Maïwenn's Polisse. *The Australian Journal of French Studies* 52(2): 162–73.

Kramsch, Claire. 2007. The traffic in meaning. *Asia Pacific Journal of Education* 26(1): 99–104.

Rosello, Mireille. 2011. Ismaël Ferroukhi's Babelized road movie. *Thamyris/Intersecting: Place, Sex and Race* 23: 257–76.

———. 2012. Plurilingual Europeans in a multilingual Europe: Incomplete and imperfect communication tactics. *European Studies* 29: 215–33.

Tarr, Carrie. 2007. The porosity of the hexagon: Border crossings in contemporary French cinema. *Studies in European Cinema* 4(1): 7–21.

———. 2009. Franco-Arab dialogues in/between French, Maghrebi-French and Maghrebi cinema, *Contemporary French and Francophone Studies* 13(3): 291–302.
Thomas, Dominic. 2014. Fortress Europe: Identity, race and surveillance. *International Journal of Francophone Studies* 17(3–4): 445–68.

Filmography

Allô Berlin? Ici Paris [Here's Berlin]. 1932. Dir. Julien Duvivier. France/Germany: Société des Films Sonores Tobis.
Code inconnu: récits incomplets de divers voyages [Code Unknown: Incomplete Tales of Various Journeys]. 2001. Dir. Michael Haneke. Austria/Germany/France: MK2, Alain Sarde.
De battre mon cœur s'est arrêté [The Beat My Heart Skipped]. 2005. Dir. Jacques Audiard. France: Why Not Productions.
Eden à l'ouest [Eden Is West]. 2008. Dir. Costa-Gavras. France/Italy/Greece: KG Productions, Novo RPI, Medusa et al.
Exils [Exiles]. 2004. Dir. Tony Gatlif. France: Princes Films, Pyramides Productions, Cofimage et al.
Inch'Allah dimanche [Sunday God Willing]. 2001. Dir. Yamina Benguigui. France/Algeria: Bandits Longs, ARP Sélection, Canal+ et al.
La Faute à Voltaire [Blame it on Voltaire]. 2001. Dir. Abdellatif Kechiche. France: Flach.
La Petite Jérusalem [Little Jerusalem]. 2005. Dir. Karin Albou. France: Gloria Films, Film Par Film, Canal+ et al.
Le Grand Voyage [The Great Journey]. 2004. Dir. Ismaël Ferroukhi. France/Morocco/Bulgaria/Turkey: Ognon Pictures, Arte France Cinéma, Soread-2M et al.
Le Mépris [Contempt]. 1963. Dir. Jean-Luc Godard. France/Italy: Rome Paris Films, Les Films Concordia, Compagnia Cinematografica Champion et al.
Le Thé au harem d'Archimède [Tea in the Harem of Archimedes]. 1985. Dir. Mehdi Charef. France: Centre National du Cinéma et de l'Image Animée, K.G., M&R Film et al.
Les Misérables. 2019. Dir. Ladj Ly. France: Srab Films.
Welcome. 2009. Dir. Philippe Lioret. France: Nord-Ouest Films, Studio 37, France 3 Cinéma et al.
Wesh-wesh, qu'est-ce qui se passe? [Wesh Wesh]. 2001. Dir. Rabah Ameur-Zaïmeche. France: Sarrazink Productions.

12

Bare Life at Sea
Mediterranean Bodies, Istanbul Limbo

Megan C. MacDonald

> What would a non-corporal punishment be?
>
> Michel Foucault, *Discipline and Punish*, 16

Stowaway

The International Maritime Organization (IMO) defines a stowaway following the Convention on Facilitation of International Maritime Traffic, 1965 (FAL Convention):

> A person who is secreted on a ship, or in cargo which is subsequently loaded on the ship, without the consent of the shipowner or the Master or any other responsible person and who is detected on board the ship after it has departed from a port, or in the cargo while unloading it in the port of arrival, and is reported as a stowaway by the master to the appropriate authorities.[1]

A more extensive version of this chapter is forthcoming in my monograph *Monsters without borders: Literary precarity and the postcolonial navette* (Liverpool University Press). Earlier versions were presented at the 'Mediterranean Cemetery' panel (ACLA 2018), organized by Edwige Tamalet Talbayev and Hakim Abderrezak and as part of the NOW research group 'Towards a political ontology of violence: reality, image and perception' (Leiden 2018), organized by Herman W. Siemens and Frank Chouraqui.

1 For more, see the IMO webpage on stowaways: http://www.imo.org/en/OurWork/Facilitation/Stowaways/Pages/Default.aspx.

In late August 2017, I made the crossing by boat from Istanbul's Haydarpaşa port to Chornomorsk, Ukraine, just west of Odessa, on the passenger ship *Kaunas Seaways*. The ship is Danish-owned, flying under a Lithuanian flag, operated by a Ukrainian ferry company, and is mainly used for transporting cargo across the Black Sea. The passengers included Turkish, Ukrainian and Russian truck drivers, Ukrainian families on holiday in Turkey with their cars and a few tourists without vehicles. On this particular crossing my fellow traveller and I noticed, shortly after boarding, a group of young men hanging out of windows on one part of the ship as if in their own cargo hold. They were yelling, had an anxious energy and speaking what sounded like North African Arabic.

A few weeks later, Reuters published an article on these men titled, 'No country for migrant stowaways caught on ferry between Ukraine and Turkey' (Thomsen, 2017a). According to the article. the 12 migrants, six thought to be Moroccan, four Algerians and two 'unknown', had been 'sailing to and fro [...] between Istanbul and Odessa for the last seven weeks locked in four cabins, with no country willing to take them' (Thomsen, 2017a: n. pag.). The men continued to cross the Black Sea, according to Bosphorus ship watcher Yörük Işık. Işık calls the maritime traffic along the Bosphorus 'a mirror for world events [...] We witness whatever is happening, right here, [...] Crises in Ukraine, or if the United States just wants to show the flag in the Black Sea' (Lord, 2017: n. pag.).

I am mobilizing Foucault's distinction between insides and outsides, exclusion and inclusion, to consider the case of a group of twenty-first-century stowaways, bodies in a period of perpetual transit, on a passenger ferry on the Black Sea, travelling between Istanbul, Turkey and Chornomorsk, Ukraine. Reading this story alongside Foucault connects this specific instance of bare life at sea to histories of incarceration, the intersection of sovereignty and bodily containment, French colonial penal colonies (*les bagnes*), postcolonial states of emergency in the Mediterranean and beyond, and, finally, archives and their traces (wakes).

This story of a failed crossing is not a metaphor. These men—without papers—are literally at sea, in between countries, and represent new migration patterns: Mediterranean crossings on the Black Sea. These northern crossings embody the Mediterranean but transplant it to a famously dead sea—one without oxygen or life beyond a few metres deep, one that preserves shipwrecks at its deepest bottom— and carry bare life which travels South to North and back again, without arrival or redress. As a conclusion to this collection on trans-Mediterranean *francosphères*, this final chapter displaces the Mediterranean, moving it to the Black Sea, bringing Istanbul into the frame of postcolonial French histories, failed crossings and stasis at sea. Morocco, Algeria, France, Turkey and Ukraine form a trans-Mediterranean constellation.

Database/Archive

The 'general legal framework' for people at sea is a combination of international maritime law, international refugee law, international human rights law 'and the emerging regime for combating transnational crime' (UNHCR, 2002: n. pag.). This consists of different agencies on the ground, namely, the UNHCR, the IMO and the International Organization for Migration (IOM). Since the boat was operated by Ukraine, under a Lithuanian flag, owned by Denmark and travelling between Ukraine and Turkey, all countries were involved in the stowaway situation.[2] And no one wanted to deal with them. The story was covered by two Danish reporters, one who wrote the Reuters article and the other who did a feature on a Danish TV news channel (Schrøder, 2017). The CEO of the Danish shipping company, DFDS, made a statement on the situation in late August, and was willing to pay for the stowaways' transportation if a country accepted them: 'But seeing as these people have no documentation with them, they have wound up in no man's land' (Grønvald Raun, 2017: n. pag.).

It is unclear if and how the men on the Black Sea ferry were smuggled or trafficked. What is clear, under international and maritime law, is that they qualified as stowaways, which requires being reported as such. There exists an archive with the traces of these stowaways via the IMO database, the Global Integrated Shipping Information System (GISIS), which (following the FAL Convention) invites governments, ships, ports and others to provide data on stowaway incidents, as well as report any measures taken. I read this database as a 'Stowaway

---

2 *Kaunas* is also the name of Lithuania's second largest city. A Red Cross refugee centre opened there in summer 2017, which has also been the site of anti-refugee protests by far-right groups. Lithuania accepted about a thousand refugees as part of an EU agreement, mostly Syrian (Refugee and Migrant Integration Center, 2017). The flag state of the boat is important, since the vessel is considered a 'floating extension' of the state. The UNHCR notes that this can be a problem with flags of convenience, as the stowaways in question will likely have no relationship to the flag state country, and often these countries would not be safe for refugees or asylum seekers (UNHCR, 2002).

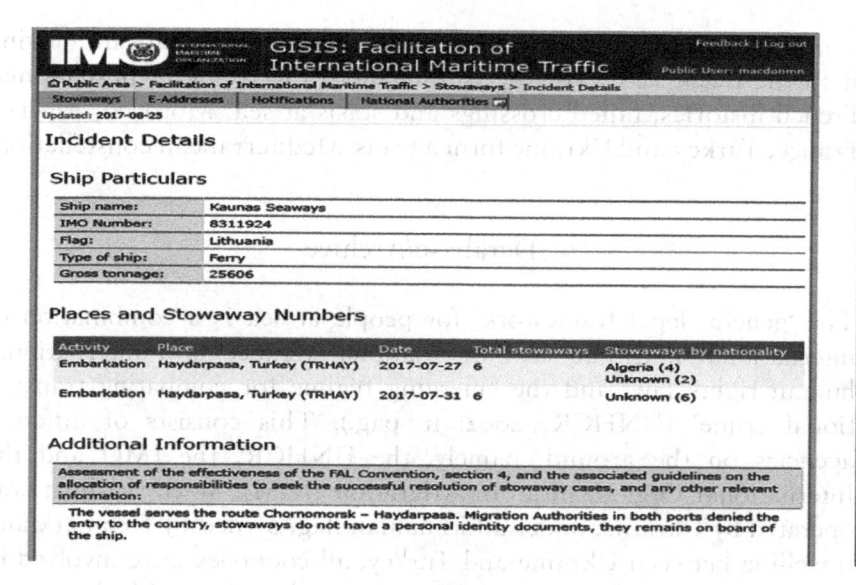

Figure 12.1. Incident report regarding the stowaways on the *Kaunas Seaways*, as reported to the GISIS/IMO.

Archive' (see Figure 12.1) that offers traces. Users can both submit data and 'conduct stowaway inquiries easily'.[3] The image above is the Stowaway Archive file for the *Kaunas Seaways* stowaways. The traces of these men live on in the database, but without names.

The fact that no country wanted to house these bodies approaches Roberto Esposito's notion of 'immunitary logic' and the *pharmakon* via containment, whereby 'Evil must be thwarted, but not by keeping it at a distance from one's borders; rather, it is included inside them. The dialectical figure that thus emerges is that of exclusionary inclusion or exclusion by inclusion' (2015; 8). This is important for archival movement. If, as Thomas Nail claims, 'the migrant is the political figure of our time' (2015: 235), what kind of figure is this, and what can it tell us about this particular time? The UNHCR 'Background Note on the Protection of Asylum-Seekers and Refugees Rescued at Sea' (2002) begins with the following truism, which bears repeating: 'The phenomenon of people taking to the seas in search of safety, refuge, or simply better economic conditions is not new'. Thomas Nail echoes this sentiment in *The Figure of the Migrant* and begins the book with the

---

3   Other companies and organizations then make use of this data, see: https://www.intercargo.org/stowaway-incidents-ports-2010-2017/.

claim (echoing Edward Said's *Reflections on Exile* (1984)) that: 'The twenty-first century will be the century of the migrant' (2015:1).

Esposito's poison/cure metaphor and the body politic come together not only in the floating container within a ship at sea. The very presence of these unwanted migrants, and their containment, is a display of the contained body, and 'blocking' the free movement of those very same bodies. The circulation of the *pharmakon* on a closed sea is also the containment of potential germ warfare (plague/leprosy), under lock and key, by guards carrying machine guns and wearing camouflaged uniforms. Esposito's *pharmakon* is a 'non-substance, a non-identity', something 'that relates to life from the ground of its reverse': death and life are held together, precarious, mobile (2015: 16). The men are misplaced (on the Black Sea rather than the typical Mediterranean passage), out of place (they got on the wrong boat) and a potential poison kept inside the body of the ship, where the ship is the symbol and concentration of a multinational body politic (flag state, owner, operator). Esposito asks: 'Can life be preserved in some other form than that of its negative protection?' (2015: 16) But preservation, according to Esposito (following Walter Benjamin), is 'not painless' (2015: 33). In this sense, the stowaways *must* be kept alive, whether or not this is what they desire.

The UNHCR's 'Note on Stowaway Asylum-Seekers' (1988) describes a situation where no involved state wants to take responsibility as a 'so-called orbit situation'. The texture of this terminology is particularly suitable to a ferry crossing a sea multiple times, and forms a visual constellation of states involved—from the southern Mediterranean to countries bordering the Black Sea, and beyond. The 'International Convention Relating to Stowaways' was created in 1957, but never implemented, since it was only ratified by nine of the ten required signatories. Denmark is a signatory and normally acts in accordance with it. The Convention requires those in charge of the ship to 'deliver the stowaway to the appropriate authority at the first port in a Contracting State at which the ship calls after the stowaway is found' (UNHCR, 1988: 348). Countries also have a duty not to leave stowaways in an unsafe country. This concern is currently relevant in Turkey. While the 2014 Turkish Law on Foreigners and International Protection ensured rights for refugees and asylum seekers after and during the Syrian refugee crisis, the law was amended in 2016 by Presidential Decree during a State of Emergency, allowing 'immediate removal' of those suspected of terrorism, or those 'deemed to pose a threat to public order, public safety or public health' (Zoeteweij-Turhan, 2018:

n. pag.). The UNHCR and the UN Refugee Agency estimate that there are 3.4 million refugees in Turkey; Turkey thinks this number is more likely 3.9 million (Zoeteweij-Turhan, 2018: n. pag.).

Camp/*Quadrillé*: The Rhetoric of Infection

Bare Life at Sea is a containment story, and the public health concerns spelled out in Turkish law connect to disease rhetoric intersecting with fear of refugees and migrants. Robert Esposito connects this to surveillance through isolation:

> The first step is to isolate places where infectious germs may develop more easily due to the storage of bodies, whether dead or alive: ports, prisons, factories, hospitals, cemeteries. But the entire territory is gradually divided intro strictly separate zones based on the need for both medical and social surveillance. (2015: 139)

Foucault uses the term 'quadrillé' to theorize the plague town under surveillance. The diseased kept from (but still with) the healthy. If leprosy in the seventeenth century demanded expulsion from the community, Foucault reads the plague which follows it, and its quarantine practices in the eighteenth century, as 'a model of political control, and [...] one of the great inventions of the eighteenth century' (2004: 48). In the specific case of these stowaways, the distinction between the expulsion characterizing leprosy and the surveillance and control that come with the plague *collapse* inside four ship cabins on the boat crossing the Black Sea. Leprosy and the plague, or, bare life at sea. I am concerned with the following questions with regard to these particular stowaways, and what I am calling bare life at sea: Is this a narrative which leaves no trace? Can an archive survive a shipwreck? Is there an archive without one? And, finally, what is the time of the stowaway?

If we turn to Agamben, 'bare life' (*homo sacer*) is that life which 'exists on a threshold that belongs neither to the world of the living nor to the world of the dead: he is a living dead man, or a living man who is actually a larva' (1998: 99). Bare life at sea is bare life made mobile, summoning the current Mediterranean 'refugee crisis', which became more visible after the so-called Arab Spring (2011), followed by intense exoduses from Syria, but which also predates it. Migration narratives cannot be thought without EU governmentality, sovereignty and the camp, refugee or otherwise. Agamben calls the camp the 'nomos' of the modern; a certain visibility of camps (dependent on the lens of an anxious 24-hour news cycle) connects northern and southern Mediterranean shores, and camps found on islands in between, but which signal Europe (such as Lampedusa) (1998: 166). For Agamben, the camp is 'the paradigm itself of political space', where 'politics becomes bio-politics and the *homo sacer* becomes indistinguishable from the citizen' (2000: 41). Camps, plural, 'were not born out of ordinary law' nor were they the result of 'a transformation and a development of prison law; rather, they were born out of the state of exception and martial law' (Agamben, 2000: 38). Michel Agier argues that due to the sheer number and kinds of camps existing today, they are becoming 'l'une des composantes majeures de la "société mondiale"' (Agier ad Lecadet, 2014: 11).

North African refugees and irregular migrants from Tunisia, Algeria and Morocco use different migration routes which often correspond to their geographical location of departure: Moroccans and some Algerians often cross the Strait of Gibraltar headed for Spain and/ or France; Algerians further east and Tunisians often aim for Italy. These patterns predate the Arab Spring and continue long after its initial unfolding, with the inclusion of sub-Saharan African refugees and others from South Asia, heading to Libya, Algeria and Morocco as intermediary points on the route to Europe.

What 'form of life' takes place at sea? (Agier ad Lecadet, 2014: 11) How is it represented? For Agamben, the nation state is no longer an adequate space, as 'growing sections of humankind are no longer representable inside the nation state'. The refugee, 'an apparently marginal figure, unhinges the old trinity of state-nation-territory, it deserves instead to be regarded as the central figure of our political history' (Agier ad Lecadet, 2014: 20–21). This quantitative increase in unrepresentable 'sections of humankind' allows Agamben to connect contemporary refugees to camp genealogies: 'We should not forget that the first camps were built in Europe as spaces for controlling refugees, and that the succession of internment camps–concentration camps–extermination camps represents a perfectly real filiation' (Agier ad Lecadet, 2014: 20–21). Zygmunt Bauman also identifies 'novelty' in contemporary refugee crises, calling refugees 'stateless in a new sense: their statelessness is raised to an entirely new level by the non-existence of a state authority to which their statehood could be referred' (2003: 76). He turns to Michel Agier, who terms refugees *hors du nomos*—outside the law—'cast in a condition of "liminal drift"', particularly apt language for stowaways at sea (qtd. in Bauman,

2003: 76). If the camp is a *nomos* of the modern, and refugees are *hors du nomos*, then stowaways on a mobile ship are in a camp within a camp, whose jurisdiction is unclear. Akbar Ahmed contends, in response to the current European migrant crisis and its intersections with far-right discourses:

> There are millions of Muslims, and they're not going anywhere. The only alternative—if their logic is correct—is to deport them all, or put them all into concentration camps, or to just throw them into the sea. And if they're not going to do that, then they are stuck with them, and they have to deal with them. It's as simple as that. (The Europeans podcast)

In terms of Bauman's recognition of the absence of a state authority, the case of North African migrants is a specific case and takes account of this in its own way. In North African Arabic (*darija*), migrants who leave the coast in boats are called *harraga*, meaning those who 'burn'. They do this in two ways, burning their way across the sea itself, and burning or burying identification papers, so that if and when they are apprehended by authorities, they cannot be readily identified.[4] Bauman's reflections on 'liminal drift' are doubly poignant for bare life at sea: 'Even if they [refugees] are stationary for a time, they are on a journey that is never completed since its destination (arrival or return) remains forever unclear, while a place they could call "final" remains forever inaccessible' (2003: 76). To Bauman's absence of a 'state authority', Achille Mbembe offers the 'ultimate expression of sovereignty': 'the power and the capacity to dictate who may live and who must die. Hence, to kill or allow to live constitutes the limits of sovereignty, its fundamental attributes' (2003: 11–12).

Staying alive and mobility are bound up with contagion in the European imagination, what Roberto Esposito calls 'contagious drift', again particularly appropriate for sea crossings, where I argue that the leper meets the plague (2015: 2). Esposito argues: 'What frightens us today is not contamination per se—which has been viewed as inevitable for some time now—as much as its uncontrolled and unstoppable diffusion throughout all the productive nerve centers of our lives' (2015: 2–3). In addition to a 'threat to public order', immigration is presented 'as a potential biological risk to the host country, according to a model that pathologizes the foreigner, the roots of which lie in

---

4 Hakim Abderrezak has written the definitive book on *harraga*s and their representation in literature, cinema and music. See Abderrezak (2016).

the European imaginary of the last century' (Esposito, 2015: 4).[5] Homi Bhabha points to a more recent shift, in a post 9/11 context, in 'which cultural differences, and the anxiety associated with alterity, is now displaced onto the stranger as a threat to life itself' (Schulze-Engler, Malreddy and Karugia, 2018). The fact that the stowaways are North African is overdetermined by social death in a French context. The stowaway is a hybrid figure, brining together Thomas Nail's kinopolitics and combining his figures of the nomad, the barbarian, the vagabond and the proletariat (Nail, 2016). The *francosphère* travels and unravels.

Bare life at sea works in at least two ways: literally people on the water, *at sea*, adrift, and the concept of bare life itself becomes unmoored, leaving one *at sea* as to where it is located. In this instance there is no anchor. Bhabha's 'scale of affect' has real-world and real-life, for lack of a better term, consequences. It can also tell us about the archive. The silent archival document in the stowaway archive is one of violence, at once image and its absence, testimony to clandestinity, and anonymous.

Part of the concern with the stowaways stems from the fear of a new Black Sea migration route, formerly used for smuggling during Soviet times (Hilton and Cupolo, 2017). Between August and September 2017, five boats carrying almost 500 asylum seekers landed in Romania, compared to 430 people in 2014, none in 2016 and 68 in 2015 (on a single boat) (Hilton and Cupolo, 2017). One reason for this increase is thought to be the terrible conditions at Greek island reception centres (known as 'hotspots'). Some refugees are willing to take the dangerous Black Sea route at any cost, declaring: 'We are already dead' (Hilton and Cupolo, 2017: n. pag.). Turkey has responded to the new routes with increased patrols and surveillance. While the stowaways may be a physical reminder of fear of a new route, their profile does not fit those crossing from Greece to Turkey then to Romania across the Black Sea, predominantly 'families and individuals from Iraq, Iran, Afghanistan, and Syria' (Hilton and Cupolo, 2017: n. pag.).

---

5 Neal Ascherson makes similar claims with regard to the ways in which Europeans viewed the nomadic people living around the Black Sea, which I will discuss below.

Extraterritorial Port/The Burning

Stowaways' time is marked via the ephemeral wake of the boat crossing the Black Sea, as well as its time in ports. A port, writes Foucault, 'is a crossroads for dangerous mixtures, a meeting-place for forbidden circulations' (1995: 144). A mobile camp that is a danger for the stowaways, and stowaways seen as a danger by countries connected to ports, 'la forme-camp' has three traits: extraterritoriality, exceptionalism and exclusion (Agier and Lecadet, 2014: 19–20). It is with regard to extraterritoriality that Agier names the camp as an 'hors-lieux', where he argues that as non-places they are set apart, and often not found on any maps (Agier and Lecadet, 2014: 20). The ferry *Kaunas Seaways* is both an *hors-lieux* and found on a map. Its temporality puts it 'on the map' each time it arrives in port, but it is also subject to GPS updated by the minute. Anyone with an internet connection can follow this ship at any given time, via sites such as Marine Traffic.[6] *Hors-lieux* are more than camps, their 'forme' is 'celle des camps bien sûr mais aussi celle des zones de transit portuaires, voire des bateaux ou même des îles' (Agier and Lecadet, 2014: 20). What is specific about this story is that the *hors-lieux* is at once a boat, a zone of/in transit, two ports, a no-place and also a space of extraterritoriality, exception and exclusion: an actual place of *enfermement* under lock and key, and armed guard. The camps highlight as well as hide, in their space/time, the stranger: 'comme déraciné, dépaysé, délocalisé, dénationalisé' (Agier and Lecadet, 2014: 24). The stowaways are constantly rejected by nations, and yet travelled (on purpose) without documentation which would provide identification. They claim two things: that they are Syrian and Palestinian (with the hope of achieving asylum) and that they 'want to go to Europe'. Silence here could be a strategy, but this too is opaque, because who can understand the young men? It was only determined where the young men came from after UN interviewers gave them phones to call home, and traced their calls to Morocco and Algeria.[7]

The floating camp, bare life at sea, is a site of radical difference. The floating other is contained (plague logic) and expelled (leprosy). In this

---

6 The ship in question, *Kaunas Seaways*, can be tracked in real time here: https://www.marinetraffic.com/en/ais/details/ships/shipid:353240/mmsi:277100000/vessel:KAUNAS%20SEAWAYS.

7 These details come from my conversation with Casper Schrøder, who visited the ferry in port in September 2017 and spoke with the captain and crew, but not the stowaways.

very camp they are kept *from* but also *with*. They are subject to radical suspension, but a suspension *while* in motion: two countries and two cities/ports. Agier notes that there are two strategies for protest in a camp: 'habiter' and 'la politique'. Neither is available to the stowaways. They acted out—fighting, flooding, burning, yelling, threatening to jump overboard—but they refused to tell their story. The stowaways were an unknown national quality/quantity until their phone calls home were traced. There was no recognition on the part of the multinational crew.[8] The stowaways wanted to go to Europe, thinking they could get there via Istanbul on a boat headed to Romania. They got on the wrong boat. Reuters followed up on the story on 1 November 2017. Six of the men identified as Algerian were sent home on 29 October; the other six were being sent back to Morocco (Thomsen, 2017b). What would happen to them upon arrival in their 'home' countries? Prison on their home soil?

In 2009, the Algerian government made it illegal to discuss clandestine migration from Algerian shores, as if by stopping the spread of words (gossip spreading like the plague), they could arrest the contagion of fleeing bodies. This became a delicate situation: talk about clandestine migration too much, and the government might have to act on the fact that young people in the country lack employment opportunities. Talk about it too much, and the virus could spread. Narratives themselves become quarantined. More recently, the Algerian government has turned to the religious ministry, asking imams to condemn clandestine migration as a sin, hoping it will appeal to religious sensibilities.[9] The men return by force, with no 'life' awaiting them. What is the *social void* created in the Maghreb? Some young people leave and die *en route*. Others experience a temporary displacement before their return. I am attempting here to write them down, to put them into an archive. To the question of identification, the stowaways preferred to remain without a country attached to them. They are subject to identification *vis-à-vis* refugee law, maritime law and an unofficial law on stowaways, as well

---

8 In an uncanny moment of recognition, when I took the journey from Istanbul to Chornomorsk, there were two individuals travelling on the ship—one with Moroccan roots, the other Algerian—as tourists. Both of these men immediately recognized the stowaways, and the stowaways recognized them as well.

9 Algerian journalist and novelist Kamel Daoud recently addressed this in a *New York Times* op-ed 'Opinion | Can it Be Illegal to Leave Your Country?' Algerians on twitter joked that perhaps the answer to the country's ills was to 'put an imam in every corner' (SΠΔiL, 2018).

as by national differences: an absolute monarchy which claims to be a parliamentary constitutional monarchy (Morocco) and a sclerotic postcolonial police state (Algeria) headed by a formerly revolutionary figure, President Bouteflika, who was then already severely incapacitated.

Moroccan sociologist Abdessamed Dialmy argues that 'in any traditional society where one is only a subject, *hogra* is a structural and structuring element' (qtd. in Abderrezak, 2016: 70). *Hogra* is North African Arabic for 'humiliation', and Hakim Abderrezak argues that a

> linguistic lens also reveals phonetic and/or transliteration proximity between the Arabic words *hrig* or *harga* (burning), *harragas* (clandestine migrants), *hogra* (humiliation), and *Hijra* (the emigration of the Prophet Muhammad and the original sacred Muslim community or *Ummah*), which in turn feeds into a historical, social, and religious legitimization of human migration in Islam-based cultures. (2016: 13)

Until recently, writes Abderrezak, depictions of clandestine migration were also illegal. Now they are everywhere—from cinema, literature and art installations to online videos of young men and women recording their attempts on cell phones (Abderrezak, 2016; Daoud, 2018).

Dead Zone/Black Sea: Where Cemetery Meets Archive

In contrast to media attention on the Mediterranean refugee crisis, almost no one is watching the Black Sea. This further displacement from the regular refugee 'script' adds an additional layer of *hors-lieux* to these stowaways. The Bosphorus, as Europeans discovered in the seventeenth century (but which was already known to locals) has two currents: 'an upper flow' and 'a deeper counterflow, running below it from the Mediterranean into the Black Sea' (Ascherson, 1996: 2). Neal Ascherson argues that this 'discovery' was 'the first step towards the study of the Black Sea for its own sake: not as a ring of shore inhabited by strange people, but as a body of water' (1996: 2). In this way, the Mediterranean and Black seas are connected, the later flowing into the former. Following Horden and Purcell's distinction between *in* and *of* the Mediterranean, I argue that Istanbul is not *in* the Mediterranean, but *of* it. Predrag Matvejević considers Mediterranean archives, noting that 'Nearly every Mediterranean city has at least one such archive, public or private, open or secret, just as each has at least one cemetery. The Mediterranean is a vast archive, an immense grave' (1999: 23). The Mediterranean urban cemetery-archive is one that travels.

The Black Sea stowaways have displaced their migration: they did not follow the regular channels: Morocco–Spain and Algeria–Italy. How did they arrive in Istanbul? Did they travel over land, using old smuggling routes, through Libya? Were they in Syria? What led them to this second, arguably more dangerous, sea? David Abulafia sees the Maghreb as 'a fascinating example of a territory caught between two Mediterraneans' (2005: 76). I would say we might see the Maghreb as caught between *three Mediterraneans*, if we count the Black Sea. Fernand Braudel, in his two-volume Mediterranean opus, wrote of the Black Sea as 'to the east [...] only partly Mediterranean', a 'dangerous sea, which was often rough and shrouded in fog' (1996 [1966]: 109–111). Neal Ascherson calls the deep Black Sea waters 'the largest mass of lifeless water in the world' where 'Talk of centre and periphery, with its implication of the centre's general superiority to the lands on the margins, sounds unconvincing' (1996: 80, 5). Bare life at sea intersects with the Black Sea's 'dead' nature, and constantly rewrites centre and periphery: it's 'unconvincing' but it's also unliveable. The sea itself is hostile to life.

Shipwreck Fiction, Archives and Wakes: Can the Stowaway Speak?

I would like to conclude with a consideration of the stowaways via the archive, its traces and the possibility of living on, if anonymously. Foucault writes of the prison in the second half of the eighteenth century as a reform institution and a place to train the body: 'punishment was seen as a technique for the coercion of individuals; it operated methods of training the body—not signs—by the traces it leaves, in the form of habits, in behavior; and it presupposed the setting up of a specific power for the administration of the penalty' (1995: 131). Are the stowaways locked at sea being punished or trained? Is being kept alive, with the desired mobility denied and a forced mobility at sea (with no real destination), a form of punishment? What traces do these anonymous men leave in the archive, or on the sea? The young men played at being tricksters, denying their voice and stories to authorities, in the hope that anonymity would get them to Europe. They also refused to be identified.

What's in a name? Who gets named, and who refuses? Liisa Malkki argues that when refugees 'are being imagined as a sea of humanity', 'No names, no funny faces, no distinguishing marks, no esoteric details of personal style enter, as a rule, into the frame of pictures of refugees' (1996: 388). Even if certain camps are visible, Michel Agier notes that many are characterized by the very opposite, 'cette invisibilité de la banalité des camps'. One must 'rendre les camps célèbres, tout comme il faut donner un nom à chaque réfugié, déplacé et migrant "illegal" qui s'y trouve confiné' (Agier and Lecadet, 2014: 17). My intention in this chapter is to create an alternative archive, and insist on the anonymity that the stowaways chose. A mark has been left for them, but is there a trace? Who gets written into the archive, and how does this come about?

Finally, this is an alternative to the fictional or literary treatment of gaps in the archives. In the stowaways' story, it is the living who are unnamed, and bare life at sea is a kind of shipwreck within a functioning vessel, where there is no choice but to stay alive. Françoise Lionnet examines colonial archives in Mauritius where names are not found, and reads them against the grain (much like the Forensic Architecture project and the Left to Die boat project). Lionnet turns to Amitav Ghosh's fiction for inspiration, where his literature is informed by his archival work, specifically encountering the presence of an Indian slave written into the Egyptian archives. Ghosh writes on the event:

> The reference comes to us from a moment in time when the only people for whom we can even begin to imagine properly human, individual existences are the literate and the consequential [...] the people who *had the power to inscribe themselves physically upon time*. But the slave [...] was not of that company; in his instance it was a mere accident that those barely discernible traces that ordinary people leave upon the world happen to have been preserved. It is nothing less than a miracle that anything is known about him at all. (qtd. in Lionnet, 2012: 452; emphasis added)

But what about archives in the present? What about those people who appear in contemporary archives, subject to governmentality and between countries, who are not named? Those who remain figures tied to a nation state, even when they themselves did not necessarily provide identity papers? This story is one of a journey, a kind of circumnavigation (with Europe as destination), interrupted, and yet still in movement. Ghosh's literary characters 'begin to develop a new way of being in the floating and fluctuating world of this ship of migrants' (qtd. in Lionnet, 2012: 455). These ways of being are not available to the young men on the Black Sea, and if new ways of being were in fact forged, they are not found in the IMO stowaway archive. Ghosh is writing fiction, pulling back the archive in order to deposit alternative histories after the fact. He writes creole subjects who are 'in no way interested in seeing Europe as either the horizon of thought or the only hope for the future' (qtd. in Lionnet, 2012: 455). For Michel Agier, refugees in camps live a life where 'leur vie est hantée par le retour' (Agier and Lecadet, 2014: 338).[10] With what I am calling 'stowaway time', the migrants are suspended—un- or misidentified, kept from the haunting of the return, or the rotten promise of arrival.

Artists, writers, film-makers and activists practise different strategies to memorialize migrants in transit, and refugees who never make it out of the sea. David Alvarez (2018) notes that in the case of the Strait of Gibraltar, there are no monuments to the dead, and if there were, where would they be placed? Where the bodies wash up? Where they wanted to land? Where they departed from? Films depicting migration from North Africa to France, notes Hakim Abderrezak, used to deploy the ferry boat as a symbol. But the ferry boat, he argues, corresponds to a time where migration from southern Mediterranean ports to northern ports was possible. As France and Spain closed their doors to immigrants coming to settle from North Africa, the ferry was 'demoted', often replaced by the cargo ship whose 'length is an interminable lifeless deck' (Abderrezak, 2016: 167). Abderrezak considers the cargo ship 'a haunted version of the ferry, a signifier of a dead connector between the two shores' (2016: 167). The passenger ferry on the Black Sea combines cargo and passengers—the 'lifeless deck' a result of being locked in cabins. These stowaways, not able to travel legally on a ferry from the southern Mediterranean (Algeria and Morocco) to the north (often Marseille), chose to act outside of the law, taking back the figure of the ferry, and displacing the Mediterranean at the same time. The image of dead ships in contemporary cinema 'reveals that regular migration is not going anywhere anymore. It is certainly not going to France' (Abderrezak, 2016: 168). This old form of transport (connected to a previous form of France's openness to North Africans due to its need for labourers) 'has since exhausted itself or has simply been put to sleep by immigration laws' (Abderrezak, 2016: 172). The ships themselves 'play the role of a rejected Other that cannot proceed further beyond the liminal space of the beach' (Abderrezak, 2016: 168). But this is only the case if we stay in a Mediterranean frame.

10 Agier remarks that both minors and asylum seekers are sometimes sent back by Italian police on the boats they came on, "enfermées dans des cellules *ad hoc* construites sur les ferries" (Agier and Lecadet, 2014: 338).

The trans-Mediterranean movement replaces North Africa–France with different boats, new routes and failed crossings marked only via the language of 'embarkation' and stowaway.

Creating an archive or naming those for whom there is no archive, or who are *deposited* into an archive despite themselves, has what result? Addressing the IMO archive at an angle, I am trying to provide a narrative of migration, but this too is anonymous. Lionnet's coming into contact with the unnamed shipwreck victim in the archive in Mauritius 'was the kind of discovery [...] for which the immediate uses are not clear, except that the urge to do something with it becomes irresistible' (2012: 458). In attempting to write on, or write over, the biopower evidenced in the archive, I am giving it a narrative, but to what use? Is the stowaway archive the institutionalization of bare life at sea?

Cell Life: The Afterlife of Naming

Bare life at sea is being reduced to the cellular level: the cell within a ship (vessel), the body on the ship as a cell in the body politic, the cellular data organized into cells on a spreadsheet. A plague ship for bare life. As Foucault has it: 'Even if the compartments it assigns become purely ideal, the disciplinary space is always, basically, cellular' (1995: 143). The time of the stowaway is archive time: anonymous, rigid, cellular.

Bibliography

Abderrezak, Hakim. 2016. *Ex-centric migrations: Europe and the Maghreb in Mediterranean cinema, literature, and music*. Bloomington: Indiana University Press.

Abulafia, David. 2005. Mediterraneans. In William V. Harris, ed., *Rethinking the Mediterranean*, 64–93. Oxford: Oxford University Press.

Agamben, Giorgio. 1998. *Homo sacer: Sovereign power and bare life*. Translated by Daniel Heller-Roazen. 1st ed. Stanford: Stanford University Press.

———. 2000. *Means without end: Notes on politics*. Minneapolis: University of Minnesota Press.

Agier, Michel and Clara Lecadet. 2014. *Un monde de camps*. Paris: La Découverte.

Alvarez, David. 2018. Maritime necropolis? Aqueous mass grave? Mortuary metaphors for Mediterranean mortalities. In *The Mediterranean cemetery*. https://www.acla.org/program-guide#/search/seminar/17308.

Ascherson, Neal. 1996. *Black Sea*. New York: Hill and Wang.
Barney, Richard A. and Helene Scheck. 2010. Introduction: Early and modern biospheres, politics, and the rhetorics of plague. *Journal for Early Modern Cultural Studies* 10 (2): 1–22.
Bauman, Zygmunt. 2003. *Wasted lives: Modernity and its outcasts*. Cambridge: Polity.
Black Sea M.A.P.—Maritime Archaeology Project. http://blackseamap.com/.
Braudel, Fernand. 1996 [1966]. *The Mediterranean and the Mediterranean world in the age of Philip II, Vol. 1*. Reprint. Berkeley: University of California Press.
Bugeja, Norbert. 2018. Haunting the Mediterranean? Orhan Pamuk's 'The Black Book' and its politics of the afterwardly. In yasser elhariry and Edwige Tamalet Talbayev, eds., *Critically Mediterranean: Temporalities, aesthetics, and deployments of a sea in crisis*, 129–46. New York: Palgrave Macmillan.
Chambers, Iain. 2008. *Mediterranean crossings: The politics of an interrupted modernity*. 1st ed. Durham, NC: Duke University Press Books.
Daoud, Kamel. 2018. Opinion: Can it be illegal to leave your country? *The New York Times*, 9 April. https://www.nytimes.com/2018/04/08/opinion/algeria-harga-emigration.html.
Esposito, Roberto. 2015. *Immunitas: The protection and negation of life*. Cambridge: Polity.
Formalities connected with the arrival, stay and departure of persons. n.d. IMO. https://gisis.imo.org/Public/FAL/Default.aspx.
The Europeans podcast. *June 5: Changing PMs at 103 BPMs*. https://europeanspodcast.com/2018/06/05/june-5-changing-pms-at-103-bpms/.
Foucault, Michel. 1995. *Discipline and punish: The birth of the prison*. Translated by Alan Sheridan. New York: Vintage Books.
———. 2004. *Abnormal: Lectures at the Collège de France, 1974–1975*. Translated by Graham Burchell. Reprint. New York: Picador.
Grønvald Raun, Katrine. 2017. DFDS CEO on migrants: This is a completely unsustainable situation. *ShippingWatch*, 28 August. https://shippingwatch.com/carriers/article9821118.ece.
Hilton, Jodi and Diego Cupolo. 2017. Old route, new dangers: Migrant smugglers revive Black Sea route to Europe. *IRIN News*, 16 October. https://www.irinnews.org/feature/2017/10/16/old-route-new-dangers-migrant-smugglers-revive-black-sea-route-europe.
Horden, Peregrine and Nicholas Purcell. 2000. *The corrupting sea: A study of Mediterranean history*. Oxford and Malden: Wiley-Blackwell.
The Left-to-Die Boat. n.d. *Forensic Architecture*. http://www.forensic-architecture.org/case/left-die-boat/.
Lionnet, Françoise. 2012. Shipwrecks, slavery, and the challenge of global comparison: From fiction to archive in the colonial Indian Ocean. *Comparative Literature* 64(4): 446–61.

Lord, Christopher. 2017. Floats your boat. *Monocle*, May.
Malkki, Liisa H. 1996. Speechless emissaries: Refugees, humanitarianism, and dehistoricization. *Cultural Anthropology* 11(3): 377–404.
MarineTraffic: Global ship tracking intelligence | AIS marine traffic. n.d. https://www.marinetraffic.com/en/ais/home/centerx:33.1/centery:43.5/zoom:6.
Matvejević, Predrag. 1999. *Mediterranean: A cultural landscape*. Translated by Michæl Heim. Berkeley: University of California Press.
Mbembe, Achille. 2003. Necropolitics. *Public Culture* 15(1): 11–40. https://doi.org/10.1215/08992363-15-1-11.
Meddi, Adlène. 2018. Algérie: la présidentielle de 2019 entre les mains de … Dieu! *Middle East Eye*, 29 March. http://www.middleeasteye.net/fr/opinions/alg-rie-la-pr-sidentielle-de-2019-entre-les-mains-de-dieu-1901298481.
Nail, Thomas. 2015a. The Barbarism of the Migrant. *Stanford University Press Blog*. https://stanfordpress.typepad.com/blog/2015/09/the-barbarism-of-the-migrant.html.
——. 2015b. *The figure of the migrant*. Stanford: Stanford University Press.
——. 2016. Kinopolitics and the figure of the migrant: An interview with Thomas Nail. *The Other Journal*, 28 November. https://theotherjournal.com/2016/11/28/kinopolitics-figure-migrant-interview-thomas-nail/.
Names of the Algerian deportees. n.d. *International Institute of Social History*. http://www.iisg.nl/collections/new-caledonia/names.php.
Paths to Europe: As a key route closes, migrants look for others. 2016. *Financial Times*, 9 March. https://www.ft.com/content/f5418000-e5f3-11e5-bc31-138df2ae9ee6.
Rawlinson, Kevin. World's oldest intact shipwreck discovered in Black Sea. *Guardian*, 22 October. https://www.theguardian.com/science/2018/oct/23/oldest-intact-shipwreck-thought-to-be-ancient-greek-discovered-at-bottom-of-black-sea.
Refugee and Migrant Integration Center Set to Open in Kaunas. 2017. *The Baltic Course | Baltic States News & Analytics*, 28 June. http://www.baltic-course.com/eng/baltic_states/?doc=130747.
Registre de l'hôtel 'La Fayette' | Musée National de l'histoire de l'immigration. n.d. http://www.histoire-immigration.fr/collections/registre-de-l-hotel-la-fayette.
Said, Edward. 2000. Reflections on exile (1984). In *Reflections on exile and other essays*. Cambridge, MA: Harvard University Press.
Schrøder, Casper. 2017. Danish TV program on stowaways. https://www.dr.dk/tv/se/tv-avisen/tv-avisen-19/tv-avisen-2017-09-13-21-29.
Schulze-Engler, Frank, Pavan Kumar Malreddy and John Njenga Karugia. 2018. 'Even the dead have human rights': A conversation with Homi K. Bhabha. *Journal of Postcolonial Writing* 54(5): 702–16. https://doi.org/10.1080/17449855.2018.1446682.
SΠΔiL. 2018. Un imam dans chaque coin: la solution miracle à tous les problèmes en Algérie pic.twitter.com/IQPWJw057h. Tweet. 19 April.

Thomsen, Julie Astrid. 2017a. No country for migrant stowaways caught on ferry between Ukraine and Turkey. *Reuters*, 14 September. https://www.reuters.com/article/us-denmark-migrants-ferry/no-country-for-migrant-stowaways-caught-on-ferry-between-ukraine-and-turkey-idUSKCN1BP28I.
———. 2017b. Twelve North African stowaways sent home after 3-month ferry ordeal. *Reuters*, 1 November. http://uk.reuters.com/article/denmark-migrants-ferry/twelve-north-african-stowaways-sent-home-after-3-month-ferry-ordeal-idUKL8N1N74SG.
UNHCR. 1988. *Note on stowaway asylum-seekers*. http://www.unhcr.org/excom/scip/3ae68cbf8/note-stowaway-asylum-seekers.html.
———. 2002. *Background note on the protection of asylum-seekers and refugees rescued at sea*. http://www.unhcr.org/protection/globalconsult/3e5f35e94/background-note-protection-asylum-seekers-refugees-rescued-sea.html.
Zoeteweij-Turhan, Margarite Helena. 2018. Turkey: Between hospitality and hostility. *Forced Migration Review*, February. http://www.fmreview.org/syria2018/zoeteweijturhan.html.

Notes on Contributors

Silvia U. Baage teaches French at the Catholic University of America. She received her PhD from the University of Maryland, College Park, in 2012. Her current research focuses on the representation of islands in contemporary literature of the French-speaking world and the ways in which writers explore the topics of islandedness, postcolonial mobilities and migration, as well as natural disasters and climate change. She has presented at national and international conferences, most recently the 2018 Borders and Crossings: International and Multidisciplinary Conference on Travel Writing in Pula, Croatia. She has also published a variety of articles and book chapters about Chantal Spitz, Jean-François Samlong, Salim Hatubou and Étienne Barilier. She is currently working on a book manuscript about transnational environmental literature in French.

Marzia Caporale is Associate Professor of French and Italian at the University of Scranton (USA). Her research specializes in French and francophone women's literature and cinema with special emphasis on issues of postcolonial identity. Some of her recent publications include 'Whose language is it? Writing the postcolonial self in Véronique Tadjo's *Loin de mon père*', which appeared in *Ecrire, Traduire, Peindre Véronique Tadjo* (Paris: Présence Africaine, 2016); 'Au-delà du silence: mémoires de la traite négrière africaine dans *La saison de l'ombre de Léonora Miano*', in *Textualité de la mémoire et de l'histoire dans les langues de la littérature africaine*, edited by Owono Zambo (Saint-Denis: Edilivre, 2018); 'Creativity and the feminine: Sexual politics and cinematic aesthetics in Nadia El Fani's documentary-making', *Esprit Créateur*, 58(2), special issue 'Femmes créa(c)tives: Women's Creatvity in its Socio-Political Contexts' edited by Giada Alessandroni, Sandra Daroczi and Gemma Edney, Summer 2018. She is currently working on an article entitled 'Résister à Ébola: écriture performative et narration écocritique dans *En compagnie des hommes* de Véronique Tadjo'.

Ipek A. Çelik Rappas is Assistant Professor of Media and Visual Arts at Koç University, Istanbul. Her research topics include the representation of refugees and migrants in European cinema, popular genre films in Europe and the role of arts and screen industries in the urban renewal of European cities. Her book, *In permanent crisis: Ethnicity in contemporary European media and cinema*, was published by the University of Michigan Press in 2015. She has also published articles in journals such as *Cinema Journal, Television and New Media, French Cultural Studies, Comparative Studies of South Asia, Africa and the Middle East* and *Revista Latinoamericana de Estudios sobre Cuerpos, Emociones y Sociedad*.

Angela Giovanangeli is a senior lecturer in the School of International Studies at the University of Technology Sydney. Angela's broad field of research is in cultural histories and intercultural engagement. In particular, she works on visual and cultural practices especially in relation to French and European cultural programmes and Australian Indigenous perspectives in tertiary education.

Mark Ingram is Professor of French at Goucher College in Baltimore, Maryland. His research has addressed the politics of the arts and heritage in France, with special attention to theatre and its role as medium for the expression of the French republican tradition. Other research examines the contested deployments of Mediterranean and European heritage in Marseille by artists and others, including EU and municipal authorities. Another recent interest centres on the use of collaborative digital map-making, in research and teaching, for illuminating the multivocal aspects of theatres as sites of social influence and solidarity. Publications include *Rites of the Republic: Citizens' theatre and the politics of culture in southern France* (University of Toronto Press, 2011), and articles in journals such as *City and*

Society, The French Review, International Journal of Heritage Studies, International Journal of Humanities and Arts Computing and the Journal of the Society for the Anthropology of Europe.

Christa Catherine Jones is Professor of French in the Department of Languages, Philosophy and Communication Studies at Utah State University. She is co-editor of *Algerian Filmmaker Merzak Allouache* (*CELAAN Review*, 2017), co-editor of *New approaches to teaching folk and fairy tales* (UP of Colorado, 2016), co-editor of *Women from the Maghreb* (*Dalhousie French Studies*, 2014) and author of *Cave culture in the Maghreb: Imagining self and nation* (Lexington Books, 2012). Her work on French and postcolonial North African francophone literature and film has appeared in *Contemporary French and Francophone Studies, Dalhousie French Studies, Expressions Maghrébines, Francofonia, French Review, Jeunesse: Young People Texts, Cultures, Nouvelles Etudes Francophones, Research in African Literatures, Women's Studies Quarterly* and elsewhere.

Gemma King is a senior lecturer in French Studies at the Australian National University. Her research explores language and cultural representation in contemporary French and francophone cinemas and museums, and her first book, *Decentring France: Multilingualism and power in contemporary French cinema*, was published with Manchester University Press in 2017. Her writing has also appeared in *Contemporary French Civilization, French Cultural Studies, Linguistica Antverpiensia*, the *Australian Journal of French Studies, The Conversation* and *Francosphères*, as well as in numerous edited volumes. She is currently working on the contracted book *Jacques Audiard* for Manchester University Press's French Film Directors series.

Claire Launchbury's research concentrates on the intersection of memory, language, resistance and the archive in post-war Lebanon. Her first monograph (2012) looked at Anglo-French hybrid cultural memory formation at the BBC during the Second World War, and she has directed special issues on 'mutating cities' in the *Journal of Romance Studies* with Cara Levey, on post-war Lebanon in *Contemporary French and Francophone Studies* with Nayla Tamraz and on the Middle Eastern francosphère in *Francosphères*. With Charles Forsdick, she is editor of

Transnational French Studies, forthcoming with Liverpool University Press. Her second monograph, *Beirut and the Urban Memory Machine*, will be published with Amsterdam University Press.

Megan C. MacDonald was 2018–19 Eurias fellow at IMéRA, Université Aix-Marseille. Her current research interests include francophone Mediterranean literatures, feminist theory and representation, archive studies and anglophone literatures from South Asia. She is co-editor with Patrick Crowley of the special issue of *Contemporary French and Francophone Studies* 'The Contemporary Roman Maghrébin: Aesthetics, Politics, Production 2000–2015'. She has published articles in journals such as the *International Journal of Francophone Studies*, *Contemporary French and Francophone Studies* and *Francosphères*. She recently co-edited a special issue of *Expressions Maghrébines* on the assassinated Algerian writer Tahar Djaout, and the 'Commentary and Criticism' section of *Feminist Media Studies* on media representations on migration from a gendered perspective. Her forthcoming monograph considers the postcolonial *navette* via transnational and postcolonial francophone literatures in transit across Mediterranean spaces.

Agnès Peysson-Zeiss is the Coordinator of the Intensive Language sequence in French at Bryn Mawr College, and Chair of International Curricular Initiatives and Middle Eastern Studies affiliated faculty. She has researched the works of the Algerian francophone writer Assia Djebar and published a number of articles on her polyphonic texts, particularly on the Algerian Quatuor. Her most recent projects deal with graphic novels and resilience, examining how the arts can fill the void trauma leaves behind and allow people to survive. She is also involved in virtual civic engagement, focusing on women's rights issues in the Democratic Republic of the Congo, translating, with her students, blogs posts and articles from the DRC to disseminate their stories. Her article 'Virtual civic engagement and translation: Empowering women through digital media and translation', came out in February 2018.

Rania Said is a postdoctoral teaching fellow at the University of Massachusetts Boston. She has a PhD in Comparative Literature from Binghamton University and an agrégation in English from the Ecole

Normale Supérieure de Tunis. Her research focuses on autobiographical writing, the city in literature and the cultural productions of the Arab uprisings.

Index

9/11 168, 221

Abderrezak, Hakim 2, 3, 213n, 220n, 224, 227
   Ex-Centric Migrations: Europe and the Maghreb in Mediterranean Cinema, Literature and Music 3
Abdou Mdahoma, Ali 171
Abulafia, David 155, 156, 157, 161, 168, 225
Abu-Lughod, Janet 20
Académie Goncourt 47n
Adnan, Etel 175, 189, 190
Afghanistan 221
Aflam 89
Agamben, Giorgio 218, 219
Agier, Michel 219, 222, 223, 226, 227
Ahmed, Akbar 220
Akian, Akel 143
Albou, Karin 209
alétheia (truth) 78
Alexakis, Vassilis 7, 8, 67–69, 71, 72, 74–80
   genre 67
   La Clarinette 7, 67, 70, 71, 72, 74, 76, 77, 78, 80
   Les mots étrangers 68, 78
   Paris-Athènes 68

Alexandria 86
Algeria 8, 10, 30n, 89, 106n, 110n, 121, 139, 141, 215, 219, 222, 224, 225
Algerian government 222
Algiers 86, 139
Ali, Ibrahim 162
alienation 28, 63, 160
Allégret, Marc 89
Al Mourabitoun 183
alterity 221
Alvarez, David 227
Amal (Lebanese political party) 181
American Comparative Literature Association 1
American University of Beirut 190
Ameur-Zaïmeche, Rabah 203
Amsterdam 48n, 139, 193
Andres, Lauren 88
Anglosphere 3
Anthologie de la nouvelle poésie nègre et malgache de langue française 171
Antolini, Andrée 130
Appadurai, Arjun 116, 164
   Modernity at Large 116
Arabic (language) 199, 202, 214
   as *lingua franca* 210
   Modern Standard (MSA) 28, 31, 204

239

Moroccan 54, 202, 204
North African 214, 220
Tunisian vernacular 28–29, 31–33
as world language 204
Arabization 32
Arab-majority city 17, 19
Arab Spring / 2011 uprising / Tunisian uprising 5, 20, 21, 25, 27, 32, 86, 218, 219
Aranctingi, Philippe 185
Bosta (2005) 185
archipelago 171
Archis 193
archive 221, 223, 225, 228
    alternative 226, 227
    colonial 226
    digital 215
    Egyptian 226
    Mauritius 228
    stowaway 215, 216, 221, 228
    time 228
Arkana, Keny 10, 95–97, 122–23, 125–26, 130
Arman 37
Armenia 106n, 193
Armes, Roy 55n
Ascherson, Neal 221, 224, 225
Athens 1, 5, 7, 67–71, 74, 76, 77, 79, 80, 86, 115, 117
    connections to Paris 68
    Exarkheia 70n
    French influence 7, 70
    Mediterranean 7
Audiard, Jacques 199
Australia 186
Auteuil, Daniel 90
autofiction 162
Autour de la maison rose (1999) 190
Avignon 122

Baage, Silvia 11–12
Bacar, Abdoulatuf 170n
BAFTA 202
Baghdad 29
Bagnes, les 214

Balibar, Etienne 106, 113
Baltic States 201
banlieue 122, 170, 200
Banque du Liban 179, 182
Barazy, Ma'an 179, 180
Bardawil, Fadi 176, 183, 184
bare life 11, 214, 218, 221, 228
    at sea 214, 218, 220, 221, 228
Barthes, Roland 54
Basso, Keith 145, 147
baths, bathing 40
Baudelaire, Charles 17, 18
Bauman, Zygmunt 219, 220
Baumann, Hannes 182, 185
Bavlier, Ariane 131
beach 39, 40
Beckmann, Max 37
Beirut 11, 12, 86, 175, 176–95
    adrift 11, 12, 175, 184, 192, 194
    Badaro 193
    beaches 176
    Bourj el Murr 187, 188
    Bourj Hammoud 193
    civil war ruins 187
    Dahiyeh 186, 193
    environmentalism 191
    everyday 186
    façadism 187
    Gemayzé 193
    Hamra 193
    Holiday Inn 183, 187, 189
    Horsch Beirut 190
    jouissance 186
    left-wing politics 183, 184
    Mar Mikhael 193, 194
    modernist architecture 176
    'Paris of the Middle East' 178
    Phoenicia Hotel 189
    as playground 176, 193, 194
    port 175
    Ras Beirut 190, 193
    rebuilding 176
    red-light district 189
    relationship with the sea 175
    Riad el Sohl Square 188
    Sodeco Square 190

Index

Solidere (Société libanaise de developpement et reconstruction) 182, 185, 187
  surveillance 11, 12, 176, 187, 188
  as trading capital 181
  Wadi Abu Jamil 187
Beirut Madinati 191
Beirut Port Company 182
Beit Beirut 190
Belle Époque 37
Ben 27
Ben Ali, Zine El Abidine 19n, 21, 24, 27, 28, 32
Benaziza, Mounir 95
Benguigui, Yamina 205
Benjamin, Walter 17, 217
Ben Jelloun, Tahar 123, 124
Bensmaïl, Malek 9, 86, 87
Bentolila, Brigitte 143
Benveniste, Émile 73
Ben Yehoyada, Naor 142
Berlin 17, 89
Berry, Richard 93
Besançon 141
Besson, Luc 92
beur 200
Beydoun, Ahmad 183
Beyroutes 11, 193
Bhabha, Homi 221
bidonville 164
bilingualism 28
bio-politics 219
biopower 228
Black Sea 2, 8, 11, 13, 214, 217, 218, 221, 224, 225, 227
  migration route 221
Blanchard, Pascal 106n
Bodard, Mags 43
body
  desexualization 59, 60
  gaze 59
  politic 217, 228
  precarity 59
  representation of female 59, 60
  sexual object 59
  transformation 59

Boeri, Stefano 128
Boëtsch, Gilles 106n
Bommelaer, Claire 131
Bonnefoy, Françoise 91
border-crossing 206
borders 113, 200
Bosphorus 13, 224
Bouazizi, Mohamed Tarek 21, 27
bouillabaisse 116
Boura, Olivier 107
Bourguiba, Habib 24
Bourial, Hatem 28
Bouteflika, Abdelaziz 224, 202
Bowles, Paul 54
Braudel, Fernand 2, 90n, 121, 135, 225
Bresson, René 38
bridging narrative 7, 9, 71, 104, 137, 155, 156, 161, 202
Brown, Jonathan 37
Brucy, Anne 138n
Bullen, Claire 95
Bulley, Dan 102, 103
Buñuel, Luis 38n
Burdett, Ricky 148
Burgel, Guy 75
Burland, Nicolas 126, 130
Buss, Robin 39
Bye-Bye 94

café 163
Caillé, Patricia 208
Cairo 21
  Tahrir Square 189
camp(s) 218–20, 226, 227
  concentration 220
Camus, Albert 123
Cannes 43
  casino 43
  film festival 43n, 55, 56, 90, 91
capital 4, 7, 11, 40, 42, 46, 49, 176, 180, 181, 182, 184, 190
  laissez-tout-faire 179
'Capitale de la rupture'(Keny Arkana) 95, 130
Caporale, Marzia 6, 7

cargo ship(s) 214, 227
Carrera Suarez, Isabella 19
Carter, Sandra Gayle 53
Casablanca 1, 55n
Cazenave, Odile 171
Çelik Rappas, Ipek 8, 9
cell, cellular 228
Cendrars, Blaise 123
Central African Republic 78
de Certeau, Michel 148, 156, 162, 163, 165, 166
Césaire, Aimé 170
César 90
Cézanne, Paul 155
Chabrol, Claude 38n
Chagall, Marc 37
Chahine, Zineb 193
Chambers, Iain 2, 4, 161
Charari, Waddah 183
Charef, Mehdi 203
Chevallier, Denis 102n
Chevaux de fortune 55
Chiha, Michel 181
Chirac, Jacques 178, 182
Chougnet, Jean-François 109, 131
Chouraqui, Frank 213n
Cichosz, Jedrzei 37
Cinémathèque française 90
citizenship, citizen 117, 219
Citroën DS 44
Cixous, Hélène 7n
Clair, René 38
class 20, 21, 28–30, 34, 44, 56, 90, 94, 122, 126,127, 129–31, 157, 158, 160, 164, 167, 201
    aristocrat, aristocratic class 40
    proletariat 221
    working class 39, 40, 47, 105, 136, 137, 139
CMA-CGM 127
Cocteau, Jean 38, 123
Code inconnu: récits incomplets de divers voyages 206
code-switching 29, 31–33
Colardelle, Michel 101, 105, 108, 109

Cole, Téju 19
colonialisme 160
Commedia dell'arte 39
Comorian 11, 12, 161, 162, 165, 170n
    literature 11, 171
    diaspora 12, 157, 159, 168, 171
Comoros Islands 4, 11, 106n, 135, 155, 157, 158, 160, 167, 170
Compagnie Algérienne (Banque Libano-Française) 181
Constantinople 80
contagion 222
container ship 217
contamination 220
Contes de ma grand-mère 162
Cordoba 86
Corsica 69, 155n
cosmopolitan, -ism 1, 5, 25, 31, 34, 37, 38, 39, 54, 56, 85, 87–89, 93, 122
Costa-Gavras 205
Côte d'Azur 44, 155n
couscous 167
Couve de Murville, Maurice 178
Crang, Mike 109, 111, 117
Crédit Foncier d'Algérie et Tunisie (Fransabank) 181
Crédit libanais 181
creole 227
cultural capital, flows 8, 71, 72 200, 202–03
cultural contact 202
Cupolo, Diego 8, 221
currency 204, 205

Damascus 175
Dana, Joseph 21
Daoud, Kamel 223n, 224
darija 220
Darwish, Mahmoud 27
De battre mon cœur s'est arrêté 199
Debré, Michel 178
décolonisation 160
dégourbification 22, 23
Deleuze, Gilles 112, 200
Dell'Umbria, Alèssi 88

Index

Demy, Jacques 6, 37, 38, 40, 42, 43, 45, 49, 50
   La Baie des anges 37, 42–46
   Les Parapluies de Cherbourg 43n2
Deneuve, Catherine 189
Denmark 215, 217
Depardieu, Gérard 91
Depierris, Jean-Louis 49
Derrida, Jacques 3n, 4, 5, 7, 7n, 8, 32, 67, 68, 71, 73, 76, 80
   L'Autre cap 4, 67, 71, 75, 80
   De l'hospitalité 7, 8, 73
Desage, Fabien 138
de Saint Phalle, Niki 37
Devin, Eric 58n
Dialmy, Abdessamed 224
diglossia 28
Dikeç, Mustafa 138
discrimination 168
Djebar, Assia 2n, 7n, 19
Dobie, Madeleine 2
Douieri, Ziad
   West Beyrouth 189
Dridi, Karim 94
Dubai 62
Dufy, Raoul 37
Dumas, Alexandre (père) 124n
Duncan, Carol 102, 110
Dupont, Claire 106n, 139, 140
Duvivier, Julien 199
Dykes, Rebecca 188

Eden à l'ouest 206
Editions du Seuil 47n
Éditions Maspero 184
education 168
   French 28
Edwards, Brian 7n
Egypt 77, 115
   Mount Sinai 115
Eid, Rana
   Panoptic 187
Eldorado 11, 159, 169
El Hallak, Mona 190
elhariry, Yasser 2
El Khoury, Jad (Potato Nose) 187

Elsheshtawy, Yasser 5, 17
Éluard, Paul 123
encounter (*rencontre*) 143
Enghien-les-Bains 42, 44
Enghien-les-Bains, casino 44
England 33
English (language) 33, 204, 210
epistolary 72
Esposito, Claudia 2
Esposito, Roberto 216, 217, 218, 220, 221
Esprit de Babel 130
Estang, Luc 49
eurocentrism 210
Euroméditerranée [L'] Euromed 9, 10, 87, 91, 93, 95, 96, 107, 108, 125–29, 131
EuropaCorp 92
Europe 2, 77, 200, 203, 209, 219, 225
   far-right politics 105
   as horizon 227
   imaginary 221
   integration 105, 106
   metropolis 18, 19
   peripheries 106, 113
Europe Capital of Culture programme (ECOC) 103, 104, 136
European Commission 121
European Union 9, 62, 75, 102–04, 107, 122, 200
exile 124, 156, 159, 206
   as poverty 160, 161
Exils 207
exodus 124

Fabian, Johanes 147
Fabre, Cédric 160
Fabre, Clarisse 122, 161
FAL Convention 213
Fanny 90
Fanon, Frantz 7n
Farah, Kenza 124
fault lines 144
Fawaz, Mona 188

Ferhati, Jilali 55
Ferroukhi, Ismaël 11, 12, 199–203, 209, 210
    Le Grand Voyage (2004) 11, 12
Ferry boat 227
Film, documentary 37, 38
Film industry 8
flâneur, flâneuse, flânerie 5, 6, 11, 17–20, 23–26, 30, 34
Flaubert, Gustave 123
FLN 162
Fogu, Claudio 2
Forensic Architecture 226
forgetting 76, 78
Forsdick, Charles 165, 170
Fortress Europe 77, 200, 201
Foster, Norman 128
Foucault, Michel 61, 214, 218, 222, 225, 228
Fourcaut, Annie 138
Fournel, Victor 17
France 8, 11, 24, 32, 54, 62, 108, 115, 117, 137, 138n, 166, 177, 178, 182, 191, 200, 201, 208, 209, 210, 215, 219, 227
    Assemblée Nationale 177
    colonial banking 181
    DROM 166
    far-right politics 69
    Metropolitan 166, 171, 206, 207
    postcolonial 11, 210
France 3 (TV station) 88
Franco-Arab identity 200
francophone, francophonie 1, 28–30, 32, 34
    trans-Mediterranean 156
francosphère 3, 13, 221
Frankenheimer, John 92
Fregonese, Sara 177, 183, 186
French 31–33
    as colonial language 32, 177, 184, 187
    history, postcolonial 215
    language 68, 168, 199, 203, 204, 210
    literature 155
    rural life 105
    soil 210
French-Algerian war 121, 135, 144
The French Connection 92
French Revolution 117
French Riviera 44
Freschel, Agnès 109
Friedkin, William 92
Front National 69, 162, 178
Front Populaire 105
Fuzibet, Frédérique 135, 142–46

gambling 42, 43, 44, 51
Gardner, Edwin 193
Gardner-Chlorus, Penelope 31
Gastaut, Yvan 89
Gates, Carolyn 181
Gatlif, Tony 207
Geagea, Samir 183
Gemayel, Amin 182
Gemayel (family) 181
Genet, Jean 54
Geneva 47
Genoa 86
Germany 201
germ warfare 217
Ghosh, Amitav 226
Ghossein, Ahmad
    White Noise 185
Gide, André 42
Gilli, Claude 37
Giono, Jean 124n
Giovangeli, Angelia 9
Girard, Emilie 116
Gironde, Michel 160, 161
Global Integrated Shipping Information System (GISIS) 215, 216
globalization 6
global South 184, 200
Godard, Jean-Luc 38n, 199
Gomes, Paulo Emílio Salles 38
Gott, Michael 204
Graham, Stuart 54n, 62n
Granoux, Olivier 130
grassroots politics 176, 181, 191

Index

Great Britain 31, 42, 54n, 62
Greece 7, 8, 69, 72–75, 78n, 79, 115, 221
   economic crisis 5, 67, 71, 72, 74, 79
   hotspots 221
   military dictatorship 71
Greek language 70, 79
   in French Language 71
Grésillon, Boris 125
de Grey, Spencer 128
Grossman, Manuel 38
Guattari, Félix 112, 200
Guédiguian, Robert 94
Guemriche, Saleh 2n
Guers, Paul 43
Guetta, David 96

Hadid, Zaha 127, 128
Hadjithomas, Joana 189, 190
Hage, Ghassan 186, 194
Haifa 175
hajj 12, 200–02, 209
Halbwachs, Maurice 146, 147
Haneke, Michael 205
Harb, Mona 193
Hariri, Rafik 178, 182, 183, 185, 189, 190
Hariri, Saad 187
harkis 167
harraga 220
Harrison, Olivia C. 2
Hartwiger, Alexander Greer 19
Harvey, David 180
Hassan, Salah 185
Hassanati: de Mayotte à Marseille 156
Hatubou, Salim 11, 155–66, 168–71
Heath, Stephen 89, 90
Henderson, Lindsay 46
Herzfeld, Michael 142
Hexagon 10, 200, 207
Hezbollah 186, 193
Higbee, Will 208, 210
Hilton, Jodi 8, 221
HIV/AIDS 157
hogra 224

homo sacer 219
Hooker, Charlotte 40
Horden, Peregrine 156, 224
hors du nomos 219, 220
hors-lieux 222, 224
hospitality 8, 68, 73
Hourani, Najib 179, 181–83
Hulshof, Janneke 193
human rights 76, 77, 103
   Cour européenne des droits de l'homme (ECHR) 77, 80
   international human rights law 215
Huntzinger, Jacques 101
Hussein, Saddam 29
Husseini, Randa 180

IAM 125
identity, dual 68
immigration, Algerian 161, 162
   hostility to 69, 74, 77
   language ability 73
immunitary logic 216
incarceration, history of 214
Inch'Allah dimanche 206
Indian Ocean 156, 157, 160n 167, 171
Indian Ocean Mediterranean 157, 167
infrastructure 102, 184, 189, 191
   water management 116
Ingram, Mark 8, 10
integration, integrate 199, 202–03, 205, 208
intercultural dialogue, relationships 160, 168, 199
intergenerational communication 203
'International Convention Relating to Stowaways' 217
international maritime law 215
International Maritime Organization (IMO) 215
International Organization for Migration (IOM) 215
international refugee law 215
intertextuality 168

Intra-Investment Company, Lebanon 182
Iran 221
Iraq 30, 181, 221
Işik, Yörük 214
Islam 20, 209
    depiction in film 209
    practices 209
Israel 25, 117
    'Grapes of Wrath' conflict 182
    Ministry of Foreign Affairs 177
Istanbul 13, 86, 213, 214, 223
    Gezi Park 189
    Haydarpaşa Port 214
Italy 37, 50, 225
Ivens, Joris 38n
Izzo, Jean-Claude 123, 124n, 158, 162, 163n

Jaffa 175
Jaggi, Maya 202
James Bond films 55
Jarman, Neil 147
Jerusalem 112
Je veux voir 189
Jimenez, Cédric 92
Jones, Christa 6
Jordan 181
Joreige, Khalil 189, 190
Jourdana, Pascal 160–62
Jousse, Thierry 43, 51
Joyce, James 31
Judaism 209
Jumblatt, Kamal 181
justice 76
Justin de Marseille 92

Karugh, John Njenga 221
Kassab, Maroun Ghassan 177
Kata'eb Party 182, 183
Kaufman, Boris 38, 39
Kaunas Seaways 215n, 216, 222
Kechiche, Abdellatif 206
Kedge Business School 131
Khalaf, Samir 175, 176, 184, 191, 193, 194

Khaldun, Ibn 24
Khannous, Touria 65
Khatir, Dalila 143
Khelifa, Ould 43n
Khlifi, Kaouthar 5, 17, 19, 20–25, 27–29, 34
Kilani, Leïla 7, 53, 55–60, 62, 65
King, Gemma 11, 12, 13, 204
King, Martin Luther 169
King Hassan II 53
kinopolitics 221
Kinoshita, Sharon 1
Klein, Melanie 194
Klein, Yves 37
Kokoreff, Michel 136
Korda, Alexander 89
Košice 122
Kosnick, Jira 89
Kramsch, Claire 203
Krankenhagen, Stefan 102, 106
Kypseli 8, 76

labour, gender 58, 59
Lacanian 8
La Ciotat 182
Lafargue de Grangeneuve, Loïc 125
La Faute à Voltaire 206
La French 92
laïcité 191, 210
Lalagianni, Vasiliki 155n, 159, 160, 161, 168
Lampedusa 219
Lamy, François 137
Landau, Rom 54n
Landau, Sigalit
    Water Meter Tree 116
Lang, Jack 121
language, portrayal on film 210
language politics 203
languages 68, 202
    lingua franca(s) 199, 203–05, 210
La Noire de ... 171
Lanovsky, Frédéric 37
La Petite Jérusalem 209
Lapeyronnie, Didier 136

Index

Lascaux 149
Latarjet, Bernard 122
Latiri, Dora 5, 17, 19, 24–29, 31, 32, 34
Launchbury, Claire 1, 11, 12
Lazarus, Neil 104
Lebanese Forces 183
Lebanon 31, 175, 177, 178, 180
    CEDRE (Conférence économique pour le développement par les réformes et avec les entreprises) 178
    cinema 189
    civil war 176, 181, 183, 189
    currency (*Livres libanaises*) 192
    domestic workers 180
    Druze 181
    Maronite 178, 183
    National Movement 183
    relationship with France 177, 178, 182, 186, 191, 195
    state absence 185
    uprising (17 October 2019) 180, 188
Lebovics, Herman 103, 107n, 110, 111
Lecadet, Clara 219, 222, 226
Le Clézio, J.M.G 124n
Lefebvre, Henri 63, 180
Legrand, Michel 43
Le Grand Voyage 199
leisure 6, 41, 161
Le Monde diplomatique 184
Le Pen, Marine 178
leprosy 218
Lesbos 77
Les Temps modernes 184
Leterrier, Louis 92
Le Thé au harem d'Archimède 203
Libération (newspaper) 137
Libya 219, 225
Lille 122, 131
L'Immortel 93
linguistic diversity 202
Lionnet, Françoise 226, 227, 228
Lioret, Philippe 199

literature, as abode 80
Liverpool 88, 131
L'Odeur du béton 156
London 17, 19, 87
Londres, Albert 89
Lord, Christopher 214
Ly, Ladj
    Les Misérables 199
Lyon 201, 206, 208, 209

Maalouf, Amin 169, 175, 192
MacDonald, Megan C. 3n, 7n, 11, 13
McGonagle, Joseph 92
Macron, Emmanuel 178
Maghreb 225
Magimel, Benoît 91
Maison de l'Histoire européenne, Belgium 102n
male gaze 18
Maliszewski, Catherine 110, 111
Malkki, Liisa 225
Malle, Louis 38n
Malreddy, Pavan Kumar 221
Mann, Claude 42
Marchal, Olivier 92
Marche pour l'égalité et contre le racisme (1983) 137
Mare Nostrum 121
marginalization 64, 206
marine traffic 222
Marius 90
Marius et Jeanette 94
Marley, Bob 92
Marrakech 163
marriage, *le grand marriage* 165, 170
Marseille 4, 8, 9, 10, 11, 85, 87–94, 96, 101, 102, 106, 109–13, 116–17, 121, 122, 125, 127, 131, 135, 136, 139, 141, 143, 155, 157–62, 165, 166, 167, 169, 170, 206, 207
    architecture 127, 128
    Belle de Mai 88, 126
    Belle Ile 164
    Belle-Ville 158
    catholic identity 110

Marseille *continued*
  cité des Flamants 145
  community building 139
  cosmopolitan 85, 87, 121, 163
  crime and corruption 91, 92, 136
  development 129
  as diaspora 11
  Fort Saint-Jean 86
  Frais-Vallon (la Colline) 130, 135, 136, 139–42, 144, 145–48
  gateway to the Orient 121, 163
  gentrification 10, 93
  ghetto 136, 158
  imagined 86, 90, 91
  immigration 136, 137, 142, 155
  J1 85
  Joliette 10
  Le Panier 88
  Le Samaritaine 164
  local 116, 188, 136
  Maghreb heritage 89, 121
  Maison des Cinématographies de la Méditerranée 86, 88
  makeover 107, 118, 126, 131, 132
  maritime imperial power 86
  media representation 87
  Mediterranean 4, 8, 85
  migration 9, 107, 169, 170
  Montolivet 144
  multiculturalism 9, 87, 138
  neighbourhood associations 140
  Notre-Dame de la Garde 110, 166
  as passage 95
  passage 109
  personification 166
  post-industrial 87–88
  public housing 135, 138, 145
  quartiers nord 135–49, 158, 164, 170
  refuge 158
  rue Thubaneau 165, 167
  solidarity 141
  'stade rouge' 145
  street 164
  Théâtre de la Mer 139, 142, 145
  timeless 91

  tourists, tourism 88, 89, 131
  transnational 8, 9, 86, 92
  urban transformation 127
  utopia 86
  Vieux Port 90, 91, 128, 129, 157, 163
Marseille-Provence, European Capital of Culture (MP13) 4, 85, 87, 103, 104, 121, 122, 123, 127–30, 139
Mas, Jean 38
Massilia 124
Matisse, Henri 37
Matvejević, Predrag 224
Mauritius 226, 228
Mayotte 157, 165, 166, 167
Mazé, Camille 102, 103, 105, 107, 117
Mazierska, Ewa 94
Mbembe, Achille 220
Mecca 11, 12, 110, 200, 201, 209
Medea 143, 144
Mediterranean
  archive 224
  bodies 11, 80
  body of water 12, 156, 210
  camps 219
  cemetery 224
  centre-periphery discourse 13, 210
  civilization 103, 104, 105, 107, 112
  cosmopolitanism 101
  crisis 80, 169, 218
  crossing 214
  displaced 215
  economic crisis 86
  epistemology 210
  Europe, relation to 106, 109
  flora 49
  food 115
  fragmentation 161, 205
  global 168
  history 167
  identity, heritage 4, 85, 101, 103, 109, 118, 140, 143, 171, 201
  interactions 12, 156, 219
  islands 219
  les brûleurs 55

Index

linguistic economy 205
literary space 13
mapping 208
meeting point 80
migrant writers 155
migration 4, 55, 77, 80 86, 140
narratives 101, 112, 115, 118
'new' 114, 117
non-Western 167
political tensions 210
refugee crisis 224
relationship to Islam 209
representation 109
shores 219
space 110, 111, 112, 113, 114, 205, 208, 210
stereotypes 49
ville-monde 156, 164, 170
Mediterraneans 157, 159, 166, 225
Mediterranean Union 10, 107, 108
Méditerranées, des grands cités d'hier aux hommes d'aujourd'hui 85
Megaton, Olivier 92
Megerle, Heidi 88
Megill, Alan 146, 147
memory 72, 75, 136, 137, 138, 142, 145, 147
    as democracy 148
    loss 8
    politics of 161
    as responsibility 76
    social 146
Mercouri, Melina 121
Mernissi, Fatima 19
Messina, Marine 138n
Metropolitan identity 4
microfinance schemes 180
Middle East Airlines (MEA)-Air Liban 182
Middle Sea 85, 86
migrant, the figure of 216, 217
    aid 80
    literature, *écriture migrante* 161
    literature, Quebecois 171
migration 11, 75, 77, 80, 194, 201
    clandestine 222

detention 76
displaced 225
failed 214
Franco-Maghrebi 205
narrative 218, 228
non-Mediterranean 155
Minnard, Liesbeth 19
mobility 93, 167, 168, 200
    economic 206
    forced 225
    modernity 167, 168
modernity, and tradition, Morocco 53, 54
Mohamed, Isabelle 170n
Monaco 37, 42, 44, 46
    capital flows 46
Monroe, Kristen 191
Monte-Carlo 179
moral depravity 50
Morcellet, Elisabeth 37
Moreau, Jeanne 42
Morin, Edgar 101, 104, 106, 113, 169, 171
Moroccan 7, 56, 200, 204
Morocco 6, 53, 54, 62, 89, 115, 201, 209, 215, 219, 222–25
    absolute monarchy 224
    cinema 53, 54
    economic policies 53
    globalization 54
    nationalism 54
Moura, Jean-Marc 155, 159, 161, 168
Mrouré, Rabih 189
Mucchielli, Laurent 136
multiculturalism 89
multilingualism 11, 12, 199, 203, 210
Mulvey, Laura 59, 60
Muqaddimah 24
Musée de l'Europe, Brussels 102n
Musée des Civilisations de l'Europe et de la Méditerranée (MuCEM) 8, 9, 10, 85, 86, 96, 101–05, 107, 108–11, 113, 114, 117, 118, 126, 129
Musée Européen Schengen, Luxembourg 102n

Musée National d'arts et Traditions
    Populaires (MNATP) 9, 104,
    105
Musée Regards de Provence 85
Museum Europäischer Kulturen,
    Berlin 102n
museum practices 101, 102, 103, 104,
    109, 110, 115, 139
    musée de société 102, 114
Music 79
    rébétiko 79
    as solidarity 79

Naas, Michael
    Positions 4
Naceri, Samy 92
Naeff, Judith 185
Nail, Thomas 216, 221
naming 225, 226
narguilé 194, 195
narrative 102
navette 2, 3
Nègre, Charles 37
neoliberalism 179, 180, 185, 189,
    190
Nepveu, Pierre 161
New York City 17, 48n
Nice 1, 5, 6, 37–39, 40, 45–47, 50
    Battle of the Flowers 42
    carnaval 6, 40, 41, 42, 51
    Cimiez 49
    as dream, as hallucination 46, 48,
        50
    Hotel Régina 37
    Majestic Eden Roc 37
    Negresco Hotel 37, 40
    Promenade des Anglais 6, 37,
        40–44, 48, 50, 51
    as bridging aspect 50
    Quai des Etats-Unis 43, 48
    as redemption 49
    street food 42
    tourism 37, 41, 44
    Vieux-Nice 39, 42–44, 46, 51
    weather 47
    Westminster 37, 40

Nigeria 79
nomad 221
nomadism 159
non-space, geographic 62
Nora, Pierre 149
North America 168
nostalgia 25, 75, 79, 88, 93, 94
Nouvel, Jean 128

Obegi, family 181
Obergöker, Timo 165–67, 170
Occident 75
Odessa 214
Odysseus 86
oral tradition 168
Organini, Bernard 129, 130
orientalism 6, 176
Orlando, Valérie 54
otherness 63
Ottoman empire 181

Pagnol, Marcel 88–94, 96, 155
Palestinian 27
    refugees 180, 186
Pan-Arabism 29, 30
Pan-Mediterranean movement 209
Paris 5, 7, 17, 38, 46, 48n, 67–71, 75,
    79, 80, 90, 104, 105, 122, 163,
    178, 184, 206, 208
    banlieue 186
    as centre of migrant experience
        208
    as distinct from France 69
    Eiffel Tower 149
    Hôtel de Ville 75
    Île de Saint-Louis 182
    indifference 69
    Institut du Monde Arabe 182
    Jardins de Luxembourg 70
    La Moquette 70
    Place de la République 189
    rue Didot 70
    Théâtre du Vieux-Colombier 38
Parisians 69
    prejudice of 69
Park, Robert 180

Index

parochial 104, 118
Pascal, Claude 37
passerelle 2, 3
passport 61, 167, 203
penal colony 214
Peraldi, Michel 106n, 107, 110, 139
Peres, Shimon 177
petit bourgeois 22, 23
petrodollars 179, 182
Peysson-Zeiss, Agnès 10
pharmakon 216
Pharoun, Henri 181
Pinoncelli, Pierre 37
pissaladière 42
plague 217, 218, 222
plague ship 228
Plus belle la vie 88
Poehls, Kerstin 102n, 117
Pôle Emploi, Agence Nationale de l'Emploi 131, 164
Pollock, Griselda 18
polysensorial 20
port(s) 155, 213, 222, 223
Portugal 62
Post-Afrique sur Seine generation 171
postcolonial
    archive 11, 13, 161
    burden 31
    city 19
    flâneur 19
    migrant literature 156
    parcours 183
    state of emergency 214
    writer 31, 168
postcolonialism 168
Pound, Ezra 31
Poupeau, Franck 138
prison 64, 225
Prix Jean Vigo 38n
Provence 10, 85, 155n
Psy4 de la rime 125
Purcell, Nicholas 156, 224

quarantine 218

racism 161, 168
Rafferty, Terrence 46
Raharimanana, Jean-Luc 170n
Ramadan 141
Ramadan, Adam 186
Rancière, Jacques 104, 115, 116
    Future of the Image 116
Rascaroli, Laura 94
Raun, Grønvald 215
Rayess Bek 185
    L'homme de gauche 186
Red Cross 215n
Reflections on Exile 217
refugee 4, 8, 76
    crisis 200, 218, 219
    fear of 218
    North African 219
    Turkey 218
    script 224
Région Provence-Alpes-Côte d'Azur (PACA) 90
Reims 149
religion 48, 50, 209
    in France 209, 210
Reno, Jean 93
Renoir, Jean 38
Renucci, Janine 155
response 76
return 170
Reuters 214, 215, 223
rhizome 200, 208
Ricciotti, Rudy 110, 111, 128
Rice, Alison 3, 7, 8
Rivette, Jacques 38n
road trip 189, 200, 208
Roberts, Jean-Marc 72
Roblès, Emmanuel 6, 37, 47–51
    La Remontée du fleuve 37, 47–50
Rodaway, Paul 20n
Rof, Gilles 109
Romania 8, 221, 223
Romans 53
Rome 86
Rosello, Mireille 201, 203, 204
Ruhr 131
rupture 8

rural space 167
ruses, urban 12, 176
Russia 42

sacred spaces 25
'Safia' 10, 139–42, 146, 148
Said, Edward 27, 28, 177, 217
Said, Rania 5, 11
Sakr-Tiernay, Julia 179, 180
Salameh, Riad 179
Samson, Michel 106n, 110, 139
Sango (CAR) 78
Sarkozy, Nicolas 9, 107, 108
Saudi Arabia 182, 201, 209
Sauvagnargues, Jean 177, 178
Sayahi, Lotfi 32
Sayegh, Nasri 187, 188
Sayegh, Yusuf 181
Schengen (zone) 122
Schilt, Thomas 204
Schlöndorff, Volker 189
    Die Falschung 189
Schroder, Casper 215, 222
Schulze-Enger, Frank 221
seas
    closed 217
    connecting 12, 13
Second World War 80
secularism, in France 210
Sehli, Yamina 163, 164
Sembène, Ousmane 171
Senegal 80
Senghor, Léopold Sédar 171
separate spheres 18
Serbia 115, 202
Shelley, Percy Bysshe 24
shipwreck 225, 228
Shub, Ester 38n
Sicily 25
Sidi Bouzid 21
Siemens, Herman W. 213n
Sif, Minna 131
Simmel, Georg 20
Singapore 19, 179
Six-Day War (1967) 25
Slovakia 122

Smythe, S.A. 11
Socca 42
social body 64
social death 221
social immobility 63
Socialist Lebanon 183
social power 203
social space 63, 148, 149
social subject 64
Sonnier, Keith 37
Sous le soleil de Marseille 124
South Bank, London 179
sovereignty 214, 220
Spain 54n, 62, 219, 225, 227
spatial practices 156, 162
Spivak, Gayatri 3n
sport 30, 40, 41
stateless, statelessness 219
state of exception 219
Stehle, Maria 91
Steiner, Stéphane 37
stereotypes 93, 94
stereotypes, gender 60
Stoughton, India 187
stowaway 11, 13, 213, 219, 220, 222,
    225, 228
    time 227
Strait of Gibraltar 2, 6, 54, 219, 227
Studio Beirut 193
Stuttgart 47
Sur la planche 55
surrealism 38, 42
Sursock, family 181
surveillance 218
Suzzarelli, Bruno 108, 109, 114
Swann, Paul 88
Switzerland 179
Sydney, NSW 19
Syria 80, 218, 221, 225

Tamalet-Talbeyev, Edwige 2, 213n
Tamraz, Roger 182
Tanger, le rêve des brûleurs 55
Tangier 5, 6, 54, 55, 57–65
    cinematic history 54, 55
    dystopia 56, 61, 64

Index

Mediterranean gateway 54
utopic space 57, 61, 63–64
Western intellectuals and artists 54
Tangier, International Zone 62n, 63–65
Tangier Exportation Free Zone 56, 60, 61, 62, 64, 65
Tarr, Carrie 200, 208
Tati, Jacques 38
Taxi 92
Teisseir, Cédric 37
Tellier, Thibault 138
Témime, Emile 121
temporality 13
terrorism 168
Terrorist attack (France, January 2015) 138n1
Tétouan, Morocco 139
TGV 93
theatre, community 139, 142, 143
theatre, North Africa 143
Théâtre de la Mer 135, 139
Thomas, Dominic 200
Thomasson, Anne-Lise 143
Thomsen, Julie Astrid 214, 223
Thomson, David 138
Tissot, Sylvie 138
Tomaney, John 104, 118
Toronto 19
Tournier, Maurice 92
Traboulsi, Fawwaz 183
trade 121
transcultural dialogue 42
translation 70, 80, 184
translingualism 71, 80
trans-Mediterranean constellation 215
  experiences 171
  flows 176, 179, 181, 182, 194, 200
  movement 228
  studies 166
transnational 103, 104, 105, 107, 109, 115, 116, 117, 189
  capital 176, 179, 180, 181, 182, 183, 184, 195
  movement 208

travel writing 165
Trésor de la langue grecque 70
Tripoli, Lebanon 175
  Sahat al Nour 189
Trippe, Micah 39
Troy 86
Truffaut, François 38n
Tunis 1, 5, 11, 17, 19–22, 29, 30, 86
  architecture 22
  banlieue nord 25
  Cathedral Saint-Vincent-de-Paul 23, 24
  downtown 22, 30
  La Goulette 25–28
  Municipal Theatre 23, 24
  suburbs 22, 23, 30
Tunisia 24, 25, 27, 29, 33, 89, 94, 95
Tunisian 23, 26–28, 32
Turkey 8, 13, 115, 117, 201, 209, 214, 215, 216, 221
Turkish Law on Foreigners and International Protection 217
Tyre 86

Ukraine 13, 214, 215, 217
  Chornomorsk 214, 223n
Ulysse le brûleur de frontières et la mer blanche du milieu 86
unemployment, chômage 70
Ungar, Steven 92
UNHCR (United Nations High Commission for Refugees) 215, 216, 217, 218
United States 30, 62, 169, 182, 184, 214
Université Libanaise 183
University of Brighton 31
urban, utopia 7
urban landscape 163
urban literature 34
urban paradoxes 12, 176
urban periphery, *banlieue* 137, 138, 148
urban planning (Tunis) 21
urban policy (France) 137, 138, 149
urban space (Tangier) 56

urban walk, *balade* urbaine 8, 135, 136, 137, 139, 144, 146, 148
urbicide 177

vagabond 221
Valéry, Paul 71
Valls, Manuel 167
Vandals 53
Varda, Agnès 38n
Venice 86, 117
    Film Festival 202
Vertov, Mikhail 38n
Vigo, Jean 6, 37–39, 40–45, 47, 50
    A propos de Nice 37, 38–42
Vigouroux, Robert 102, 107

Wainwright, Oliver 128
Wake, the 225
walls 167
Welcome 199

Wesh-wesh, qu'est-ce qui se passe? 203
Weston, Daniel 31
Westphal, Bertrand 20, 25
Williams, Adebayo 19
Williams, Tennessee 54
Wilson, Elizabeth 18
Wolff, Janet 18
women, emancipation 45, 46

xenophobia, *xénophobie* 7, 8, 72, 73, 74, 161

Yuen, Corey 92

Zawarib 192
Ziad and the Wings 194
Zoeteweij-Turhan, Margarite Helena 217, 218
Zola, Emile 29, 124